Guide to INDIAN PHILOSOPHY

The Asian Philosophies and Religions Resource Guides

Guide to INDIAN PHILOSOPHY

KARL H. POTTER

with

Austin B. Creel

and

Edwin Gerow

G.K.HALL &CO.

70 LINCOLN STREET, BOSTON, MASS.

LIBRARY OF CONGRESS
Library of Congress Cataloging-in-Publication Data

Potter, Karl H.
Guide to Indian philosophy / Karl H. Potter with Austin B. Creel and Edwin Gerow.
p. cm.—(The Asian philosophies and religions resource guides)
Includes index.
ISBN 0-8161-7904-2
1. Philosophy, Indic—Bibliography. 2. India—Religion—Bibliography. I. Creel, Austin B. II. Gerow. Edwin. III. Title. IV. Series.
Z7129.I5P68 1988
[B5131]
016.181'4—dc19 88-7031

This publication is printed on permanent/durable acid-free paper
MANUFACTURED IN THE UNITED STATES OF AMERICA

Project on Asian Philosophies and Religions

Sponsoring Organizations

Center for International Programs and Comparative Studies of the New York State Education Department/University of the State of New York
Council for Intercultural Studies and Programs, Inc.

Steering Committee

Kenneth Morgan	Emeritus, Colgate University *Chairman*
Wing-tsit Chan	Chatham College Emeritus, Dartmouth College
David J. Dell	Foreign Area Materials Center Columbia University *Project Manager, 1975-77*
Edith Ehrman	Foreign Area Materials Center *Project Manager, 1971-74*
Robert McDermott	Baruch College, City University of New York
Bardwell Smith	Carleton College
H. Daniel Smith	Syracuse University
Frederick J. Streng	Southern Methodist University

Editorial Coorindators

David J. Dell
Edward S. Haynes

Preparation of this series of guides to resources for the study of Asian philosophies and religions was made possible by a grant from the National Endowment for the Humanities, supplemented through the Endowment's matching funds scheme, with additional financial support from the Ada Howe Kent Foundation, C. T. Shen, and the Council on International and Public Affairs, Inc. None of the above bodies is responsible for the content of these guides, which is the responsibility of those listed on the title page.

This project has been undertaken by the Foreign Area Materials Center, State Education Department, University of the State of New York, under the auspices of the Council for Intercultural Studies and Program, 60 East 42nd Street, New York, NY 10017.

IN MEMORY OF
EDITH EHRMAN
1932-1974

Straightway I was 'ware
So weeping, how a mystic shape did move
Behind me, and drew me backward by the hair
And a voice said in mastery while I strove, . . .
'Guess now who holds thee?—'Death', I said, but there
The silver answer rang . . . 'Not Death, but Love.'

Elizabeth Barrett Browning

Contents

Series Preface xi

Preface. xvii

Guide to Indian Philosophy 1

Name Index 133

Subject Index. 147

Series Preface

<u>Asian Philosophies and Religions and the Humanities in America</u>

This guide is one of a series of books on resources for the study of Asian philosophies and religions. The series includes volumes on Chinese, Indian, Islamic, and Buddhist philosophies and religions. Since the preparation of the series has been undertaken as a contribution to advancing humanistic learning in America, it is important to place the study of these traditions in that larger context.

Humanistic scholarship and teaching in America has understandably concentrated on Western civilization of which we are a part. Yet Western civilization has historically drawn significantly upon the humanistic accomplishments of other traditions and has interacted with these traditions. Given the increasing mobility of the scholars and students in the second half of the twentieth century and the rapidly advancing technological capacity of communicating ideas in the modern world, this interaction is accelerating as we approach the twenty-first century.

Liberal education for American students in the 1970's and 1980's must reflect not only our human heritage in all of its diversity as it has accumulated through past centuries, but also the nature of the future in its intellectual and cultural as well as economic, social and political dimensions. By the year 2000, a logical future reference point for today's college students who will spend most of their adult lives in the next century, four out of five human beings will live in the "Third World" of Asia, Africa, and Latin America about which we study least in our colleges and universities today.

Numerical distribution of humanity is certainly not the only criterion which should determine the content of humanistic learning in our institutions of higher education. But when orders of magnitude achieve the proportions which, according to most demographic projections, will exist in the year 2000, geographical location of humanity is certainly one criterion which will be applied by today's students in assessing the "relevance" of their undergraduate education to the real world of the future.

The argument becomes all the more compelling when the qualitative aspects of civilizations other than our own are considered. Western man can claim no corner on creative accomplishment, as Herbert Muller has rightly recognized in this passage from The Uses of the Past.

> Stick to Asia, and we get another elementary lesson in humility. Objectively its history looks more important than the history of Europe. . .It has produced more civilizations, involving a much greater proportion of mankind, over a longer period of time, on a higher level of continuity. As for cultural achievement, we have no universal yardstick; but by one standard on which Western Christendom has prided itself, Asia has been far more creative. It has bred all the higher religions, including Christianity.*

There is little doubt that the rapid growth of student interest in the study of these traditions is the result in part of their search for new value systems in contemporary society. But this interest is also a recognition of other civilizations as being intrinsically worthy of our attention.

Origins of the Project on Asian Philosophies and Religions

The project was initiated in response to this growth of student interest, which began in the 1960's and has persisted in the 1970's, notwithstanding a current general decline in the growth rates in American colleges and universities. Faculty members with specialized training in Asian philosophical and religious traditions, however, are still limited in number and most courses in these subjects are being taught by non-specialists. While the proportion of those with specialized training has certainly increased in recent years, the situation is unlikely to improve greatly due to the ceilings on faculty size which many institutions have imposed because of financial stringency.

The need for a series of authoritative guides to literature in these fields for use in both undergraduate and beginning graduate study of Asian philosophies and religions, which first prompted us to seek support from the National Endowment for the Humanities for the project in 1971, remains just as compelling as the project draws to a close.

Organization of the Project

The project on Asian philosophies and religions was conceived from the beginning as a cooperative venture involving scholars and

*The Uses of the Past, New York: New American Library, 1954, p. 314.

teachers of these subjects. The key element in the organization of the project has been the project team or working group, a deliberately informal structure with its own leader, working autonomously but within a general conceptual framework developed early in the project by all of those who were involved in the project at that time.

The individual working groups have been linked together by a project steering committee, which has been concerned with the overall organization and implementation of the project. The members of the project steering committee, working group leaders, and other key project personnel are as follows:

Kenneth Morgan, Emeritus, Colgate University (Chairman of the Project Steering Committee)

Wing-tsit Chan, Chatham College and Emeritus, Dartmouth College (Member, Project Steering Committee; Leader of Working Group on Chinese Philosophy and Religion)

Bardwell Smith, Carleton College (Member, Project Steering Committee and Working Group on Buddhist Religion)

H. Daniel Smith, Syracuse University (Member, Project Steering Committee and Working Group on Hinduism)

Robert McDermott, Baruch College, City University of New York (Member, Project Steering Committee and the Working Group on Hinduism)

Thomas Hopkins, Franklin and Marshall College (Leader of the Working Group on Hinduism)

David Ede, Western Michigan University and McGill University (Leader of the Working Group on Islamic Religion)

Karl Potter, University of Washington (Leader of the Working Group on Indian Philosophy)

Frank Reynolds, University of Chicago (Leader of the Working Group on Buddhist Religion)

Kenneth Inada, State University of New York at Buffalo (Leader of the Working Group on Buddhist Philosophy)

Frederick J. Streng, Southern Methodist University (Member, Project Steering Committee and Working Groups on Buddhist Religion and Philosophy)

David Dell (Project Manager, 1957-77 and a Member of the Working Group on Hinduism)

Two characteristics of the project's organization merit mention. One has been the widespread use of other scholars and teachers, in addition to the members of the project steering committee and working groups, in the critical review of preliminary versions of the guides. Reviewers were asked to comment on both commissions and omissions, and their comments were used by the compilers in making revisions. A far more extensive exercise than the customary scholarly review of manuscripts, this process involved well over 200 individuals who contributed immeasurably to improving the quality of the end product.

A similar effort to enlarge participation in the project has been made through discussions at professional meetings about the project among interested scholars and teachers while it was in progress. Over the past four years a dozen such sessions, involving over 300 participants, have been held at both national and regional meetings of the American Academy of Religion and the Association for Asian Studies.

The Problem of Availability of Resources in the Guide and the Microform Resource Bank

We realized from the beginning that a series of guides of this character would have little value if the users could not acquire materials listed in the guides. We therefore sought the cooperation of the Institute for the Advanced Studies of World Religions, which is engaged in a major effort to develop a collection of resources for the study of world religions in microform, and through the Institute, have established a microform resource bank of material in the guides not readily available from other sources.

Subject to the availability of the material for microfilming and depending upon its copyright status, the Institute is prepared to provide in microfilm any item included in any of the guides out-of-print or otherwise not readily available, in accordance with its usual schedule of charges. Where an item is already included in the Institute's microform collection, those charges are quite modest, and an effort is being made by the Institute to increase its holding of materials in the guides. Material can also be provided in hard xerographic copy suitable for reproduction for multiple classroom use at an additional charge.

Under the terms of a project agreement with the Institute, the Institute is undertaking the microfilming of some 30,000 pages of material included in these guides. In addition, the Institute already has in its microform collection a substantial number of titles in the fields of Buddhist and Chinese philosophy and religion.

The Institute will from time to time issue lists of material in microform from the guides available in its collections, but as its microform collections are continually being expanded, users are urged to contact the Institute directly to see if a particular title in which they are interested is available:

Series Preface

Institute for Advanced Studies of World Religions
Melville Memorial Library
State University of New York
Stony Brook, New York 11794

Acknowledgements

An undertaking of this scope and magnitude, involving such widespread participation, is bound to accumulate a long list of those who have contributed in one way or another to the project. It would be impossible to identify by name all of those who have contributed, and it is hoped that those who are not so identified will nonetheless recognize themselves in the categories which follow and understand that their help, interest, and support are also appreciated.

To begin with, primary thanks must be extended to the members of the project steering committee, the leaders of the various project working groups, and the members of each of the groups. Those responsible for each guide in the series are separately listed on the title page of that volume.

Thanks should also be expressed to the large number of scholars and teachers who served as critical reviewers of preliminary versions of the guides and the many who participated in sessions at regional and national meetings where the guides were subject to further scrutiny and where many constructive suggestions for their improvement were made.

We wish to acknowledge with grateful thanks the generous financial support of the National Endowment for the Humanities, and through its matching fund scheme, additional support from the Ada Howe Kent Foundation, C.T. Shen, and Council for International and Public Affairs, Inc. The patience and understanding of the Endowment's Education Division during the long and protracted period of completion of this project has been particularly noteworthy.

Many institutions have provided support to the project indirectly by making possible participation of their faculty in the various project working groups. In addition, both the South Asia Center at Columbia University and the Institute for Advanced Studies of World Religions have provided special assistance.

The project has been undertaken under the auspices of the Council for Intercultural Studies and Programs by the Foreign Area Materials Center, a project office of the Center for International Programs and Comparative Studies, State Education Department, University of the State of New York. The last-named institution, acting as the agent of the Council for Intercultural Studies and Programs, has been responsible for administering the National Endowment for Humanities grant and other financial support received for the project and has contributed extensively out of its own resources throughout the project, particularly in the concluding months, to assure its proper completion. Without the interest and support of key officials in the Center for International Programs and the New York State Education Department, the project could not have been completed.

A particular word of appreciation is in order for Norman Abramowitz of the Center, who succeeded me as Project Director after my resignation from the directorship of the Center in October, 1976 and to whom fell the unenviable task of overcoming administrative and financial obstacles in the final three years of the project. Appreciation should also be expressed to G.K. Hall and Company, the publishers of this series, and to its editorial staff. Their forebearance, as the manuscripts have been completed over a far longer time than we anticipated, has been exemplary.

Last but certainly not least are the project managers who have carried responsibility from day to day for implementing the project. Perhaps the most difficult and demanding role has been played by David J. Dell who came into the project at mid-stream and who struggled to assure its orderly completion. He and Edward Haynes have shared responsibility for final preparation of manuscripts for publication as editorial coordinators for the series, with the former handling two (Chinese Philosophy and Hindu Religion) and the latter, the remaining five titles in the series.

Different, but in many ways no less difficult, was the task confronting the interim project director, Josephine Case, whose services were kindly made available to the project by the New York Public Library in 1974 and 1975. She responded with dignity and sensitivity to the demands of this task.

But in many ways the most important figure in the project is one who is no longer with us. Edith Ehrman was the Manager of the Foreign Area Materials Center from its inception in 1963, a key figure in the conceptualization of this project, and its manager from the beginning until her untimely death in November, 1974. She was the moving spirit behind the project during its first three years. It is to her memory that this series of guides is dedicated by all those involved in the project who witnessed the extraordinary display of courage borne of her love of life during her last difficult illness.

Ward Morehouse, Chairman
Editorial and Publications Committee

Preface

By "Indian philosophy" in this volume we mainly intend the subject of bondage and liberation and the methods of gaining the latter. This basic orientation has been extended in a few ways. The range of what results can easily be seen by surveying the main subjects listed in the Subject Index. The reader will see that, in addition to standard philosophical topics such as epistemology, logic, metaphysics and ethics, works on aesthetics, philosophy of religion, and social, legal, and political philosophy, philosophy of history and education have been included.

A study of this sort becomes quickly dated. We have tried to survey works published up to 1985, and in one or two cases even more recently. There has been something of an emphasis placed on works published within the last ten years, as being both more easily available as well as providing improvements on work done previously.

Certain other conditions were placed on what is included, since the literature on these matters is vast. With rare exceptions, articles were only included if they were more than ten pages long. Everything listed involves some English exposition, although frequently an English interlaced with Sanskrit terms. We have attempted to include only works of philosophical (as opposed to religious, literary, etc.) relevance, although our conception of "philosophy" may not fit everyone's. We have tried to avoid listing publications that duplicate material found in other entries. Finally, however, we realize that many favorite works of readers may have been omitted, and we can only submit that this is our list, for better or worse.

To use this work most efficiently one should look at the Name Index if one is trying to find entries about or by a specific author, philosopher or work. There is also a subject index. The user should note that when seeking material on a given topic he should consult both entries listed under the relevant specific headings as well as under the more general headings within which the specific heading(s) fall. Thus, for example, if looking for works on substance one should also consider works listed under the more general "metaphysics" category.

Preface

The process that led to the production of this volume involved quite a few hands additional to those of the three editors mentioned. This volume has been in preparation for many years under varying administrative guidance. Under the circumstances it would be tendentious to pick out some of them by name. The present editorial team is not in a position now to know everyone who was involved, and it seems virtually impossible to reconstruct a list. We should like to extend heartfelt thanks to those who participated, and an apology that under the circumstances it does not seem possible to fairly specify individuals at this time.

Special thanks are due to Laura Townsend, who put in a large part of the drudgery required to produce this volume.

Guide to Indian Philosophy

1 Agrawal, Madan Mohan. "Origin and Development of the Doctrine of Difference and Nondifference." Philosophy East and West 32 (1982):46-64.
Reviews little-studied authors on the topic.

2 Agrawal, Madan Mohan. "Relation of Jīva and Brahman to the Philosophy of Nimbārka." Philosophy East and West 29 (1979):163-76.
A clear discussion of a difficult topic in an area underexamined by philosophers.

3 Akhilananda, Swami. Hindu Psychology: Its Meaning for the West. New York and London: Harpers, 1946, 241 pp.
Contains chapters on cognition, emotion, will, subconscious mind, sub- and superconscious experience, and extrasensory perception. A readable, nontechnical introduction to the topic.

4 Alper, Harvey P. "Śiva and the Ubiquity of Consciousness: The Speciousness of an Artful Yogi." Journal of Indian Philosophy 7 (1979):345-407.
A long but generally illuminating analysis. Alper argues that tantric Saivism, unlike many Vedāntas, accepts change as ultimately characterizing the world.

5 Ames, William L. "Buddhapālita's Exposition of the Mādhyamaka." Journal of Indian Philosophy 14 (1986):313-48.
Translations of selected passages from the first twenty-two chapters of the work (the rest, identical with the Akutobhayā commentary on Nāgārjuna's Kārikās, seems to be a different work).

6 Ames, William L. "Svabhāva in the Thought of Candrakīrti." Journal of Indian Philosophy 10 (1982):161-77.
Explains how Candrakīrti can consistently affirm, deny, and dismiss as nonsense the existence of any svabhāvas.

7 Amma, Visweswari. Udayana and His Philosophy. Delhi: Nag Publishers, 1985, xv + 200 pp.

A thorough review of what is known about the great medieval Nyāya philosopher. While breaking no new ground, this is a handy summary of knowledge to date.

8 Anacker, Stefan. Seven Works of Vasubandhu. Delhi: Motilal Banarsidass, 1984, x + 492 pp.

The definitive treatment of Vasubandhu and his works, this volume contains translations of Vādavidhi, Pañcaskandhaprakaraṇa, Karmasiddhiprakaraṇa, Viṃśatikā, Triṃśikā, Madhyāntavibhāgabhāṣya, and Trisvabhāvanirdeśa. The introduction clarifies historical and other scholarly problems about Vasubandhu, and the entire treatment is written with charm, even flair.

9 Anacker, Stefan. "Vasubandhu's Karmasiddhiprakaraṇa and the Problem of the Highest Meditations." Philosophy East and West 22 (1972):247-58.

The "problem is how, in the absence of a fixed entity self . . . one can account for the retribution of past acts. Vasubandhu's Yogācāra is finally as Śūnyavāda as is Nāgārjuna's Mādhyamika." Excellent analysis of Vaibhāṣikas, Vasubandhu on saṃtāna, memory, and attainment of highest meditations.

10 Anand, Kewal Krishna. Indian Philosophy (The Concept of Karma). Delhi: Bharatiya Vidya Prakashan, 1982, 396 pp.

This doctoral dissertation appears to be the most complete review of the theory of karma available. It covers all the classical philosophical systems, as well as the epics.

After a review of the different types of karma, the author concludes with a classification of important aspects of the theory and an estimate of its worth as a metaphysical system.

11 Ānandapūrṇa Vidyāsāgara. Ānandapūrṇa Vidyāsāgara, Nyāyacandrikā, with Svarūpānandamunīndra's Nyāyaprakāśikā. Edited by N.S. Anantakrishna Sastri and K. Ramaswami Sastri. Madras: Government Oriental Manuscripts Library, 1959, x + 148 + 80 + 563 + 118 + 15 pp.

A large part of this volume is taken up with an exhaustive bibliography of Advaita Vedānta by Anantakrishna Sastri covering every Advaitin anyone ever heard of. Concludes with a table of dates of Advaita and Dvaita disputants.

12 Anantharangachar, N.S. The Philosophy of Sādhana in Viśiṣṭādvaita. Mysore: University of Mysore, 1967, 304 pp.

A survey of Viśiṣṭādvaita thought following Vedānta Deśika's expositions, with chapters on the seeker (sādhaka), the goal (sādhya), and the path (sādhana); on karma-, jñāna-, and bhakti-yoga; and prapatti. Contains an appendix on epistemology. Because of its attention to detail, it is one of the most informative sources on Viśiṣṭādvaita presently available.

13 Anderson, Tyson. "Wittgenstein and Nāgārjuna's Paradox." Philosophy East and West 35 (1985):157-69.

Takes to task the tendency of recent writers to find analogies between Nāgārjuna and the later Wittgenstein. Makes the (startling?) point that the "two-truths" theory is incoherent and falls to Nāgārjuna's own critique. A better analogy is found with the conclusions of the Tractatus.

14 Annambhatta. Tarkasaṃgraha. Edited with Dīpikā and Govardhana's Nyāyabodhinī by Y.V. Athalye, and translated with English notes by M.R. Bodas. Bombay Sanskrit and Prakrit Series, no. 55, 1897. 2d ed., rev. and enl., 2d impression by A.D. Pusalker. Poona: R.N. Dandekar, 1963, lxiii + 384 pp.

The introduction (by Bodas) provides a historical survey of Indian logic. Athalye's copious notes to the editions are helpful, though hard to use for non-Sanskritists. Annambhaṭṭa's work is one of the most-studied beginners' handbooks on Nyāya-Vaiśeṣika.

15 Appadorai, Angadipuram. Political Ideas in Modern India: Impact of the West. Bombay: Academic Books, 1971, 111 pp.

A brief introduction to the main currents of thought on democracy, the state, and socialism in modern India.

16 Archer, J.C. "Śaṃkara and the Hindu One." Review of Religion 1 (1937):238-48.

Was Śaṃkara a monist? No! Well written, this article straightens out prevalent misconceptions.

17 Aronson, Harvey B. Love and Sympathy in Theravāda Buddhism. Delhi: Motilal Banarsidass, 1980, 127 pp.

Collects and analyzes Pāli canon (with Buddhaghoṣa's commentary) treatment of the concepts of love, sympathy, and the four "sublime attitudes" (brahmavihāras).

18 Arora, V.K. The Social and Political Philosophy of Swami Vivekananda. Calcutta: Punthi Pustak, 1968, xi & 134 pp.

A useful review of Vivekananda's perspective, although a critical assessment is absent.

19 Āryadeva. Catuḥśataka. Edited in Tibetan and translated by Karen Lang. Indiske studier, no. 7. Copenhagen: Akademisk Förlag, 1986, 208 pp.

A carefully argued introduction fixes Āryadeva's date between 225 and 250 A.D., shows which works Āryadeva wrote, and provides a helpful, brief summary of the work. The translation is supported with copious footnotes to assist understanding.

20 Aurobindo, Sri. The Human Cycle. Pondicherry: Sri Aurobindo Ashram, 1949, 334 pp. Reprint. New York: Sri Aurobindo Library, 1950, vii + 312 pp.

Essays written (and published in Ārya) between 1916 and 1918, which articulate Aurobindo's views on various issues pertaining to social existence and its ultimate context. (Also included in the volume entitled Social and Political Thought; see entry 21.)

21 Aurobindo, Sri. Social and Political Thought. Sri Aurobindo Birth Centenary Library, no. 15. Pondicherry: Sri Aurobindo Ashram, 1971, xix + 616 pp.

Contains articles originally published in the philosophical journal Ārya in the period from 1915 to 1920, subsequently published in book form as "The Human Cycle," "The Ideal of Human Unity," and "War and Self-Determination" (Pondicherry: Sri Aurobindo Ashram, 1962, 912 pp.). Earlier, in 1962, the Sri Aurobindo International Centre of Education published these three in one volume, which has been reprinted in the Centenary series.

22 Aurobindo, Sri. The Spirit and Form of Indian Polity. Calcutta: Arya Publishing House, 1947, 91 pp.

A defense of traditional polity, centering on the ideal of dharma. Originally appeared in his series "A Defense of Indian Culture," contra William Archer's articles in Ārya 1918-1921.

23 Bagchi, Sitansusekhar. Inductive Reasoning: A Study of Tarka and Its Role in Indian Logic. Calcutta: Sri Munishchandra Sinha, 1953, 312 pp.

Far and away the most exhaustive survey on an extremely interesting topic. Tarka or "reasoning" covers many of the methods used by philosophers in refuting opposing positions--for example, begging the question, infinite regress, simplicity. The work surveys the views of many classical writers in specific detail, especially those of the Nyāya and Dvaita Vedānta schools. No other effort comes close on this topic.

24 Baijnath, Bahadur Lal. "The Philosophy of Advaita." International Congress of Orientalists 11 (1897):99-142.

This traces the history of Vedānta from the Vedas and divides post-Śaṃkara Advaita into dṛṣṭisṛṣṭivāda (solipsists), bimbapratibimbavāda (reflectionists), avacchedyāvacchedakavāda (limitationists) and ajātivāda (no-causeists).

25 Balasubramanian, R. "Sureśvara." Journal of the Madras University (1968):105-47.

A study of the differences between Śaṃkara and his pupil Sureśvara in their writings on the Bṛhadāraṇyaka Upaniṣad and in Sureśvara's Naiṣkarmyasiddhi.

26 Balslev, Anindita Niyogi. A Study of Time in Indian Philosophy. Wiesbaden: Otto Harrassowitz, 1983, 172 pp.

A bit too brief to be able to fulfill the promise of the title, this study is nevertheless somewhat out of the ordinary in the texts surveyed and the aspects of the question distinguished.

27 Bandyopadhyay, Nandita. "The Buddhist Theory of Relation between Pramā and Pramāṇa." Journal of Indian Philosophy 7 (1979):43-78.

Although the Buddhist logicians are supposed to be unique in their identification of knowledge (pramā) and the means to it (pramāṇa), this paper argues that Sāṃkhya, Yoga, Advaita, some Mīmāṃsā, and even the Jain philosophers must admit identification; and that only the Nyāya-Vaiśeṣika insists that they are different.

28 Bandyopadhyay, Nandita. The Concept of Logical Fallacies: Problems of Hetvābhāsa in Navya-Nyāya in the Light of Gaṅgeśa and Raghunātha Siromaṇi. Calcutta: Sanskrit Pustak Bhandar, 1977, x + 206 pp.

Though somewhat disorganized, this volume should be helpful to students of Navya-Nyāya, especially those who wish to assess Raghunātha's contribution. Portions of text are quoted and translated, and there are helpful appendixes on Buddhist logic.

29 Bandyopadhyay, Nandita. "The Concept of Similarity in Indian Philosophy." Journal of Indian Philosophy 10 (1982):239-75.

A needed analysis of the notion of similarity (sādṛśya) as it is treated in the Nyāya-Vaiśeṣika and Mīmāṃsā, Alaṃkārika and Vaiyākaraṇa systems.

30 Bandyopadhyaya, Jayantanuja. Social and Political Thought of Gandhi. Bombay: Allied Publishers, 1969, 415 pp.

A substantial study, from a social-science vantage point, that gives attention to Gandhi's thought, analyzed in terms of the rubrics of ultimate values, social structure, and social control.

31 Banerjea, Krishna Mohan. Dialogues on the Hindu Philosophy. London: Williams and Norgate, 1861, 538 pp.

Dialogues between Satyakāma (truth-lover), Tarkakāma (logic-lover), and Āgamika (authoritarian)! Discussions range over the relevance of the Vedas, dharma, preexistence, saṃsāra, causation, God, creation, atomic theory, ethics, liberation, idealism, and māyā. Definitely usable for classes, the book provides a lively introduction to Indian philosophy.

32 Banerjee, Anukul Chandra. Sarvāstivāda Literature. Calcutta: Calcutta Oriental Press, 1957, vii + 271 pp.

Summaries of the basic Sarvāstivādin works--the Jñānaprasthāna, Vijñānakāya, etc.--as well as others, together with a thorough review of the history of the Buddhism of the period. Definitive study of the school.

33 Banerjee, Kali Krishna. "The Doctrine of Triple Negation in Neo-Nyāya Logic." In Logic, Ontology, and Action. Jadavpur Studies in Philosophy, no. 1. Delhi: Macmillan Co., 1979, pp. 146-94.

While early Nyāya holds that the absence of an absence is a positive entity, later or "new" Nyāya takes it to be a different absence. The new school views a triple absence as identical with the single absence. The reasons for this are explained in detail.

34 Banerjee, Kali Krishna. "Wittgenstein versus Naiyāyika." Calcutta Review 147 (1958):27-44.

Dialogue between them. An example of constructive comparison. May be a bit too long.

35 Banerjee, Nikunja Bihari. Glimpses of Indian Wisdom. New Delhi: Munshiram Manoharlal, 1972, 100 pp.

Chapter 3 asks, what is living and what dead in Advaita Vedānta: is liberation a relevant ideal now? Sensible thoughts by one of India's senior academic philosophers.

36 Barlingay, S.S. Beliefs, Reasons, and Reflections. Amalner: Indian Philosophical Quarterly Publications, 6, 1983, xii + 252 pp.

This collection of papers by a senior academic philosopher of contemporary India ranges through many topics, mostly logical and metaphysical, but with some exploration of value theory as well.

37 Barlingay, S.S. A Modern Introduction to Indian Logic. Delhi: National Publishing House, 1965, 238 pp.

A slightly disappointing attempt at a much-needed task. Chapters on history of logic, knowledge and language, judgments, propositions and functions, truth functions, definitions and upādhi, theory of negation, theory of sāmānya or jāti, logic of relations, theory of inference, inductive elements, symbols, formalized language, and metalanguage. Explanations are not always as clear or helpful as might be wished.

38 Basham, Arthur L. History and Doctrines of the Ājīvikas. London: Luzac, 1951, 304 pp.

The definitive account of a forgotten sect, usually described as fatalistic, which flourished about the time of the Buddha. Basham spends ample time expounding the Ājīvikas' philosophy, especially their notion of niyati (fate?), their cosmology, atomic theory, and attitudes toward the soul, the gods, and logic.

39 Basham, Arthur L. The Wonder That Was India: A Survey of the Indian Sub-Continent before the Coming of the Muslims. New York: Macmillan Co., 1954, xxiii + 568 pp. (Previously published by Grove Press, 1939; 3d ed. Taplinger, 1968.)

A useful review of social institutions and ideas is given in chapter 6 (pp. 137-88).

40 Bechert, Heinz. "Notes on the Formation of Buddhist Sects and the Origins of Mahāyāna." German Scholars in India. Vol. 1. Varanasi: Chowkhamba Sanskrit Series Office, 1973, pp. 6-18.

Insightful suggestions shedding beams of light on what went on in the early period of Buddhism.

41 Bedekar, D.K. "Revelatory Character of Hindu Epistemology." Annals of the Bhandarkar Oriental Research Institute 28 (1949):64-84.

Looks for understanding of the authority of revealed knowledge in magical practices. Thoughtful, innovative; emphasizes disparity between assumptions of Indian and Western philosophy.

42 Bedekar, V.M. "The Development of the Sāṃkhya and the Problem of the Ṣaṣṭitantra." Journal of the University of Poona 11 (1959):37-49.

Summarizes the influential work of Erich Frauwallner on the history of Sāṃkhya, especially the lost work called Ṣaṣṭitantra, which presumably expounded the essential form of the classical Sāṃkhya system.

43 Bedekar, V.M., ed. Philosophy in the Fifteen Modern Indian Languages. Pune: Continental Prakashan, 1979, xix + 342 pp.

Filling an evident gap, this volume helps those who cannot read all fifteen of the modern Indian languages (which is just about everyone) to understand what philosophers writing in those languages are saying.

44 Behanan, Kovoor T. Yoga: A Scientific Evaluation. New York: Dover, 1959, 27 pp. (Orig. pub. 1937.)

A dispassionate appraisal of Yoga from a psychological standpoint. Readers not used to Indian methods of exposition may appreciate this author's approach. The book covers essentials of Sāṃkhya philosophy, rebirth, yogic practices (breathing, postures, concentration), and draws comparisons with psychoanalysis and psychic research.

45 Belvalkar, S.K. Vedānta Philosophy. Poona: Bilvakunja Publishing House, 1929, xv + 240 pp.

Part. 1, Lectures 1-6 pertain to Vedānta in the Upaniṣads, the Bhagavadgītā, the Brahmasūtras, pre-Śaṃkara Vedānta, and Śaṃkara's life and times. Last lecture has extensive discussion of the authenticity of works traditionally ascribed to Śaṃkara.

46 Belvalkar, S.K., and R.D. Ranade. History of Indian Philosophy. Vol. 2, The Creative Period. Poona: Bilvakunja, 1927, xxxix + 512 pp. Reprint. New Delhi: Oriental Books Reprint Corp., 1972.

Detailed coverage of the philosophy of the Brāhmaṇas and early Upaniṣads.

47 Betty, L. Stafford. "Nāgārjuna's Masterpiece--Logical, Mystical, Both, or Neither?" Philosophy East and West 33 (1983):123-38.

Betty's position is that Nāgārjuna's Mādhyamakakārikās "'undercut themselves' and are therefore not philosophically cogent." Rather, "they are like a fabulous picture without a wall to hang on." Far from decrying Nāgārjuna's contribution, Betty's effort is to do justice to it. He launches telling attacks in the direction of many respected scholars.

48 Bhaduri, Sadananda. Studies in Nyāya-Vaiśeṣika Metaphysics. Poona: Bhandarkar Oriental Research Institute, 1947, xvi + 331 pp.

A philosophically insightful account of Vaiśeṣika ontology, which clarifies many obscure points about the theory without using Sanskrit terms. An outstanding but little-known piece of research.

49 Bhandarkar, R.G. "The Sāṃkhya Philosophy." Indian Philosophical Review 2 (1919):193-209. Reprinted in Collected Works of R.G. Bhandarkar, vol. 1 (Poona: Bhandarkar Oriental Research Institute, 1933), pp. 62-78.

Compares Sāṃkhya's "idealism" with that of Buddhism and Fichte.

50 Bharadwaja, V.K. "The Jaina Concept of Logic." Indian Philosophical Quarterly 9 (July 1982):363-75.

The Jain theories of instruments of knowledge (pramāṇas), aspects (nayas), and sevenfold predication (saptabhaṅgī or syādvāda) have different areas of operation and do different jobs. Bharadwaja uses this insight in criticizing Matilal's attempts to defend Jain logic.

51 Bharadwaja, V.K. "Rationality, Argumentation, and Embarrassment: A Study of Four Logical Alternatives (catuṣkoṭi) in Buddhist Logic." Philosophy East and West 14 (July 1984):303-19.

"However embarrassing it might be to the philosophers, neither formal logic nor the methodology of empirical knowledge can be said to be relevant for an adequate understanding of the so-called problem of the catuṣkoṭi."

52 Bharadwaja, V.K. "A Theory of Tarka Sentence." Philosophy and Phenomenological Research 41 (1980-81):532-46.

This interesting piece argues that reductio-ad-absurdum (tarka) -type arguments have nothing to do with vyāpti, despite the attempts by some Nyāya logicians to utilize them that way.

53 Bharati, Agehananda. A Functional Analysis of Indian Thought and Its Social Margins. Chowkhamba Sanskrit Studies, no. 37. Varanasi: Chowkhambe Sanskrit Series Office, 1964, 175 pp.

Lessons in how to study Indian thought and practice, by a remarkable critic (see his autobiography, The Ochre Robe [New York: Doubleday, 1970]). The work is generally about Indian philosophy, though the last two chapters consider the place of nature in Indian poetics and the place of woman in Indian thought. The author is full of iconoclastic ideas that the reader may not find acceptable, but they keep the book unfailingly interesting and challenging.

54 Bhartiya, Mahesh Chandra. Causation in Indian Philosophy (with Special Reference to Nyāya-Vaiśeṣika). Ghaziabad: Vimal Prakashan, 1973, xiii + 297 pp.

Doctoral dissertation bringing together the views of many Indian systems on causality.

55 Bhartṛhari. Vākyapadīya. Translated by K.A. Subramania Iyer. Chapter 1, with the Vṛtti, Poona: Deccan College Postgraduate and Research Institute, 1965, xl + 136 pp. Chapter 2, with notes based on the Vṛtti and on Puṇyarāja's commentary, Delhi: Motilal Banarsidass, 1977, li + 205 pp. Chapter 3, Part 1, with notes based on Helārāja's Prakāśa, Poona: Deccan College Postgraduate and Research Institute, 1971, x + 243 pp. Chapter 3, Part 2, with notes based on Helārāja's Prakāśa, Delhi: Motilal Banarsidass, 1974, xiii + 412 pp.

Finally we have a complete translation of Bhartṛhari's great work, thanks to the lifetime application of Professor Subramania Iyer, who has also published the complete text elsewhere. Now it remains to make sense out of this vast piece of grammatico-philosophical analysis, a job that will take several more lifetimes, one suspects.

56 Bhatia, Kamala, and Baldev Bhatia. The Philosophical and Sociological Foundations of Education. Delhi: Doaba House, 1974, xv + 275 pp.

An eclectic review of a number of perspectives and problems. The chapter on "The Gandhian Philosophy of Education" (pp. 55-82) briefly surveys Gandhi's position and notes various criticisms that have been raised.

57 Bhatt, G.H. "The System of Vallabhācārya." In The Cultural Heritage of India. Vol. 3, The Philosophical Systems. 1st ed. Calcutta: Ramakrishna Mission Institute of Culture, 1937, pp. 597-608.

A technical but solid account of this system, probably the best brief description available.

58 Bhatt, Govardhan P. Epistemology of the Bhāṭṭa School of Pūrva Mīmāṃsā. Chowkhamba Sanskrit Series, no. 17. Varanasi: Chowkhamba Sanskrit Series Office, 1962, 436 pp.

Probably the most thorough treatment of Mīmāṃsā theory of knowledge. Bhatt's approach is noteworthy for the attention given to the arguments offered by Mīmāṃsakas, especially Prabhākara and Kumārila, for their various views.

59 Bhattacharya, A. "Brahman and the World." Journal of the Department of Letters, University of Calcutta 28 (1935): 100 pp.

A book-length monograph exploring the relation of Brahman to the world as expounded in Advaita, Viśiṣṭādvaita, Bhāskara, and Nimbārka.

60 Bhattacharya, A.C. Sri Aurobindo and Bergson: A Synthetic Study. Varanasi: Jagabandhu Prakashan, 1972, xx + 282 pp.

An interesting comparison. The writer concludes by defending his two philosophers from various charges of confusion.

61 Bhattacharya, Ashutosh. Studies in Post-Śaṃkara Dialectics. Calcutta: University of Calcutta, 1936, 322 pp.

Explores the most intricate parts of post-Śaṃkara Advaita epistemology, especially as found in such works as Citsukhī, Khaṇḍanakhaṇḍakhādya, and Advaitasiddhi. The literature surveyed is technical and difficult, but philosophers may find this one of the most important resources on Advaita, since it deals with the system in its fully matured form.

62 Bhattacharya, B.P. "A Peep into the Later Buddhism." Annals of the Bhandarkar Oriental Research Institute 10 (1930):1-24.

An attempt to identify factors which led to the decline of Buddhism--the idea of bliss as a property of nirvāna; the strictness of monastic rules, which produced an inevitable reaction; the theory of the Bodhisattva's compassion, which was too much for the masses and provided an excuse for immorality; and the Indian fondness for magic.

63 Bhattacharya, Candrodaya. "Transcendental Consciousness in the Philosophy of Samkara." Journal of the Indian Academy of Philosophy 1 (1961-62):89-112.

A serious, difficult, long paper on an important problem.

64 Bhattacharya, Dinesh Chandra. History of Navya-Nyāya in Mithila. Darbhanga: Mithila Institute of Post-Graduate Studies and Research, 1958, viii + 205 pp.

A valuable piece of historical scholarship, with little philosophical analysis, although a number of works are summarized.

65 Bhattacharya, Dinesh Chandra. "Yoga Psychology of Patañjali and Some Other Aspects of Indian Psychology." Our Heritage 26, no. 2 (1978):30, no. 2 (1982):100 pp.

These intelligent accounts span a variety of topics in Indian psychological theory, including sections on the unconscious, emotions, intuition, Āyurveda, dreams, error, education, and pleasure. The result is a small book on classical Indian psychology, by no means restricted to Yoga.

66 Bhattacharya, Gaurinath. "A Study in the Dialectics of Sphoṭa." Journal of the Department of Letters, University of Calcutta 29 (1937):115 pp.

Bhartṛhari's theory of sphoṭa expounded at length, with appropriate comparisons to other systems.

67 Bhattacharya, Gopikamohan. Navya Nyāya: Some Logical Problems in Historical Perspective. Delhi: Bharatiya Vidya Prakashan, 1978, xii + 113 pp.

A collection of the late Dr. Bhattacharya's papers on Navya-Nyāya. He presents one of the most readable approaches to a difficult system.

68 Bhattacharya, Gopikamohan. Studies in Nyāya-Vaiśeṣika Theism. Calcutta Sanskrit College Research Series, no. 14. Calcutta: Sanskrit College, 1961, 170 pp.

A study of arguments for and against the existence of God, closely following Udayana's Nyāyakusumāñjali, but ranging over many Indian systems. It may be partly superseded by Chemparathy (see entry 153).

69 Bhattacharya, Hari Mohan. "The Jaina Conception of Truth." Philosophical Quarterly 3 (1927):201-16.

Covers the subject given in the title.

70 Bhattacharya, Hari Satya. Reals in the Jaina Metaphysics. Bombay: Seth Santi Das Khetsy Charitable Trust, 1966, 412 pp.

Contains chapters on the problem of reals and the principles of motion, rest, space, time, matter, and soul. The last two chapters are the longest, and the final section offers a thorough review of the theories of each and every Indian school on the question of the omniscience of the self and its relation to liberation.

71 Bhattacharya, Janakivallabha. Negation. Indian Studies Past and Present, 6. Calcutta: Indian Studies Past and Present, 1965, 168 pp.

Lengthy study of negation in all the systems, with detailed attention to individual philosophers. Doesn't spare the reader any technicalities, but is more faithful to the texts than other books on the subject.

72 Bhattacharya, Janakivallabha. "Vācaspati Miśra's Misinterpretation of the Sāṃkhya Theory of Perception." Sri Venkatesvara University Oriental Journal 8 (1965):9-20.

Vācaspati assimilates Sāṃkhya philosophy toward Nyāya-Vaiśeṣika, but it is really very different. The point has been noticed by other scholars, but this is a helpful exposition of it.

73 Bhattacharya, Kalidas. "Classical Philosophies of India and the West." Philosophy East and West 8 (1958):17-36.
A very general overview, but thought-provoking and containing excellent insights; this could well be used as an introductory essay for many kinds of courses.

74 Bhattacharya, Kalidas. "Concept of Cause as in India and the West." Our Heritage 1 (1953):30-45, 163-92; 2 (1954):111-42.
One of the best publications on theories of causation in Indian philosophy.

75 Bhattacharya, Kalidas. Gopinath Kaviraj's Thoughts--Towards a Systematic Study. Calcutta: University of Calcutta, 1982, 176 pp.
Both Bhattacharya and Kaviraj are important recent philosophers of India, and the effort by the former to explain the not always clear thoughts of the latter provides a valuable insight into contemporary philosophy, developed in an original way. In addition, Kaviraj's philosophy is perhaps the most important contribution of Saivism to recent thought in India.

76 Bhattacharya, Kalidas. "The Indian Concepts of Knowledge and Self." Our Heritage 2 (1954):221-48; 3 (1955):20-63, 181-210; 4 (1956):21-50, 177-216.
Fine analysis of epistemologies of most major systems by one of India's most original contemporary philosophers and one of its most acute scholars.

77 Bhattacharya, Kalidas. On the Concepts of Relation and Negation in Indian Philosophy. Calcutta Sanskrit College Research Series, no. 109. Calcutta: Sanskrit College, 1977, 45 pp.
These are invaluable, though all too brief, treasures of analysis by the late master philosopher. Mostly the attention is to Nyāya categories and distinctions, analyzed in graceful, clear, but by no means simplistic exposition.

78 Bhattacharya, Kalidas. "The Status of the Individual in Indian Philosophy." Philosophy East and West 14 (1964): 131-44. Reprinted in The Indian Mind, ed. Charles A. Moore (Honolulu: University of Hawaii Press, 1967), pp. 299-319. Also reprinted in The Status of the Individual in East and West, ed. Charles A. Moore (Honolulu: University of Hawaii Press, 1968), pp. 47-64.
This article is filled with interesting questions and answers as the author tries to clarify common confusions about

Indian attitudes towards individuals, freedom of the will, and related matters.

79 Bhattacharya, Kalidas. "Studies in Comparative Indian Philosophy." Bulletin of the Ramakrishna Mission Institute of Culture 32 (1981):7, 27, 59, 83, 107, 133, 152, 174, 200, 230.

A series of lectures that neatly divides all Indian philosophers into naturalists or transcendentalists, argues that these systems "are all basically different accounts of the final essence of man," and that to try to refute a detail of one from the standpoint of another is "no refutation at all, unless with the refutation of any such detail the whole system is meant to be refuted."

80 Bhattacharya, Kalidas. "Towards a Systematic Study of Gandhian Thought." Visvabharati Quarterly 44, no. 1-2 (1978):47-100.

Famous modern philosopher's assessment of Gandhi's views.

81 Bhattacharya, Kamaleswar. "Nāgārjuna's Arguments against Motion." Journal of the International Association of Buddhist Studies 8, no. 1 (1985):7-16.

What exactly is the argument against motion that Nāgārjuna offers in the second chapter of his Mādhyamakakārikās? Bhattacharya provides a clear explanation, basing himself on Candrakīrti and criticizing other interpretations.

82 Bhattacharya, Karuna. "Śaṃkara's Criticism of Nāgārjuna." Journal of the Indian Academy of Philosophy 1 (1961-62): 53-65.

Studies passages in Brahmasūtrabhāṣya, of interest because of recurrent suggestions that Śaṃkara owes much of his inspiration to Buddhist thought.

83 Bhattacharya, Krishna Chandra. "Studies in Sāṃkhya Philosophy." In Studies in Philosophy. Vol. 1. Calcutta: Progressive Publishers, 1956, pp. 127-214.

A solid, technical, but highly important, analysis by the teacher of many of India's most important professional philosophers.

84 Bhattacharya, Krishna Chandra. "Studies in Vedantism." In Studies in Philosophy. Vol. 1. Calcutta: Progressive Publishers, 1956, pp. 1-92.

1. Approach through psychology. 2. Vedāntic metaphysics. 3. Vedāntic logic. Among the more critical assessments of Vedānta, important for its comparisons of Vedānta with kindred systems such as Sāṃkhya and Yoga. Should be read together with entries 83 and 85.

85 Bhattacharya, Krishna Chandra. "Studies in Yoga Philosophy." In Studies in Philosophy. Vol. 1. Calcutta: Progressive Publishers, 1956, pp. 215-38.

Despite this writer's tortured style, this piece provides the most penetrating account of the Yoga system ever written in English, and makes incisive contributions to its understanding. It is "must" reading for any serious scholar of Pātañjala Yoga philosophy.

86 Bhattacharya, Narendra Nath. History of Researches in Indian Buddhism. New Delhi: Munshiram Manoharlal Publishers Private, 1981, 239 pp.

Like our study, this attempts to pick out the more important publications. However, it goes well beyond philosophy and considers only monographs, not articles, in its purview.

87 Bhattacharya, Narendra Nath. History of the Tantric Religion. New Delhi: Manohar, 1982, xviii + 507 pp.

An exhaustive survey of Tantric literature, in Buddhism as well as Hinduism. There are also comparisons of Tantra with Vaiṣṇava, Śaiva and other religious sects, and a chapter on Tantric art.

88 Bhattacharya, Tarasankar. The Nature of Vyāpti according to the Navya-Nyāya. Calcutta: Sanskrit College, 1970, 306 pp.

This work explores the knottiest philosophical literature of India, dealing with the definitions of pervasion (vyāpti) discussed by Gaṅgeśa and expanded with infinite variety by other Navya-naiyāyikas.

89 Bhattacharya, U.C. "A Neglected School of Vedānta." Philosophical Quarterly 6 (1930):191-219.

The "neglected school" is that of Vijñānabhikṣu, whose philosophy is expounded here.

90 Bhattacharya, Vidhusekhara, trans. The Āgamaśāstra of Gauḍapāda. Calcutta: University of Calcutta, 1943, cxlvi + 308 pp.

The standard translation.

91 Bhattacharya, Vidhusekhara. The Basic Conception of Buddhism. Calcutta: University of Calcutta, 1934, x + 103 pp.

I have not been able to see this book, but judging from the literature it has provoked it should be among those consulted by scholars of Buddhist philosophy who are eager for "a bit of action."

92 Bhattacharya, Vidhusekhara. "The Māṇḍūkya Upanishad and the Gauḍapāda Kārikā." Indian Historical Quarterly 1 (1925):116-25, 295-302.

A provocative argument that the Māṇḍūkya Upaniṣad is based on Gauḍapāda and thus is later than him.

93 Bhave, Vinobha. Swaraj Śāstra: The Principles of a Nonviolent Social Order. Translated by Bharatan Kumarappa. 2d ed. Wardha: Akhil Bharat, 1955, 95 pp.

In pamphlet form, many of the refrains of the sarvodaya approach to politics are outlined in this early (1942) statement, written during imprisonment.

94 Biderman, Shlomo. "A 'Constitutive' God--an Indian Suggestion." Philosophy East and West 32 (1982):425-37.

Utilizing the contemporary distinction between constitutive and regulative rules, Biderman seeks to justify Saṃkara's thesis that God created the world in play (līlā). He argues that God is bound by the constitutive rules of creation, that this solves the problem of evil and fits Saṃkara's views about the authority of scripture.

95 Bishop, Donald H., ed. Thinkers of the Indian Renaissance. New Delhi: Wiley Eastern, 1982, xii + 408 pp.

Besides the standard figures surveyed in such books, one finds here treatments of Keshub Chunder Sen, Dayananda Saraswati, Annie Besant, M.N. Roy, and J. Krishnamurti. A lively group of contemporary Indian scholars help the editor get a grasp on this array of no less than nineteen different philosophers of the past two centuries.

96 Biswas, Sri Bijan. "Some Reflections on Sāmānyalakṣaṇa pratyakṣa." Our Heritage 30, no. 2 (1982):61-84; 31, no. 1 (1983):35-40.

Nyāya posits an extraordinary type of perception by which one can cognize all members of a class in virtue of cognizing by normal means (such as perception) the universal feature common to those members. That is, by being aware of the property of potness we also are aware, by this extraordinary perception, of all pots past, present and future. The present paper ranges over a wide and unstudied range of material dealing with this kind of perception.

97 Blackwood, R.T., and A.L. Herman, eds. Problems in Philosophy West and East. Englewood Cliffs, N.J.: Prentice-Hall, 1975, xvi + 474 pp.

A standard introductory textbook in philosophy, of the anthology variety. The difference is that the selections range around the world rather than, as is customary, being confined to the Western hemisphere. Selections include both segments of translations from Indian texts and sections of writings about Indian philosophy.

98 Bochenski, I.M. A History of Formal Logic. New York: Chelsea, 1970, xxii + 567 pp. (Orig. pub. University of Notre Dame Press, 1961.)

For once, an important book on the history of logic takes account of Indian contributions to the subject. A chapter toward the conclusion provides a sketchy account, and some interesting observations by this famous scholar.

99 Bodhi, Bhikkhu. "Aggregates and Clinging Aggregates (Khandha/Upādānakkhanda)." Pali Buddhist Review 1 (1976):91-102.

Carefully explains Abhidharma views about "clinging" (upādāna). Is even the arhat composed of clinging aggregates? Yes, since they can be desired by others, and even for the arhat in comparison with his blissful state in phalasamāpatti and in nirvāṇa-without-residue (anupadiśeṣa).

100 Bond, George D. "The Development and Elaboration of the Arahant Ideal in the Theravāda Buddhist Tradition." Journal of the American Academy of Religion 52 (1984):227-42.

"The arahant concept seems to have developed from an ideal readily attainable in this life . . . into an ideal remote and impossible to achieve in one or even many lifetimes."

101 Bond, George D. "Theravāda Buddhism's Meditations on Death and the Symbolism of Initiatory Death." History of Religions 19 (1980):237-58.

Argues "that the meditations on death" in Abhidharma Buddhism "parallel and are analogous to the symbolism of initiatory death in archaic and primitive religions." In Theravāda death at once represents "the essence of the human predicament and a primary solution to this predicament."

102 Bondurant, Joan V. Conquest of Violence: The Gandhian Philosophy of Conflict. Berkeley and Los Angeles: University of California Press, 1965, xxxiii + 271 pp. (Orig. pub. Princeton University Press, 1958.)

A study that is both historical and analytic of the Gandhian technique of social change, with some comparative attention to figures and issues in Western political theory.

103 Bondurant, Joan V. "Traditional Polity and the Dynamics of Change in India." Human Organization 22 (1963):5-10.

An analysis of the concept of dharma, suggesting that Indian polity, when properly understood, is oriented toward change. Many students of dharma will question elements of this interpretation.

104 Bos, Mike. "After the Rise of Knowledge (Some Remarks Concerning Śaṃkara's Views on Jīvanmukti)." Wiener Zeitschrift für die Kunde Südasien 27 (1983):165-84.

Śaṃkara is known for saying that when knowledge arises liberation immediately ensues, but there are passages where he admits that a trace of ignorance persists and that liberation only comes at death. Bos considers passages of the latter sort. Passages of both sorts appear in the Brahmasūtrabhāṣya as well as the Bṛhadāraṇyakopaniṣadbhāṣya.

105 Brahmachari, Mahanama Brata. Vaiṣṇava Vedānta (The Philosophy of Sri Jīva Gosvāmi). Calcutta: Ḍas Gupta & Co., 1974, xxi + 240 pp.
Jīva Gosvāmi is one of the three great devotional philosophers of the 16th century who spread Caitanya's tradition throughout northern India. Though a bit wordy and inspirational, this study helps bring the Vaiṣṇava philosophy into the awareness of Western readers.

106 Bronkhorst, Johannes. "God in Sāṃkhya." Wiener Zeitschrift für die Kunde Südasien 27 (1983):149-64.
Sāṃkhya was theistic until the end of the first millenium A.D.

107 Bronkhorst, Johannes. "Nāgārjuna and the Naiyāyikas." Journal of Indian Philosophy 13 (1985):107-32.
The Nyāyasūtras must have antedated Nāgārjuna, since he knows them, as Bronkhorst demonstrates. It is also shown that Nyāya got the important notion that only one mental act at a time can occur in one person from Sarvāstivāda.

108 Bronkhorst, Johannes. "Yoga and Seśvara Sāṃkhya." Journal of Indian Philosophy 9 (1981):309-20.
If the evidence mustered here is correct, "we must conclude that there never was a separate Yoga philosophy." Yoga meant "one form of Sāṃkhya philosophy, owing to Saṃkara's incorrect understanding of some Brahmasūtras." Sāṃkhya with God (seśvara) seems to be the view of Pāñcarātra.

109 Brooks, Richard. "The Meaning of 'Real' in Advaita Vedānta." Philosophy East and West 19 (1969):385-98.
Clarifies definitions of "real" and "unreal" in Advaita, levels of reality, and significance of these distinctions for the system.

110 Brown, D. Mackenzie. The Nationalist Movement: Indian Political Thought from Ranade to Bhave. Berkeley and Los Angeles: University of California Press, 1970, x + 244 pp.
Modern Indian leaders who are reflective in their approaches to political life are introduced through short representative statements.

111 Brown, D. Mackenzie. "The Philosophy of Bal Gangadhar Tilak. Karma vs. Jñāna in the Gītā Rahasya." Journal of Asian Studies 17 (1958):197-206.
A brief introduction which sets the context for Bal Gangadhar Tilak's major work, presenting salient aspects of his contribution to the modern interpretation of the Gītā.

112 Brown, D. Mackenzie. The White Umbrella--Indian Political Thought from Manu to Gandhi. Berkeley and Los Angeles: University of California Press, 1953, xv + 205 pp.

A basic tool, ably providing "a concise survey of Hindu political ideas" by means of short introductions and excerpts from ancient texts and modern leaders.

113 Brown, W. Norman. Man in the Universe: Some Continuities in Indian Thought. Berkeley and Los Angeles: University of California Press, 1966, xi + 112 pp.

Chapter 3 ("Time Is a Noose") provides a short treatment of texts and ideas in traditional India concerning mundane existence; other portions of the book are indirectly relevant to issues of historical life.

114 Bucknell, Rod. "The Buddhist Path to Liberation: An Analysis of the Listing of Stages." Journal of the International Association of Buddhist Studies 7, no. 2 (1984):7-40.

The "noble eightfold path" is "but one of several differently worded statements of Gotama's course of practice leading to liberation." Between forty and fifty other such courses are discoverable in the Suttapitaka alone. Five such lists are compared.

115 Budhananda, Swami. "Ethical and Spiritual Values as the Basis for National Integration of India." Vedānta Kesarī 54 (1968):387-92, 437-42.

A plea for the grounding of modern development in the traditional priority for spiritual values.

116 Buhler, G., trans. The Laws of Manu. Sacred Books of the East, no. 25. Delhi: Motilal Banarsidass, 1964, cxxviii + 620 pp. (Orig. pub. Oxford: Clarendon Press, 1886.)

Manu is a code rather than a philosophical treatise, but the work is of monumental importance in Indian history as an expression of Hindu social philosophy. A student of Indian social history should also attend to other legal treatises, although Manu is preeminent.

117 Bulcke, Camille, S.J. The Theism of Nyāya-Vaiśeṣika: Its Origin and Early Development. Delhi: Motilal Banarsidass, 1968, 58 pp. (Orig. pub. Calcutta, 1947.)

A study of the few Nyāyasūtras which may have theistic implications. Chapter 8 poses the tension between karma theory and theism, and explores Uddyotakara's and Vācaspati's attempts at a solution.

118 Cairns, Grace E. "Aurobindo's Conception of the Nature and Meaning of History." International Philosophical Quarterly 12 (1972):205-19.

A review of the major aspects and categories of Aurobindo's view of history, in the context of his metaphysics. A concluding section notes some Western parallels.

119 Cairns, Grace E., and T.M.P. Mahadevan, eds. Contemporary Indian Philosophers of History. Calcutta: World Press Private, 1977, x + 311 pp.

Philosophy of Indian history is relatively unexplored. This volume brings the thinking of a number of well-known present-day Indian philosophers to the subject, including Kalidas Bhattacharya, D.M. Datta, A.G. Javadekar, T.M.P. Mahadevan, B.K. Matilal, J.N. Mohanty, N.A. Nikam, S.K. Saksena, and Dhirendra Sharma.

120 Cairns, Grace E. Philosophies of History: Meeting of East and West in Cycle-Pattern Theories of History. Westport, Conn.: Greenwood, 1971, xxiii + 496 pp. (Orig. pub. New York: Philosophical Library and Citadel Press, 1962.)

Part 1 includes treatment of classical Indian "recurrent cosmic cycle" perspectives, and Part 2 examines the views of Aurobindo and Radhakrishnan as contemporary "one-cycle patterns." As noted in the subtitle, various Western positions on historical cycles are also examined.

121 Cairns, Grace E. "Social Progress and Holism in T.M.P. Mahadevan's Philosophy of History." Philosophy East and West 20 (1970):73-82.

An exploration of the emergence of views of social progress in modern Indian thought, as in Mahadevan's "spiritually oriented holistic philosophy."

122 Cairns, Grace E. "Time, Eternity, and Social Progress in the Advaita Vedānta of T.M.P. Mahadevan." Darshana International 8 (July 1968):64-68.

A brief examination of Mahadevan's continuity with and expansion of Śaṃkara's perspective. Principal attention is to the yuga theory.

123 Candragomin. Difficult Beginnings: Three Works on the Bodhisattva Path. Translated, with commentary, by Mark Tatz. Boston: Shambhala, 1985, 121 pp.

Translation of Candragomin's Bodhisattvasaṃvaraviṃśaka from the Tibetan of Candragomipraṇidhāna and Deśanastava, with Buddhaśānti's Vṛtti on the last.

124 Cardona, George. "On Reasoning from Anvaya and Vyatireka in Early Advaita." In Studies in Indian Philosophy. A Memorial Volume in Honour of Pandit Sukhalalji Sanghvi, edited by Nagin J. Shah. L.D. Series, 84. [Ahmedabad, 1981], pp. 79-104.

A vigorous argument defending Śaṃkara's use of the arguments from presence (anvaya) and absence (vyatireka) against alleged misinterpretations of it by Hacker, Van Buitenen, and Mayeda.

125 Carman, John Bransted. The Theology of Rāmānuja: An Essay in Interreligious Understanding. New Haven: Yale University Press, 1974, xi + 333 pp.

An expanded version of Carman's doctoral thesis. There is a helpful summary of Rāmānuja's life and writings, followed by an extended study of Rāmānuja's contribution to religion and his relation to his successors. Beautifully written, this is one of the first pieces Rāmānuja-seekers should read.

126 Casey, David F. "Nāgārjuna and Candrakīrti--A Study of Significant Differences." Transactions of the International Conference of Orientalists in Japan 9 (1964):34-45.

An excellent review of scholarship on the Mādhyamikakārikās of Nāgārjuna, and its most famous interpretation.

127 Chakrabarti, A. "Is Liberation (Mokṣa) Pleasant?" Philosophy East and West 33 (1983):167-82.

A careful analysis of the question whether the liberated self enjoys happiness or not. The author concludes that practically happiness should not be sought, but leaves open the question of whether liberation involves feelings.

128 Chakraborty, Nirod Baran. The Advaita Concept of Falsity--A Critical Study. Calcutta: Sanskrit College, 1967, xvi + 90 pp.

Discusses the concept of falsity, why and how far it is necessary for the Advaita Vedānta. Chakraborty takes up Rāmānuja's criticisms seriatim and reviews different definitions of falsity found in later Advaita. The final chapter discusses the falsity of falsity!

129 Chakravarti, Appaswami. "Jainism, Its Philosophy and Ethics." In The Cultural Heritage of India. Vol. 3, The Philosophical Systems. 1st ed. Calcutta: Ramakrishna Mission Institute of Culture, 1937, pp. 414-33.

A helpful summary of Jain philosophy.

130 Chakravarti, P.C. The Linguistic Speculations of the Hindus. Calcutta: University of Calcutta, 1933, 496 pp.

This work covers a wider spectrum than the author's The Philosophy of Sanskrit Grammar. It includes chapters on philosophy of language, origin of speech, evolution of sound, sentence, parts of speech, division and denotation of words, roots, the Sanskrit language, Prakrit and Apabhraṃśa, sound and sense, history of word and meaning, and logic and language, and brings together many and varied textual authorities.

131 Chakravarti, P.C. The Philosophy of Sanskrit Grammar. Calcutta: University of Calcutta, 1930, 344 pp.

A sound survey of the subject, with chapters on the evolution of Sanskrit grammar, technical notions of Pāṇini's system, sphoṭa, sentences and parts of speech, kāraka, compounds, and grammar in Mīmāṃsā, Nyāya, and Ālaṃkāra.

132 Chakravarti, Pulinbihari. Origin and Development of the Sāṃkhya System of Thought. Calcutta Sanskrit Series, no. 30. Calcutta: Metropolitan Printing and Publishing House, 1952, 325 + xiv pp.

Examines questions about the origins and nature of Sāṃkhya, on the basis of study of Yuktidīpikā and Yogabhāṣya. An important work for historians.

133 Chand, Tara. "The Individual in the Legal and Political Thought and Institutions of India." In The Indian Mind: Essentials of Indian Philosophy and Culture, edited by Charles A. Moore. Honolulu: University of Hawaii Press, 1967, pp. 374-93. Reprinted in The Status of the Individual in East and West, ed. Charles A. Moore (Honolulu: University of Hawaii Press, 1968), pp. 411-28.

An examination of legal and social philosophy and practice in reference to goal of "consummation of the free self."

134 Chandra Roy, Pratap, trans. Mahābhārata. 13 vols. Rev. ed. Calcutta: Oriental Publishing Co., 1952-62.

Awkward either to include or exclude here. While not a philosophical text, much understanding of Hindu society is expressed. Of special note is the "Śānti Parva," given in vols. 8, 9, and 10 of this translation.

135 Chatterjee, Ashok Kumar. "Facets of Buddhist Thought." Our Heritage 19 (1971), no. 1:1-32; no. 2:33-54. Reprint. Calcutta: Calcutta Sanskrit College Research Series, 107, 1975, 54 pp.

Lectures in pratītyasamutpāda, Mādhyamika and the philosophy of language, and the way the Buddhist synthesizes idealism and absolutism, offered by a senior Indian teacher.

136 Chatterjee, Ashok Kumar. The Yogācāra Idealism. Varanasi: Banaras Hindu University, 1962, xii + 309 pp.

The best of the very few works in English dealing with Yogācāra as a whole.

137 Chatterjee, K.N. Word and Its Meaning: A New Perspective (in the Light of Jagadīśa's Śabda-Śakti-Prakāśikā). Chaukhambha Oriental Research Series, no. 18. Varanasi: Chaukhambha, 1980, lviii + 704 pp.

Not a translation, this volume "aims at a critical analysis of all the topics discussed" by Jagadīśa, which include most of the grammatical issues on which Nyāya has positions to defend.

138 Chatterjee, Satischandra. Fundamentals of Hinduism. Calcutta: Das Gupta, 1950, 179 pp. Reprint. 1960.

This little work covers the fundamental concepts of Indian thought (the nontechnical ones) in just the fashion the student needs if he is to understand the standard Indian approach to these matters. There are chapters on God, self, world, rebirth, law of karma, bondage and liberation, dharma, rāja-, karma-, bhakti-, and jñāna-yoga. Many have tried to produce a similarly fashioned introduction, but few, if any, have succeeded as well. Should be made available outside of India.

139 Chatterjee, Satischandra. The Nyāya Theory of Knowledge. Calcutta: University of Calcutta, 1939, 387 pp. Reprint. 1950.

An invaluable introduction to Nyāya epistemology, covering all the important topics concerning the pramāṇas. It is easy to read, although the author does not hesitate to use Sanskrit terms where he deems it necessary. Undoubtedly the best book on the subject.

140 Chatterjee, Satischandra, and Dhirendramohan Datta. An Introduction to Indian Philosophy. 4th ed., rev. and enl. Calcutta: University of Calcutta, 1950, 443 pp.

A highly popular textbook by two of the great scholar-philosophers of recent times in India. Covers Cārvāka, Jainism, Buddhism, Nyāya and Vaiśeṣika, Sāṃkhya and Yoga, Mīmāṃsā, Advaita and Viśiṣṭādvaita Vedānta. Intended for students preparing for university examinations, whether "B.A. Pass or Honours," it does not spare the reader any technicalities. The authors are content, however, to expound without much criticism.

141 Chatterjee, Tara. "The Concept of Śākṣin." Journal of Indian Philosophy 10 (1982):339-56.

The peculiar Advaita notion of the "witness" is explored in this well-written account, inviting comparisons with other Indian systems as well as contrasts with Sartre.

142 Chatterji, Jagdish Chandra. Kashmir Śaivism. Śrinagar: Research and Publication Department, Government of Jammu and Kashmir, 1962, 168 pp.

Covers history, literature, and main doctrines of the system. Now superseded by R.K. Kaw (see entry 364), but still usable.

143 Chatterji, Margaret. Gandhi's Religious Thought. London: Macmillan & Co., 1983, xiv + 194 pp.

In this well-planned and well-written volume, Margaret Chatterji, long a leader in the philosophical world of modern India, looks at Mahātma Gandhi's thoughts about religion though, as she recognizes, Gandhi himself would not have separated that topic from others. This little gem is not so much a philosophical analysis as a sympathetic expression of Gandhi's thought as he would have offered it if he had written in our language and our times.

144 Chattopadhyaya, Debiprasad. History, Society, and Polity: Integral Sociology of Srī Aurobindo. New Delhi: Macmillian Co. of India, 1976, xvii + 281 pp.

Aurobindo's social thought is examined with reference to Marxist perspectives; affinities and contrasts are noted.

145 Chattopadhyaya, Debiprasad. Indian Atheism. Calcutta: Manisha, 1969, 328 pp.

The Marxist approach cuts through a number of traditional bits of preciousness in the interpretation of Indian thought; arguing for Indian philosophy's atheistic, nonspiritual origins as its essential genius. Unfortunately, the author's predilections lead him into other equally precious inaccuracies.

146 Chattopadhyaya, Debiprasad. Lokāyata. New Delhi: People's Publishing House, 1959, xxvii + 696 pp.

Mostly a sociological analysis of myths. The author views "materialism" as a wide enough rubric to encompass early Sāṃkhya and early Buddhism as well as Cārvāka. It is a scholarly, thought-provoking approach.

147 Chattopadhyaya, Debiprasad. What Is Living and What Is Dead in Indian Philosophy. New Delhi: People's Publishing House, 1976, xv + 656 pp.

The radical position of this writer is evident from his book's title to its closing peroration. But just because of it this approach to Indian philosophy is a challenging alternative to standard, noncommittal attempts, which some, and not only sympathizers, will find fascinating.

148 Chattopadhyaya, Narayan Kumar. Indian Philosophy--Its Exposition in the Light of Vijñānabhikṣu's Bhāṣya and Yogavārttika: A Modern Approach. Calcutta: Sanskrit Pustak Bhandar, 1979, 272 pp.

The only general exposition in English to date of Vijñānabhikṣu's philosophy.

149 Chaudhuri, Anil Kumar Ray. The Doctrine of Māyā. 2d ed. Calcutta: Das Gupta, 1950, 212 pp.

Chaudhuri defends ignorance (ajñāna) as a legitimate concept in philosophy and explores post-Śaṃkara literature. Also included are extensive comparisons with Western philosophers, and other Indian systems, on the topic.

150 Chaudhuri, Anil Kumar Ray. Self and Falsity in Advaita Vedānta, with an Appendix on Theories of Reality in Indian Philosophy. Calcutta: Progressive Publishers, 1955, 262 pp.

The author explores post-Saṃkara literature with great expertise.

151 Chaudhuri, Roma. Doctrine of Śrīkaṇṭha. 2 vols. Pracyavan Research Series, no. 11. Calcutta: Prācyavān Research Series, 2 (1959):xix + 309 + xii pp.; 1 (1962):479 + 8 pp.

Most of volume 1 is devoted to a careful exposition of the thought of this generally ignored Vedāntin. Part 3 contains some of the best material available anywhere on basic Indian concepts such as nonattached action (niṣkāmakarma), egoism vs. altruism, objections to the "law of karma" answered, problem of evil, etc. Volume 2, published earlier, is a translation of Śrīkaṇṭha's Brahmasūtrabhāṣya.

152 Chavan, Y.B. Winds of Change. New Delhi: Somaiya Pub., 1973, viii + 235 pp.

Chavan draws upon his experiences as Defence Minister, Home Minister, and Finance Minister of the government of India to discuss three major issues involved in technological change and development: (1) Growth and Social Justice, (2) Ideology and Commitment, and (3) Domestic Strategy and Development.

153 Chemparathy, George. An Indian Rational Theology: Introduction to Udayana's Nyāyakusumāñjali. Vienna: De Nobili Research Library, 1972, 202 pp.

A thorough, careful, and penetrating analysis of the classic Indian account of arguments concerning God's existence. Important research on an important author and his greatest achievement.

154 Chemparathy, George. "The Nyāya-Vaiśeṣika as Interpreters of Śruti." Journal of Dharma 3 (1978):274-91.

How Nyāya-Vaiśeṣika went about interpreting the Vedas.

155 Chethimattam, John B. Consciousness and Reality. Bangalore: Dharmaram College, 1967, ix + 259 pp. Reprint. London: G. Chapman, 1971, x + 228 pp.

Contains epistemological explorations.

156 Chi, Richard S.Y. Buddhist Formal Logic. London: Luzac, 1969, 222 pp.

Concerns Dignāga's hetucakra and the doctrine of the "threefold mark," studied through a Chinese translation of the Nyāyapraveśa. There is much highly technical use of symbolic apparatus, which makes for confusing reading.

157 Christie, Elizabeth. "Indian Philosophers on Poetic Imagination (Pratibhā)." Journal of Indian Philosophy 7 (1979):153-207.

"The original attempt to define perception . . . gave rise to problems concerning [its] untrustworthiness, . . . leaving only the self-spontaneous consciousness which reveals the world by its own self-contemplation." This consciousness, called pratibhā in Sanskrit, appears regularly in Indian philosophy and literature. This article brings out its special place in Bhartṛhari's philosophy, along with that of others.

158 Clooney, Francis X. "Jaimini's Contribution to the Theory of Sacrifice as the Experience of Transcendence." History of Religions 25 (1986):199-212.

Shows how Jaimini presents a kind of transcendence that precludes the supernaturalism of anthropocentrism.

159 Cole, Colin A. Asparśa-Yoga: A Study of Gauḍapāda's Māṇḍūkya Kārikā. Delhi: Motilal Banarsidass, 1982, xiii + 158 pp.

The author adopts what he calls a "soteriological" perspective on Gauḍapāda's text, suggesting it gives a new perspective and implying that the perspective is more accurate than that of pure philosophy.

160 Collins, Steven. Selfless Persons: Imagery and Thought in Theravāda Buddhism. Cambridge: Cambridge University Press, 1982, ix + 323 pp.

Probably the best book written on Theravāda to date, though it requires consistent attention to get the most out of it. The explanations move at a high level of abstraction, but in that fashion Collins is able to say a lot while speaking comparatively little. By the same token, it is difficult to state succinctly the thesis of this work.

161 Conio, Caterina. The Philosophy of Māṇḍūkya Kārikā. Varanasi: Bharatiya Vidya Prakashan, 1971, ii + ii + 238 pp.

Conio carefully studies Gauḍapāda's philosophy, reviews critical literature (which is voluminous), and also examines Samkara's commentary and Viśiṣṭādvaita, Dvaita, and Suddhādvaita interpretations at the hands of Kuranārāyaṇa, Madhva, and Puruṣottama respectively.

162 Conze, Edward. "Buddhist Philosophy and Its European Parallels," and "Spurious Parallels to Buddhist Philosophy." Philosophy East and West 13 (1963):9-24, and 105-16.

Conze criticizes common comparisons between Buddhists and those such as Hume and Kant. Compare also Alex Wayman, "Conze on Buddhism and European Parallels" (Philosophy East and West 21 [1971]:237-54).

163 Conze, Edward. Buddhist Thought in India. London: Allen and Unwin, 1962, 302 pp.

Despite, or perhaps because of, the author's tendentious style, this work is possibly the most attractive introductory work dealing with Buddhist philosophy. This is due to Conze's unflagging imaginativeness in exposition and his ability to infuse scholarship with a sense of human concern. Billed as a history of Buddhist philosophy, the work is divided into three parts: archaic Buddhism, the Sthaviras, and the Mahāyāna.

Attention is primarily to the basic concepts rather than to the philosophers themselves.

164 Conze, Edward. The Prajñāpāramitā Literature. 2d ed., rev. and enl. Tokyo: Reiyukai, 1978, 138 pp.

The definite guide to the Prajñāpāramitā works and their commentaries. Materials in Sanskrit, Tibetan, Chinese, Japanese, and Mongolian are listed; short summaries of the contents of each are provided.

165 Coomaraswamy, Ananda Kentish. Hinduism and Buddhism. New York: Philosophical Library, 1943, 86 pp.

A specimen of scholarship that finds a "philosophia perennis" in every system of thought. Coomaraswamy was the master of this trade, and these essays range in incomparable fashion through Upaniṣads, Gītā, and various early Buddhist works, with great attention to mythology and little to technical philosophy.

166 Coomaraswamy, Ananda Kentish. The Religious Basis of the Forms of Indian Society. New York: Orientalia, 1946, 27 pp.

A lecture which outlines the metaphysical correlates of the Indian social system, with many comparisons to Western philosophy.

167 Coomaraswamy, Ananda Kentish. Spiritual Authority and Temporal Power in the Indian Theory of Government. American Oriental Series, no. 22. New Haven: American Oriental Society, 1942, 87 pp.

Technical, somewhat abstruse. Argues that self-control is the essence of government, as of all existence. Coomaraswamy was influential in the United States, less so in India.

168 Cousins, L.S. "Nibbāna and Abhidhamma." Buddhist Studies Review 1, no. 2 (1983-84):95-109.

How do the nikāyas and the early Abhidhamma literature view nirvāṇa? It is "neither temporal nor spatial, neither mind . . . nor matter, but certainly not the mere cessation of other dhammas."

169 Creel, Austin B. Dharma in Hindu Ethics. Calcutta: Firma KLM Private, 1977, 178 pp.

A thoughtful critique of Hindu ethics--or, as the author argues, the lack of it. This book is not a review of things Indian but a cogent, sympathetic criticism of Hindu shortcomings in the field of moral philosophy.

170 Damle, P.R. "Study of Indian Philosophy." Journal of the University of Bombay 4 (1936):139-48.

This piece on the general features of the study may be the best of its genre.

171 Dandekar, R.N. "Hinduism." In Historia Religionum, edited by C. Jouco Bleeker and Geo Widengren. Vol. 2, Religions of the Present. Leiden: E.J. Brill, 1971, pp. 237-345.
One of India's greatest scholars gives us his view of the subject to which he has devoted his life's work.

172 Dandekar, R.N. "Man in Hindu Thought: A Broad Outline." Annals of the Bhandarkar Oriental Research Institute 43 (1963):1-57.
A philosopher's explanation of the major facets of the Hindu social system.

173 Danielou, Alain. Yoga: The Method of Re-Integration. London: C. Johnson, 1949, 165 pp.
Expounds yoga by translations of juxtaposed texts, the assumption apparently being that the authoritativeness of the texts guards against misunderstanding. The texts cover various types of yoga: haṭha, rāja, mantra, laya, śiva, karma, jñāna, bhakti, etc. It is rather an odd type of approach.

174 Das, A.C. "Advaita Vedānta and Liberation in Bodily Existence." Philosophy East and West 4 (1954):113-24.
Examines critically Advaita views on karma, jīvanmukti. There are responses by Malkani in Philosophy East and West 5 (1955):69-74, and K.S. Joshi, Philosophy East and West 18 (1968):77-81.

175 Das, Manmath Nath. The Political Philosophy of Jawaharlal Nehru. New York: John Day Co., 1961, 256 pp.
An examination of the philosophical perspective on political life embodied in Nehru's writings and speeches.

176 Das, Saroj Kumar. Towards a Systematic Study of the Vedānta. Calcutta: University of Calcutta, 1931, 292 pp.
This work, the Mallik lectures for 1929, provides a rather attractive introduction to Advaita Vedānta, covering all important aspects. It is full of comparisons between Advaita and Western philosophers, not all of the latter any longer known in the West.

177 Das, Sudhendu Kumar. Śakti or Divine Power. Calcutta: University of Calcutta, 1934, 298 pp.
Traces development of the idea of śakti from the Vedas, with particular attention to its use in Kashmir Saivism and Vīraśaivism. Useful for students of Indian philosophy of religion.

178 Dasgupta, Shashi Bhusan. An Introduction to Tantric Buddhism. Calcutta: University of Calcutta, 1950, x + 11 + 235 pp.
This work describes later, tantric Buddhist texts and relates them to their appropriate philosophical schools in

Mahāyāna. The schools of Tantric Buddhism are distinguished and key concepts and technical terms are analyzed.

179 Dasgupta, Surama. Development of Moral Philosophy in India. Bombay: Orient Longmans, 1961, 226 + xiv pp.

Written "under close personal supervision of the late Professor Surendra Nath Dasgupta," this work by his widow is probably the best history available, although Ishwar Chandra Sharma's Ethical Philosophies of India (see entry 717) may be preferable as philosophy. Survey is limited to Vedas, Upaniṣads, Mīmāṃsā, Smṛtis, Pāñcarātra, Vedānta, Sāṃkhya, Yoga, Nyāya, Vaiśeṣika, Buddhism, and Jainism.

180 Dasgupta, Surendranath. Hindu Mysticism. New York: Frederick Ungar, 1959, 168 pp. (Orig. pub. Chicago, 1927.)

Lectures on mysticism in the Vedas, Upaniṣads, Yoga, Buddhism, and devotional sects from various parts of India.

181 Dasgupta, Surendranath. A History of Indian Philosophy. 5 vols. Cambridge: Cambridge University Press, 1922-55. (Abridged ed., Allahabad, 1969.)

This stands in a class by itself. Of the very few histories of Indian philosophy Dasgupta's excels because of its impeccable English style, ground-breaking accounts of classical texts, and general good philosophical sense. There are some drawbacks: careless proofreading makes for frequent and exhausting repetitions, and occasional large-scale omissions (e.g., on Navya-Nyāya) had to be rectified later. Nevertheless, this five-volume set is the one indispensable item in the library of the would-be student of Indian thought. Contents are as follows: Volume 1: Introductory. The Vedas, Brāhmaṇas and their Philosophy. The earlier Upaniṣads (700 B.C.-600 B.C.). General observations on the systems of Indian philosophy. Buddhist philosophy. Jaina philosophy. The Kapila and the Pātañjala Sāṃkhya (Yoga). The Nyāya-Vaiśeṣika philosophy. Mīmāṃsā philosophy. The Śaṃkara school of Vedānta. Volume 2: Śaṃkara school of Vedānta continued. Philosophy of the Yogavāsiṣṭha. Speculations on the medical schools. Philosophy of the Bhagavad-Gītā. Volume 3: The Bhāskara school of philosophy. The Pāñcarātra. The Arvars. A historical and literary survey of the Viśiṣṭādvaita school of thought. The philosophy of Yāmunācārya. Philosophy of the Rāmānuja school of thought. The Nimbārka school of philosophy. The philosophy of Vijñāna Bhikṣu. Philosophical speculations of some of the selected Purāṇas. Volume 4: The Bhāgavata Purāṇa. Madhva and his school. Madhva's interpretation of the Brahmasūtras. A general review of the philosophy of Madhva. Madhva logic. Controversy between the dualists and the monists. The philosophy of Vallabha. Caitanya and his followers. The philosophy of Jīva Gosvāmi and Bāladeva Vidyābhūṣaṇa, followers of Caitanya. Volume 5: Literature of southern Śaivism. Vīra-Śaivism. Philosophy of Śrīkaṇṭha. The

Śaiva philosophy in the Purāṇas. Śaiva philosophy in some of the important texts.

182 Dasgupta, Surendranath. Indian Idealism. Cambridge: Cambridge University Press, 1933, 206 pp.
A useful survey by a great scholar and master stylist which covers idealism in the Vedas, Upaniṣads, Buddhism, and Vedānta.

183 Dasgupta, Surendranath. Yoga as Philosophy and Religion. London: Kegan Paul, Trench, Trubner; New York: E.P. Dutton, 1924, 200 pp.
The definitive work on Yoga philosophy by one of India's greatest scholars. Discussions tend to be somewhat complex but, unlike many Indian expositors, the author is able to get away from his textual sources and generate some independently exciting philosophical analyses (not, however, as profound as those of K.C. Bhattacharya; see entry 85).

184 Dasgupta, Surendranath. "Yoga Psychology." Quest 13 (1921-22):1-19. Reprinted in Proceedings of the All-India Oriental Conference 3 (1924):427-38.
An outstanding exposition of the subject.

185 Datta, Dhirendra Mohan. The Philosophy of Mahātma Gandhi. Madison: University of Wisconsin Press, 1953, xiv + 154 pp.
An excellent, brief study. Chapter 3, "Morals, Society, and Politics" (pp. 73-145), is the most pertinent.

186 Datta, Dhirendra Mohan. "Political, Legal, and Economic Thought in Indian Perspective." In Philosophy and Culture East and West: East West Philosophy in Practical Perspective. Honolulu: University of Hawaii Press, 1962, pp. 569-98. Reprinted as "Some Philosophical Aspects of Indian Political, Legal, and Economic Thought," in The Indian Mind: Essentials of Indian Philosophy and Culture, ed. Charles A. Moore (Honolulu: University of Hawaii Press, 1967), pp. 267-98.
A brief summary of traditional ideals, examined in the light of modern issues.

187 Datta, Dhirendra Mohan. The Six Ways of Knowing: A Critical Study of the Vedānta Theory of Knowledge. Rev. ed. Calcutta: University of Calcutta, 1960, 360 pp. (Orig. pub. London: G. Allen and Unwin, 1932.)
A classic treatment of the six pramāṇas of the Advaita system, with generous references to other schools as well. Has especially extensive materials on perception and testimony.

188 Davis, Lawrence. "Tarka in the Nyāya Theory of Inference." Journal of Indian Philosophy 9 (1981):105-20.
Why doesn't Nyāya classify tarka as a pramāṇa? Davis considers a number of wrong answers to this. His own solution involves clarification of the meanings of pramāṇa (which is not

just an instrument of knowledge, but one involving no false awareness), and of anumāna (which is not true, but more particularly, sound inference).

189 Day, Terence P. "The Concept of Punishment in Early Indian Literature." SR (Waterloo, Ontario) 2 (1982).

One of the few serious attempts to analyze specific moral notions in classical Indian literature.

190 Daye, Douglas D. "Some Epistemologically Misleading Expressions: 'Inference' and 'Anumāna,' 'Perception' and 'Pratyakṣa.' In Analytical Philosophy in Comparative Perspective, edited by Bimal Krishna Matilal and Jaysamkar Lal Shaw. Dordrecht, Holland: D. Reidel, 1985, pp. 231-52.

Though not easy to read, this paper points out the dangers involved in taking standard translations of two Sanskrit philosophical terms without the usual grain of salt.

191 De, Sushil Kumar. Early History of the Vaiṣṇava Faith and Movement in Bengal. Calcutta: K.L. Mukhopadhyay, 1961, ix + 703 pp.

The standard source for the history of Bengal Vaiṣṇavism from Caitanya to the present, with analyses of the writings of Sanātana, Rūpa and Jīva Gosvāmin. It covers all aspects of the subject, religious as well as philosophical.

192 De Bary, William Theodore, et al., comps. Sources of Indian Tradition. New York: Columbia University Press, 1958, xii + 962 pp. Reprint (paperback). 1967, 2 vols., 1:xxiv + 535 pp.; 2:xvi + 384 pp.)

Excerpts from texts, with brief introductions, including passages pertinent to social and political philosophy (especially chapters 9-11). Also contains material on Jain (chapter 5) and Theravāda Buddhist (chapter 6) interpretations. Chapters 17 and 24 introduce Islamic perspectives.

193 Della Santina, Peter. Mādhyamaka Schools in India. Delhi: Motilal Banarsidass, 1986, xxiii + 242 pp.

The first book to concentrate on the general topic of the division between the Prāsaṅgika and Svātantrika schools of Mādhyamaka Buddhism. The author shows that the major points of distinction include both differences in the sorts of arguments allowed as well as differences between their interpretation of the nature of conventional reality, the Svātantrikas regularly dividing phenomenal truths into "true" and "false."

194 Derrett, J. Duncan M. Introduction to Modern Hindu Law. London: Oxford University Press, 1963, xciv + 653 pp.

Chapter 1, "History, Sources, and Application of Hindu Law" (pp. 1-31) is a sound general survey of traditional and modern developments.

195 Derrett, J. Duncan M. Religion, Law, and the State in India. New York: Free Press, 1968, 615 pp.

An examination of many factors that are necessary background and context for the philosophy of law, giving convenient access to some papers published earlier elsewhere.

196 Desai, S.M. Haribhadra's Yoga Works and Psychosynthesis. L.D. Series, no. 94. Ahmedabad: L.D. Institute of Indology, 1983, vi + 96 pp.

Summarizes Haribhadra's yogic views, especially as found in Yogabindu and Yogadṛṣṭisamuccaya.

197 Deshpande, D.Y. "Māyāvāda." Journal of the University of Bombay 14 (1945):57-68.

A good, hard-nosed critique.

198 Deshpande, Madhav. "Sentence-cognition in Nyāya Epistemology." Indo-Iranian Journal 20 (1978):195-216.

A clear account of Jagadīśa's thoughts about our knowledge of the meaning of a sentence. Jagadīśa gives convincing reasons why verbal cognition must count as a distinct instrument of knowledge.

199 Deussen, Paul. The Philosophy of the Upaniṣads. Edinburgh: T. and T. Clark, 1906, xiv + 429 pp.

The classic exposition of Upaniṣadic philosophy by the famous German scholar. It contains much that is pertinent to the study of Vedāntic systems.

200 Deussen, Paul. The System of the Vedānta. Translated by Charles Johnston. Chicago: Open Court, 1912, 513 pp. Reprint. New York: Dover Publications, 1973.

Famous, exhaustive study of Śaṃkara's philosophy. Draws from Upaniṣads, Brahmasūtras, and Saṃkara's commentaries on them. Chapters devoted to theology or the doctrine of Brahman; cosmology or the doctrine of the world; psychology or the doctrine of the soul; saṃsāra or the doctrine of the transmigration of the soul; mokṣa or the teaching of liberation. Appendixes give short survey of Vedānta system, index of all quotations in Saṃkara's Brahmasūtrabhāṣya, index of the proper names in that work, terms of the Vedānta.

201 Deutsch, Eliot. Advaita Vedānta: A Philosophical Reconstruction. Honolulu: East-West Center Press, 1969, 119 pp.

Deutsch's intent is to "approach Asian philosophy as material for creative thought," and he is quite successful. Excellent book for a first course in serious philosophy dealing with Advaita thought, for despite its brevity, most central Advaita themes are intelligently developed.

202 Deutsch, Eliot, and J.A.B. Van Buitenen, eds. A Source Book of Advaita Vedānta. Honolulu: University of Hawaii Press, 1971, 335 pp.

Selections from Upaniṣads (translated by Van Buitenen), Bhagavadgītā (translated by Deutsch), and Śaṃkara and his followers (translations by a variety of scholars, in some cases prepared expressly for this publication). One of the few collections of source materials available, this book is priced so high as to make its use in courses difficult, but it contains some excellent material.

203 Dev, Govinda Chandra. "Notion of Falsity of the World in Gauḍapāda and Śaṃkara." Journal of the Asiatic Society of Pakistan 5 (1960):148-63.

Is māyā a subjectivist doctrine? No, or at least not solely. "[The] mark of falsity in Vedānta . . . [is] not . . . actual cancellation of content . . . but its cancellability."

204 Devanandan, Paul David. The Concept of Māyā. London: Butterworth Press, 1950, 234 pp.

Dissertation tracing the development of the concept in Hindu thought (Buddhism intentionally excluded).

205 Devaraja, N.K. An Introduction to Śaṃkara's Theory of Knowledge. Delhi: Motilal Banarsidass, 1962, 225 pp.

A very lively, reasonably critical work, based on a doctoral dissertation, that pays particular attention to criteria to which Śaṃkara resorted in justifying his views.

206 Devaraja, N.K. The Mind and Spirit of India. Delhi: Motilal Banarsidass, 1967, xviii + 403 pp.

A contemporary philosopher's examination of the historic patterns of the treatment of the ethical dimensions of social life; Devaraja advocates a humanism that is spiritual. While there are other pertinent passages, the concentrated attention to social philosophy is in chapter 4, "Moral Consciousness and the Principles of Social Harmony" (pp. 157-95).

207 Devasenapathi, V.A. "Basic Concepts of Śaiva Siddhānta." Indian Philosophical Annual 14 (1980-81):39-80.

A highly respected senior scholar of south India delivers his authoritative interpretation of Śaiva Siddhānta tenets.

208 Devasenapathi, V.A. Śaiva Siddhānta as Expounded in the Śivajñānasiddhiyār and Its Six Commentaries. Madras University Department of Indian Philosophy Publications, no. 7. Madras: University of Madras, 1960, xiii + 322 pp.

The best recent work on Śaiva Siddhānta, by a leading South Indian scholar.

209 Devasthali, G.V. Mīmāṃsā: The Vākya Śāstra of Ancient India. Bombay: Booksellers' Publishing Co., 1959, x + 248 pp.
On Mīmāṃsā philosophy of language.

210 Dhar, Niranjan. "The Rule of Law and the Indian Tradition." Quest 58 (1968):37-41.
A study of contrasts between elements of traditional structure and authority and the presuppositions of the "rule of law" in the modern era.

211 Dharmakīrti. Dharmakīrti, Pramāṇavārttika, Kārikās 1-51 of Svārthānumāna Section. Edited and translated by Satkari Mookerjee and Hojun Nagasaki. Nalanda: Nava Nalanda Mahavihara, 1964, 134 pp.
A vital need for study of Buddhist philosophy, and Indian thought generally, is a complete translation of the Pramāṇavārttika, the pinnacle of achievement by the school of Buddhist logic initiated by Dignāga. Translation of the chapter on perception is expected (by M. Nagatomi, forthcoming in the Harvard Oriental Series). At present, this rendition of a portion of the chapter on inference-for-oneself is all we have. Even so truncated, it is a book which repays careful study.

212 Dharmakīrti. "Dharmakīrti, Saṃtānāntarasiddhi." Translated by Th. Stcherbatsky. Indian Studies Past and Present 10 (1969):335-83.
Argues that there are many saṃtānas or streams of consciousness, not just one.

213 Dharmatrāta. "Pañcavastukavibhāṣā of Bhadanta Dharmatrāta," translated and edited by N. Aiyaśvami Sastri. Adyar Library Bulletin 20 (1956):231-37.
A good discussion of the views of Dharmatrāta (a Vaibhāṣika Buddhist) on fundamental notions of Abhidharma Buddhism.

214 Dhavamony, Mariasusai. Love of God According to Śaiva Siddhānta. Oxford: Clarendon Press, 1971, xvi + 402 pp.
The quintessential piece for one who wants to know and understand Saiva Siddhānta. Besides an illuminating examination of the historical development of bhakti, the work provides a careful account of the contents of all the fundamental Tamil texts. An invaluable document.

215 Dhawan, Gopinath. The Political Philosophy of Mahātma Gandhi. Ahmedabad: Navajivan Publishing House, 1962, viii + 365 pp.
A pioneering study, first published in 1946 and subsequently revised in 1951 and 1957, that undertakes to articulate the various strands of Gandhi's thought that comprise his political philosophy.

216 Dignāga. Ālambanaparīkṣā. Edited by Aiyasvami Sastri. Adyar Library Series, no. 32. Adyar: Adyar Library, 1942, xxiii + 7 + 125 pp.

Restored into Sanskrit and translated, with Dharmapāla's commentary and extracts from Vinītadeva's commentary, by N. Aiyasvami Sastri. A few verses with commentary on the status of the object of cognition.

217 Dignāga. "Dignāga, Hetucakraḍamaru or -Nirṇaya." Translated by D.C. Chatterji. Indian Historical Quarterly 9 (1933):511-14.

Dignāga's famous "wheel of reasons," in which he expounds the fundamentals of the theory of the trairūpya or three-fold mark of a (valid) reason in argument.

218 Dixit, Krishna Kumar. Jaina Ontology. Lalbhai Dalpatbhai Series, no. 31. Ahmedabad: L.D. Institute of Indology, 1971, 203 pp.

Title is a bit misleading, as work is more of a history of Jain epistemology and metaphysics than an ontology. Particularly helpful in placing contributions of Jain āgamas in perspective and relating them to later developments.

219 Doctor, Adi Hormusji. Sarvodaya: A Political and Economic Study. Bombay and New York: Asia Publishing House, 1967, 229 pp.

Attempts "a comprehensive exposition and evaluation of the entire Sarvodaya philosophy, in both its political and social aspects."

220 Dravid, N.S. "The Problem of Relation in Indian Philosophy." Indian Philosophical Quarterly 5, no. 1 (October 1977):39-63.

A crystal-clear account of Buddhism and Vaiśeṣika on relations, with cogent comparisons between these systems and those of certain recent Western philosophers.

221 Dravid, Raja Ram. The Problem of Universals in Indian Philosophy. Delhi: Motilal Banarsidass, 1972, 473 pp.

The only thorough study of this problem in print. Covers the territory. Written in the usual Indian thesis format, sticks carefully with original sources. A helpful resource. Chapters on Nyāya-Vaiśeṣika, Mīmāṃsā, Buddhist, Jaina, Advaita, Grammarian, and Western theories of universals.

222 Dube, S.C. India since Independence. New Delhi: Vikas Publishing House, 1976, 560 pp.

Primarily concerned with economic and political affairs; however, Indian science and technology are considered in their social context.

223 Dube, S.N. Cross Currents in Early Buddhism. New Delhi: Manohar, 1980, xvi + 375 pp.

A lengthy analysis of the positions and arguments found in the Kathāvatthu. The author also considers later Buddhist developments.

224 Dumont, Louis. "World Renunciation in Indian Religions." Contributions to Indian Sociology 4 (1960):33-62. Reprinted in Religion, Politics, and History in India: Collected Papers in Indian Sociology (Paris and The Hague: Mouton, 1970), ix + 166 pp.

An analysis of the implications of the role of the renouncer as it pertains to the life of society. The 1970 volume contains other papers pertinent to the framework of social philosophy in the Hindu tradition.

225 Dunuvile, Rohan A. Śaiva Siddhānta Theology: A Context for Hindu-Christian Dialogue. Delhi: Motilal Banarsidass, 1985, xii + 231 pp.

As the author announces at the start, this pioneering work surveys the theological literature of Saiva Siddhānta, then concentrates on the work of Aghoraśiva, summarizing and analyzing his thought and offering an edition and translation of the introductory section of his Tattvaprakāśikā. He concludes with an essay comparing Christian and Śaiva Siddhānta tenets.

226 Durai, J. Chinna. "Hindu Law and Western Ideas." Asian Review 54 (1958):39-44.

In this article the legal implications of the Hindu joint family are contrasted with Western views of welfare and the primacy of "the well-being of the individual."

227 Dutt, Nalinaksha. "Buddhist Meditation." Indian Historical Quarterly 11 (1935):710-40.

A summary of Buddhaghosa's Viśuddhimagga on cittaviśuddhi that discusses kinds of samādhis, hindrances to the practice of samādhis, objects of meditation, the spiritual preceptor, the candidate, and successive steps in meditation.

228 Dutt, Nalinaksha. "Place of the Āryasatyas and the Pratītyasamutpāda in Hīnayāna and Mahāyāna." Annals of the Bhandarkar Oriental Research Institute 11 (1930):101-27.

Āryasatyas and the Pratītyasamutpāda are "real according to the Hīnayānists," "unreal and matters of convention according to the Mahāyānists." Distinguishes three senses of "convention" (saṃvṛti).

229 Dwivedi, C.B. "Sāṃkhya Framework of Mind, Senses, and Intellect and Its Relationship with Language and Thought." Prajna 16 (1970-71):171-84.

A psychologist looks at Sāṃkhya.

230 Eckel, M. David. "Bhāvaviveka's Critique of Yogācāra Philosophy in Chapter XXV of the Prajñāpradīpa." In

Miscellanea Buddhica, edited by Christian Lindtner. Indiske studier, no. 5. Copenhagen: Akademisk Förlag, 1985, pp. 25-75.

An illuminating translation of a chapter by Bhāvaviveka which Eckel argues "is the beginning of a body of literature whose specific purpose is to distinguish the Mādhyamaka from the Yogācāra." Eckel's introductory remarks take us a long way beyond Stcherbatsky and into an attempt to understand the sense in which Mādhyamaka negativism has to be taken.

231 Edgerton, Franklin, trans. The Beginnings of Indian Philosophy: Selections from the Rig Veda, Atharva Veda, Upaniṣads, and Mahābhārata. Cambridge: Harvard University Press, 1965, 362 pp.

A useful collection of source materials, including a particularly welcome set of passages from the Mokṣadharma portion of the Mahābhārata. Comments by one of America's greatest Indologists.

232 Edgerton, Franklin, trans. The Bhagavad Gītā. Harvard Oriental Series, vols. 38 and 39. Cambridge: Harvard University Press, 1944, 38:xiv + 190 pp.; 39:180 pp. Reprint (paperback). New York: Harper and Row, 1964, 202 pp.

Part 1: Transliterated Sanskrit text with translation on facing pages. Part 2: Series of interpretative essays and Sir Edwin Arnold's verse translation, "The Song Celestial." Arnold's translation is omitted and the preface and notes are revised in the 1964 reprint.

233 Edgerton, Franklin. "The Meaning of Sāṃkhya and Yoga." American Journal of Philology 45 (1924):1-46.

Examines pre-Kārikās Sāṃkhya, as it occurs in Mahābhārata and later Upaniṣads. Discusses early Sāṃkhya, arguing that it was not atheistic; relation of epic Brahmanism to later Sāṃkhya and Vedānta; Yoga in Mokṣadharma; two different interpretations of the Yoga method.

234 Eliade, Mircea. Patañjali and Yoga. Translated by C.L. Markmann. New York: Funk and Wagnalls, 1969, 216 pp.

Good introduction to yoga--both Hindu and Buddhist--by famous historian of religion. Excellent bibliography. Illustrated. Chapters on yogic techniques; ascetics, ecstatics, and contemplatives in ancient India; Buddhism; Tantrism; Haṭhayoga.

235 Eliade, Mircea. Yoga: Immortality and Freedom. Princeton, N.J.: Princeton University Press, 1967, xxii + 536 pp.

Eliade's best-known work, a classic in-depth exploration of yoga from a standpoint which mingles, and perhaps transcends, the philosophical, psychological, textualist, religionist, and mythological approaches.

236 Embree, Ainslie T., ed. The Hindu Tradition. New York: Random House, Modern Library, 1966, xv + 363 pp.

An accessible and extremely useful anthology which includes excerpts from texts dealing with society.

237 Faddegon, Barend. The Vaiśeṣika-System Described with the Help of the Oldest Texts. Amsterdam: J. Muller, 1918, 606 pp.

The magnum opus of one of the great Indological scholars of Europe is still one of the classic books on Vaiśeṣika, ranging over much else in Indian thought in the course of its detailed exposition of Kaṇāda, Praśastapāda, and Śrīdhara.

238 Farqhar, J.N. "Karma: Its Value as a Doctrine of Life." Hibbert Journal 20 (1921-22):20-34.

Farqhar's article is followed by articles by Ozanne and Welland. The three together provide an excellent discussion (from a Western standpoint) of the pros and cons of karma.

239 Farqhar, J.N. An Outline of the Religious Literature of India. Delhi: Motilal Banarsidass, 1967, 541 pp. (Orig. pub. Oxford: Oxford University Press, 1920.)

Traces the development of philosophical literature from the beginning to 1800 A.D., and is especially good for its detailed breakdown of the numerous sects of northern Vaiṣṇavism which flourished between 1350 and 1800 A.D. There is an exceptionally helpful bibliography of materials published prior to 1920. A valuable resource.

240 Fenner, Peter G. "A Reconstruction of the Mādhyamakāvatāra's Analysis of the Person." Journal of the International Association of Buddhist Studies 6, no. 2 (1983):7-34.

This paper is one of the best attempts to show how emptiness is to be established through logical analysis. It is emphasized how important it is to be convinced that the self is both/neither the same as/nondifferent from the aggregations (skandhas).

241 Fenner, Peter G. "A Study of the Relationship between Analysis (Vicāra) and Insight (Prajñā) based on the Mādhyamakāvatāra." Journal of Indian Philosophy 12 (1984):139-97.

Despite being written in a very dry and abstract style, this paper asks and convincingly answers in the affirmative an interesting question: Does logical analysis play any part in gaining liberation?

242 Feuerstein, George A. The Essence of Yoga: A Contribution to the Psychohistory of Indian Civilization. New York: Grove Press, 1974, 224 pp.

"Yoga . . . embraces two great tendencies which must be strictly distinguished. The one pertains to what I will refer to as the magic-mythical structure of consciousness, whilst the other shows distinct holistic traits."

243 Filliozat, Pierre Sylvain. "A Dualistic School of Śaivism." Quarterly Journal of the Mythic Society 69 (1978):180-90.
A useful clarification of the complex divisions of Śaiva philosophy.

244 Franco, Eli. "Studies in the Tattvopaplavasiṃha." Journal of Indian Philosophy 11 (1983):147-66; 12 (1984):105-38.
Jayarāśi's work is the only Lokāyata text so far discovered, but it is still largely ignored. Franco discusses two issues, the criterion of truth (1983), and the theory of error (1984), arguing that this work is "the only text where a full-fledged scepticism is propounded." He also shows that the text is highly informative due to its negative criticism of Hindu, Buddhist, and Jaina schools.

245 Frauwallner, Erich. History of Indian Philosophy. Translated by V.M. Bedekar. 2 vols. Delhi: Motilal Banarsidass, 1973, 1:454 pp.; 2:276 pp.
The most celebrated history since Dasgupta's (see entry 180) now available to English readers. Volume 1 covers the philosophy of the Vedas and epics, the Buddha and Mahāvīra, and Sāṃkhya and the classical Yoga system. Volume 2 deals with the schools of natural philosophy: Nyāya, Vaiśeṣika, Jainism, and materialism.

246 Frauwallner, Erich. "Landmarks in the History of Indian Logic." Wiener Zeitschrift für des Kunde Süd- und Ostasiens 5 (1961):125-48.
Methodology of dating Indian philosophers. Establishes dates of a number of Buddhist philosophers of the fourth through ninth centuries A.D.

247 Frenkian, A.M. "Sextus Empiricus and Indian Logic." Philosophical Quarterly 30 (Amalner 1957):115-26.
The stock illustrations of the rope and the snake, smoke and fire (in inference), and the catuṣkoṭi are found in Sextus and other early Greek writers.

248 Gächter, Othmar. Hermeneutics and Language in Pūrva-Mīmāṃsā: A Study in Śabara Bhāṣya. Delhi: Motilal Banarsidasas, 1983, x + 164 pp.
The first extended study to concern itself particularly with Śabara's views. Attention is directed toward Śabara's views on language (śabda). The analysis is sometimes obscured by "hermeneutics," derived from Gadamer, the significance of his obsession with which is never really clarified.

249 Gadādhara Bhaṭṭācārya. Viṣayatāvāda. Edited and translated by Sibajiban Bhattacharyya. Journal of Indian Philosophy 14 (1986):109-302.

A viṣaya is any object of awareness. The Viṣayatāvāda is a section of Gadādhara's voluminous commentary on Gaṅgeśa's Tattvacintāmaṇi, and represents the most difficult philosophical material in the whole Indian corpus, impossible to turn into readable English. Bhattacharyya comes as close to doing that as is humanly possible, using symbolic logic, diagrams, but most of all, great clarity and good sense.

250 Gajendragadkar, K.V. Neo-Upanishadic Philosophy. Bombay: Bharatiya Vidya Bhavan, 1959, 164 pp.

Surveys the many Upaniṣads written since the great old dozen or so on which Śaṃkara and other classical philosophers commented. Most of those rendered here are redolent of Tantra, which is what the book is mostly about, though by no means confined to it.

251 Gajendragadkar, Prahlad Balacharya. The Constitution of India: Its Philosophy and Basic Postulates. Nairobi: Oxford University Press, 1969, xvi + 107 pp.

A brief review of the constitution with attention to its formulation and to the fundamental rights, but few would consider "philosophy" a major component.

252 Galanter, Marc. "The Displacement of Traditional Law in Modern India." Journal of Social Issues 24 (1968):65-91.

A helpful, brief introduction to key aspects of traditional and modern legal patterns.

253 Gambhirananda, trans. Eight Upanishads. 2 vols. Calcutta: Advaita Ashrama, 1 (1957):iv + 427; 2 (1958):515 pp.

Volume 1 contains translations of Śaṃkara's commentaries on the Īśā, Kaṭha, Kena, and Taittirīya Upaniṣads, and Volume 2, Śaṃkara on the Aitareya, Māṇḍūkya, Muṇḍaka, and Praśna Upaniṣads.

254 Gandhi, Kishor. "Political Thought of Sri Aurobindo." Cultural Forum 14 (1972):59-67.

A judicious introduction to (and summary of) Aurobindo's social and political philosophy.

255 Gandhi, Kishor. Social Philosophy of Sri Aurobindo and the New Age. Pondicherry: Sri Aurobindo Society, 1965, 273 pp.

A follower seeks to give systematic presentation to ideas that Aurobindo advanced in various contexts without himself providing a systematic formulation. Some of these introductory studies encompass other topics than social philosophy.

256 Gangadhara, S. "Epistemological Ideas in the Jñānāmṛtam." Indian Philosophical Annual 14 (1980-81):203-14.

A brief summary of the epistemology propounded in this Tamil Saiva work.

257 Gangopadhyaya, Mrinalkanti. Indian Atomism: History and Sources. Bagchi Indological Series, no. 1. Calcutta: K.B. Bagchi & Co., 1980, xii + 377 pp.

Debiprasad Chattopadhyaya writes in his informative introduction that this work "is the compilation of practically all the important sources discussing Indian atomism." Jain, Buddhist, Nyāya-Vaiśeṣika, Mīmāṃsā and Vedānta passages are translated. A model for future treatments of Indian philosophy.

258 Ganguli, B.N. Gandhi's Social Philosophy: Perspective and Relevance. New York: John Wiley & Sons, 1973, xiii + 453 pp.

A social scientist's exploration (frequently in a comparative manner) of Gandhi's views and their continuing implications.

259 Ganguli, Hemanta Kumar. Philosophy of Logical Construction. Calcutta: Sanskrit Pustak Bhandar, 1963, 251 pp.

A wild but wonderful caper through Buddhist and Grammarian epistemologies, with many knowledgeable glances toward Wittgenstein, Russell, and Western analyses. Many thought-provoking topics are aired.

260 Gard, Richard A., ed. Buddhism. New York: G. Braziller, 1961, 256 pp.

Part 1 contains seventeen pages on ways, schools, and paths in Buddhism, useful for beginners. Part 3 offers selections from Prasannapadā, Madhyāntavibhāga, and Viśuddhimagga.

261 Ghoshal, Upendra Nath. A History of Indian Political Ideas: The Ancient Period and the Period of Transition to the Middle Ages. London: Oxford University Press, 1959, xxii + 589 pp. Reprint (with corrections). 1966.

A distinguished historian surveys the texts dealing with polity in Hindu tradition (to A.D. 1200).

262 Gillon, Brendan S., and Martha Lila Love. "Indian Logic Revisited: Nyāyapraveśa Reviewed." Journal of Indian Philosophy 8 (1980):349-84.

Unlike most treatments of Indian logical texts, this article combines imaginative exegesis with negative criticism. The result is one of the most illuminating attempts yet to convey the way that Indian logic works, combining game theory, Sanskrit analysis, symbolic logic, and careful criticism.

263 Glasenapp, Helmuth von. Immortality and Salvation in Indian Religions. Translated by E.F.J. Payne. Calcutta: Susil Gupta, 1963, 112 pp.

Surveys with care and understanding Indian views on immortality, retribution, and salvation. An invaluable resource for beginning students, who often find it very difficult to understand the basic starting point of the Indian systems in the quest for liberation.

264 Goekoop, C. The Logic of Invariable Concomitance in the Tattvacintāmaṇi. Dordrecht, Holland: D. Reidel, 1967, 162 pp.
Text and translation of the Anumiti and Vyāpti sections of the Tattvacintāmaṇi, together with an introduction and copious notes using symbolic logic and diagrams to clarify the difficulties involved.

265 Gokhale, Balkrishna G. Indian Thought through the Ages: A Study of Some Dominant Concepts. New York: Asia Publishing House, 1961, xi + 236 pp.
An historian's examination of concepts relevant to social philosophy.

266 Gore, N.N.S. A Rational Refutation of the Hindu Philosophical Systems. Translated by Fitzedward Hall. Calcutta: Christian Tracts and Books Society, 1862, x + 284 pp.
Unique--a serious, internal criticism of Hindu thought as a whole.

267 Griffin, Ralph T.H., trans. The Hymns of the Ṛgveda. 2 vols. Chowkhamba Sanskrit Series Studies, no. 35. Vāranasi: Chowkhamba, 1963, 1:4 + xvi + 706 pp.; 2:4 + 672 pp. (Orig. pub. Benares: E.J. Lazarus, 4 vols., 1889-92.)
Still the best complete translation available in English.

268 Griffiths, Paul J. "Buddhist Hybrid English: Some Notes on Philology and Hermeneutics for Buddhologists." Journal of the International Association of Buddhist Studies 4, no. 2 (1981):17-32.
A cogent complaint against the barbarous rendition of Buddhist texts which is prevalent nowadays. The author refreshingly suggests that a large part of Buddhist texts are better left untranslated, and for the rest "translation is only occasionally the most appropriate method."

269 Griffiths, Paul J. "Concentration on Insight: The Problematic of Theravāda Buddhist Meditation Theory." Journal of the American Academy of Religion 49 (1981):605-24.
There are two radically different types of meditative practice: of samādhi, leading to cessation, and of prajñā or vipassanā, leading to wisdom. Without attempting to resolve the problem of the apparent incompatibility of these, Griffiths suggests how they might be viewed as related to the desire to be liberated from desire and ignorance, respectively.

270 Griffiths, Paul J. "Notes towards a Critique of Buddhist Karmic Theory." Religious Studies 18, no. 3 (September 1982):277-91.

Unusual in writings on Buddhism, or indeed on Indian philosophy in general, Griffiths asks of Buddhist karma theory: (1) is it contradictory?, (2) is there evidence for it?, (3) does it explain what it was intended to explain?, (4) is it unable to explain things it proposes to? These questions are addressed to seven Buddhist philosophical claims, with mixed results. A remarkably clear-cut analysis.

271 Griffiths, Paul J. On Being Mindless: Buddhist Meditation and the Mind-Body Problem. La Salle, Ill.: Open Court, 1986, xxii + 220 pp.

This work deals with a particular problem in Buddhism, the attainment of cessation (nirodhasamāpatti). Chapters are devoted to Theravāda, Vaibhāṣika, and Yogācāra treatments of the topics with appendixes providing detailed analyses of passages in the Abhidharmakośabhāṣya and Abhidharmasamuccayabhāṣya. A combination of care and insight in both Sanskrit scholarship and philosophical analysis make this something of a breakthrough in this area.

272 Guenther, Herbert V. Philosophy and Psychology in the Abhidharma. Lucknow: Buddha Vihara, 1957, 404 pp. Reprint. Delhi: Berkeley, 1974.

A helpful account of Abhidharma views on mind, meditation, the world, and the path to liberation, based on the writings of Buddhaghosa, Asaṅga, and Vasubandhu. Some tables at the end encapsulate the accounts of these authors and one or two Tibetan accounts stemming from the same schools.

273 Guha, Dinesh Chandra. Navya Nyāya System of Logic: Some Basic Theories and Techniques. Varanasi: Bharatiya Vidya Prakasan, 1968, xvi + 335 pp.

Extremely difficult material explored with about as much success as could be expected. Special expository procedures are required to render Navya-Nyāya. However, this is one of the few works to follow up on Ingalls' pioneering efforts to deal with Navya-Nyāya in English. (See entry 315).

274 Gupta, Rita. "The Buddhist Doctrine of Momentariness and Its Presuppositions." Journal of Indian Philosophy 8 (1980):47-68.

A close analysis of the section of Dharmakīrti's Hetubindu in which he argues for the doctrine of momentariness.

275 Gupta, Sanjukta. Studies in the Philosophy of Madhusūdana Sarasvatī. Calcutta: Sanskrit Pustak Bhandar, 1966, iii + xxii + 230 + vii pp.

A doctor's thesis covering Madhusūdana's place in the history of Advaita, his epistemology, metaphysics, and theory of liberation and of devotion, with frequent comparisons with contemporary and other relevant writers.

276 Gupta, Shanti Nath. The Indian Concept of Values. New Delhi: Manohar, 1978, x + 197 pp.

Perhaps the most thorough study of the four puruṣārthas to appear under one cover. The author argues that while the four values are arranged axiologically, each is independent ontologically.

277 Gupta, Sisir Kumar. Madhusūdana Sarasvatī on the Bhagavad Gītā. Delhi: Motilal Banarsidass, 1977, xvi + 343 pp.

Madhusūdana brings to his commentary all his considerable knowledge of Indian philosophical systems other than Advaita, as well as a mastery of Advaita dialectical method. The result is one of the greatest interpretations of Saṃkara, a masterpiece of interpretation.

278 Hacker, Paul. "Śaṃkarācārya and Śaṃkara-bhagavatpāda." New Indian Antiquary 9 (1947):175-86.

A world-renowned authority's views on the authenticity of various works ascribed to Saṃkara.

279 Hacker, Paul. "The Sāṃkhyization of the Emanation Doctrine Shown in a Critical Analysis of Texts." Wiener Zeitschrift für die Kunde Süd- und Ostasiens 5 (1961):75-112.

Studies the Śāntiparvan of the Mahābhārata for Sāṃkhya ideas and also various Purāṇas. Concludes with the reconstruction of the contents of an old Sāṃkhya text differing somewhat from the Sāṃkhyakārikās and predating them.

280 Halbfass, Wilhelm. Studies in Kumārila and Śaṃkara. Studien zur Indologie und Iranistik, 9. Reinbek: Verlach für Orientalistische Fachpublikationen, 1983, v + 140 pp.

A collection of papers: "Kumārila on Ahiṃsā and Dharma," "Human Reason and Vedic Revelation in the Philosophy of Saṃkara," and "Saṃkara and Kumārila on the Plurality of Religious Traditions." In an appendix of notes on the Yogasūtrabhāṣyavivaraṇa, Halbfass retains a judicious ambivalence, remaining unconvinced that Saṃkara wrote the Yoga commentary, while admitting himself unable to prove it.

281 Halbfass, Wilhelm. "The Vaiśeṣika Concept of Guṇa and the Problem of Universals." Wiener Zeitschrift für die Kunde Süd- und Ostasiens 24 (1980):225-38.

Criticizes and improves on Potter's thesis of the unrepeatability of guṇas in Nyāya-Vaiśeṣika.

282 Haldar, Aruna. Some Psychological Aspects of Early Buddhist Philosophy Based on Abhidharmakośa of Vasubandhu. Asiatic Society Monograph Series, no. 25. Calcutta: Asiatic Society, 1981, xxv + 200 pp.

More works of this sort on Abhidharma are needed. This one reviews what the Abhidharmakośa tells us about the four "internal" skandhas of vedanā, saṃjñā, vijñāna, and saṃskāra, but is especially useful since it brings to bear comparisons with Western psychological notions.

283 Hanayama, Shoyu. "A Summary of Various Research on the Prajñāpāramitā Literature by Japanese Scholars." Acta Asiatica 10 (1966):16-93.

Supplements and in some instances controverts Conze's similar survey in The Prajñāpāramitā Literature (see entry 164). Unless one reads Japanese, one has only this and a small number of similar guides to work with.

284 Haribhadra Suri. Saddarśanasamuccaya. Translated by K. Sacchidananda Murty. Tenali: Tagore Publishing House, 1957, 143 pp.

A work by a Jain philosopher surveying the schools existing in his time, providing brief synopses of their tenets, and indicating the superiority of the Jain position.

285 Hariharananda Aranya. Yoga Philosophy of Patañjali. Translated by P.N. Mukherji. Calcutta: University of Calcutta, 1963, iv + 472 pp.

Yogasūtras and Vyāsa's Bhāṣya in Sanskrit, with the English explanation by Hariharananda, one of the great modern exponents of the Yoga system.

286 Harvey, Peter. "'Signless' Meditations in Pāli Buddhism." Journal of the International Association of Buddhist Studies 9, no. 1 (1986):25-52.

Normal states of consciousness cling to "signs" (nimitta). As insight arises consciousness is first directed away from external signs as śamatha meditation. From the fourth meditative state a meditation can enter the four "signless" (animitta) attainments, eventually achieving signless objects until finally, when an arhat, "consciousness is no object, not even a signless one, but is nibbāna."

287 Hasurkar, S.S. "Maṇḍana Miśra's Views on Error." Adyar Library Bulletin 23 (1959):19-38.

Attempts to discover Maṇḍana's views on khyātivāda (theory of error) in Brahmasiddhi and Vibhramaviveka. Hasurkar thinks Maṇḍana did not accept anirvacanīyakhyāti.

288 Hasurkar, S.S. Vācaspati Miśra on Advaita Vedānta. Darbhanga: Mithila Institute, 1958, 257 pp.

This work is not easy to read, but is full of information on early Advaita--Śaṃkara, his pupils, Maṇḍana and the early commentators, especially, of course, Vācaspati.

289 Hattori, Masaaki. "Apoha and Pratibhā." In Sanskrit and Indian Studies. Essays in Honour of Daniel H. Ingalls, edited by Masatoshi Nagatomi, B.K. Matilal, J.M. Masson, and Edward Dimock. Dordrecht, Holland: D. Reidel, 1980, pp. 61-73.

The clearest explanation of the Buddhist theory of apoha available. Hattori indicates how Dignāga borrows from Bhartṛhari in his theory of pratibhā, as well as why Śāntarakṣita interpreted apoha anew in a positive way to meet a criticism of Kumārila's.

290 Hattori, Masaaki. Dignāga on Perception. Harvard Oriental Series, no. 47. Cambridge: Harvard University Press, 1968, 265 pp.

Section of Dignāga's Pramāṇasamuccaya dealing with perception, edited (in Tibetan) and translated by an outstanding Japanese scholar. The book has massive amounts of footnotes and interpretative materials of great interest to students of Buddhist thought.

291 Hayes, Richard P. "Diṅnāga's Views on Reasoning (Svārthānumāna)." Journal of Indian Philosophy 8 (1980):219-77.

Translation of a portion of the inference-for-oneself (svārthānumāna) section of Pramāṇasamuccaya, accompanied by a clear (though not especially innovative) interpretative essay on it.

292 Hayes, Richard P. "The Question of Doctrinalism in the Buddhist Epistemologists." Journal of the American Academy of Religion 52 (1984):645-70.

Did Buddhist epistemologists like Vasubandhu, Dignāga, Dharmakīrti, and Śāntarakṣita view their study as scientific--like grammar or medicine--or as defense of traditional dogma? Hayes argues that the four Buddhist philosophers mentioned come to represent a "full circle" on this question.

293 Hegde, R.D. "The Nature and Number of Pramāṇas according to the Lokāyata System." Annals of the Bhandarkar Oriental Institute 63 (1982):99-120.

Jayanta Bhaṭṭa gives generous space to the materialist opinions of a Bhaṭṭa Udbhaṭa, apparently the well-known rhetorician dated 779-813. This paper unpacks what can be gleaned from the two works that appear to refer to him.

294 Heimann, Betty. Facets of Indian Thought. New York: Schocken, 1964, 177 pp.

Posthumous essays by one of the most original of Indological scholars. Chapter headings include "India's Biology," "Indian Metaphysics," "Indian Eschatology," "Indian Logic," and "Indian Grammar and Style." Shows very individualistic treatment of all subjects.

295 Heimann, Betty. The Significance of Prefixes in Sanskrit Philosophical Terminology. Royal Asiatic Society Monographs, no. 25. Hertford: Royal Asiatic Society, 1951, 99 pp.

Has an unusual approach, which may be helpful for those students who undertake Sanskrit for the purpose of reading Indian philosophical texts.

296 Herman, Arthur L. An Introduction to Buddhist Thought: A Philosophic History of Indian Buddhism. Lanham, Md.: University Press of America, 1983, xx + 457 pp.

Herman applies his chatty approach, so successfully used in his previous general introduction to Indian philosophy, here to Buddhism. Useful as a first reading for the uninitiated, the approach here takes for granted the relevance of Buddhism to philosophy as taught in the Western world, an avenue not so common in present times.

297 Herman, Arthur L. An Introduction to Indian Thought. Englewood Cliffs, N.J.: Prentice-Hall, 1976, xv + 301 pp.

Intended to introduce students to philosophy and to Indian thought at the same time, this textbook spends a lot of time analyzing arguments culled from (or imputed to) passages in the Vedas, Upaniṣads, and Bhagavadgītā, making little attempt to bring the student into the debates among the classical systems on technical issues.

298 Herman, Arthur L. "Two Dogmas of Empiricism." Journal of the Ganganatha Jha Research Institute 18-19 (1982-83):87-108.

The two dogmas are (1) "that the impermanence (anitya) of existence leads to pain or sorrow (duḥkha) and (2) that impermanence and sorrow can both be ended." Herman argues that (1) and (2) are (a) false and (b) mutually inconsistent.

299 Hino, Shoun. Sureśvara's Vārtika on Yājñavalkya-Maitreyī Dialogue: Bṛhadāraṇyakopaniṣad 2.4 and 4.5. Delhi: Motilal Banarsidass, 1982, xiv + 327 pp.

Sureśvara's vast commentary is virtually unavailable in translation. The present book makes a beginning toward its translation. An introduction brings out certain important features of Sureśvara's thought and its relation to other Advaitins such as Gauḍapāda, Śaṃkara, and Ānandagiri.

300 Hiriyanna, Mysore. "Bhartṛprapañca: An Old Vedāntin." Indian Antiquary 53 (1924):77-94. Reprinted in Indian Philosophical Studies 1 (Mysore: Kavyalaya, 1957), pp. 79-94.

Reconstructs the philosophy of an old Vedāntin against whom Śaṃkara explicitly jousts in many of his writings. Bhartṛprapañca was an early advocate of what is now called bhedābhedavāda, as well as of the theory that knowledge and action are together required to achieve liberation: both theories are rejected by Śaṃkara.

301 Hiriyanna, Mysore. "The Doctrine of Niyoga." Journal of Oriental Research 15 (1945):37-47.

Offers views of Prabhākara and his school on karma and dharma. A clear exposition of technical Mīmāṃsā notions.

302 Hiriyanna, Mysore. The Essentials of Indian Philosophy. London: Allen and Unwin, 1949, 216 pp.

Shorter, and with less detail than his Outlines (see entry 304), but contains added sections on original Buddhism and on Dvaita Vedānta.

303 Hiriyanna, Mysore. "Fragments of Bhartṛprapañca." Proceedings of the All-India Oriental Congress 3 (1924):439-50.

Extant passages attributed to Bhartṛprapañca translated.

304 Hiriyanna, Mysore. Outlines of Indian Philosophy. London: Allen and Unwin, 1932, 419 pp.

One of the most successful introductory works on Indian thought. Somewhat larger than Hiriyanna's later Essentials (see entry 302) but covering the same ground, it is a sound, honest account broached in a relatively nontechnical language.

305 Hiriyanna, Mysore. "Prābhākaras--Old and New." Journal of Oriental Research 4 (1930):99-140.

The new school of Prābhākara Mīmāṃsā differs in several respects from the old, in (a) new categories, (b) the introduction of tripuṭi doctrine, (c) the theory of error, and (d) the view that affective qualities require cognition to reveal them.

306 Hiriyanna, Mysore. "The Problem of Truth." In Indian Philosophical Studies 1. Mysore: Kavyalaya, 1957, pp. 1-18.

This essay, together with the next four printed in the book, cover several of the major theories of error found in Indian philosophy.

307 Hoffman, Bengt R. Christian Social Thought in India: 1947-1962; An Evaluation. Social Concerns Series, no. 14. Bangalore: Christian Institute for the Study of Religion and Society, 1967, vii + 224 pp.

Based on a dissertation. A thematic approach to modern social issues by Christian writers.

308 Hoffman, F.J. "Rationality in Early Buddhist Fourfold Logic." Journal of Indian Philosophy 10 (1982):309-37.

A sensible solution to the vexing problem of interpreting the catuṣkoṭi. Hoffman reviews the suggestions of others, then proposes a very natural reading of the third koṭi as "there exists an x such that y applies (in part) and z applies in part" (where y and z are characteristics of a thing). He argues that no contradictions arise from this reading.

309 Hopkins, E. Washburn. Ethics of India. New Haven: Yale University Press, 1924, 265 pp.

Studies mainly moral ideas as found in the Vedas, Upaniṣads, legal literature, and Buddhism. Concluding chapters on ethical aberrations, pro and contra. Readable, now superseded by more thorough books on same topic.

310 Hopkins, E. Washburn. "Yoga-Technique in the Great Epic." Journal of the American Oriental Society 22 (1901):333-79.

The development of yoga as a philosophical concept in the Mahābhārata.

311 Hume, R.E. The Thirteen Principal Upanishads. London: Humphrey Milford, 1931, xvi + 588 pp.

Standard translations of Bṛhadāraṇyaka, Chāndogya, Taittirīya, Aitareya, Kauṣītakī, Kena, Kaṭha, Īśā, Muṇḍaka, Praśna, Māṇḍūkya, Śvetāśvatara and Maitrī Upaniṣads. Contains also an introductory essay on the philosophy of the Upaniṣads and a helpful annotated bibliography.

312 Huntington, C.W., Jr. "The System of the Two Truths in the Prasannapadā and the Mādhyamakāvatāra: A Study in Mādhyamika Soteriology." Journal of Indian Philosophy 11 (1983):77-106.

Huntington thoughtfully and clearly analyzes Candrakīrti's interpretation of the Mādhyamika approach to things, drawing useful comparisons with Wittgenstein. His purpose is to refute facile interpretations of what we are asked to believe to be neither an ontological nor an epistemological concern, but a very pragmatic one.

313 Iida, Shotaro. Reason and Emptiness: A Study in Logic and Mysticism. Tokyo: Hokuseido Press, 1980, vi + 321 pp.

The main contribution of this book is an edition and translation of a portion of Bhāvaviveka's Mādhyamakahṛdaya and its autocommentary Tarkajvālā. In addition we are provided a thorough scholarly résumé of the literary history and bibliography of Bhāvaviveka, a translation of a Tibetan work espousing Bhāvaviveka's school, and some scholarly reflections on the "two-truths" and "three-truths" theories in Buddhism.

314 Ingalls, Daniel Henry Holmes. "Authority and Law in Ancient India." Journal of the American Oriental Society, supp. 17 (1954):34-45.

A short but probing analysis of the character of the ancient legal tradition.

315 Ingalls, Daniel Henry Holmes. Materials for the Study of Navya-Nyāya Logic. Harvard Oriental Series, no. 40. Cambridge: Harvard University Press, 1951, 182 pp.

A pioneering work, expounding Navya-Nyāya concepts in English, that makes limited use of symbolism and proceeds mostly by painstaking explanations of technical notions. The work takes careful study, but repays the effort handsomely. It is absolutely essential for students of Indian logic.

316 Ingalls, Daniel Henry Holmes. "Śaṃkara on the Question: Whose is Avidyā?" Philosophy East and West 3 (1954):291-306.

Suggests methodology for studying Saṃkara: using Bhāskara (a contemporary) as a foil. Concludes that the Bṛhadāraṇyakopaniṣadbhāṣya is a more original piece of writing than the Brahmasūtrabhāṣya.

317 Ingalls, Daniel Henry Holmes. "The Study of Śaṃkarācārya." Annals of the Bhandarkar Oriental Research Institute 33 (1952):1-14.

Ingalls characterizes different kinds of approaches to the study of Saṃkara--those of the believer, the philosopher, the historian. In the spirit of the last, he discusses the authenticity of certain works usually ascribed to Saṃkara.

318 Iyengar, P.T. Srinivasa. Outlines of Indian Philosophy. Benares: Theosophical Publishing Society, 1909, vii + vi + x + 302 pp.

The common ideas of Indian thought are: man as a complex of consciousness, mind, and matter; ātman, mind, free will, sense-organs, subtle body, pralaya, guṇas, kalpas, tanmātras, vital breaths, karma, beginninglessness, liberation. Iyengar surveys all the systems.

319 Iyer, K.A. Subramania. Bhartṛhari: A Study of the Vākyapadīya in the Light of the Ancient Commentaries. Poona: Deccan College Postgraduate and Research Institute, 1969, xiv + 597 pp.

Explores all aspects of Bhartṛhari's life, works, and thought and reviews scholarship on these topics.

320 Iyer, M.K. Venkatarama. Advaita Vedānta according to Saṃkara. Bombay: Asia Publishing House, 1964, xii + 213 pp.

Straightforward introduction to this system.

321 Iyer, N. Raghavan. The Moral and Political Thought of Mahātma Gandhi. New York: Oxford University Press, 1973, xiii + 449 pp.

A more substantial treatment than provided in earlier works, the book seeks to clarify and occasionally to assess "the solid conceptual foundations" of Gandhi's moral and political thought.

322 Jacobi, Hermann. "Dates of the Philosophical Sūtras of the Brahmans." Journal of the American Oriental Society 31 (1910):1-29.

The basic, indispensable work on the subject.

323 Jacobi, Hermann. Studies in Jainism. Ahmedabad: Jaina Sahitya Samsodhaka Karyalay, 1946, 92 pp.

Three lectures on Jainism by a famous European scholar. The third essay develops an interesting comparison between

Sāṃkhya and Jainism, finding that they play a parallel role in the development of Indian thought.

324 Jagirdar, P.J. Studies in the Social Thought of M.G. Ranade. New York: Asia Publishing House, 1963, vii + 148 pp.
An examination of the philosophical perspective of a distinguished modern social reformer.

325 Jaimini. The Mīmāṃsā Sūtras of Jaimini. Translated by Mohan Lal Sandal. Sacred Books of the Hindus, no. 27. Allahabad: Panini Office, 1923-25, 1 + 122 pp.
The original sūtras of Pūrvamīmāṃsā.

326 Jain, Champat Rai. The Key of Knowledge. New Delhi: Today & Tomorrow's Printers & Publishers, 1975, 788 + cix + xlviii.
This book will not please the impartial scholar, but it is worthy of notice as a unique effort to compare Jainism with other religious views, notably Christianity. The author is frankly an enthusiast, but this makes his approach the more attractive, and his explanations of Jain views must be among the most generous and detailed available.

327 Jain, S.C. Structure and Function of Soul in Jainism. Murtidevi Jaina Granthamala English Series, no. 7. New Delhi: Bharatiya Jnanpith, 1978, xv + 239 pp.
A philosophically knowledgeable, well-written, and not heavily textual study of Jainism.

328 Jaini, Padmanabh S., ed. Abhidharmapradīpa with Vibhāṣaprabhāvṛtti. Tibetan Sanskrit Works Series, no. 4. Darbhanga: Mithila Institute, 1959, xiv + 144 + 499 pp.
Jaini's introduction has a sixteen-page summary of the contents of the work; a useful series of tables giving the dharmas of such works as Abhidharmasamuccaya, Abhidharmakośa, etc.; a survey of Buddhaghoṣa's list of dharmas; and a discussion of some major controversies between the author of the Abhidharmapradīpa and Vasubandhu the Kośakara.

329 Janacek, A. "The Methodological Principle in Yoga according to Patañjali's Yogasūtras." Archiv Orientalni 19 (1951):514-67.
The method of yoga is "cultivation of opposite (of perverse-considerations)." It shows how to replace qualitative change by quantitative increase, repetition by dispassion. Concentration on God fits this pattern, opposes the kleśas. This work is interesting and worthwhile, but technical and long.

330 Jayatilleke, K.N. Early Buddhist Theory of Knowledge. London: G. Allen and Unwin, 1963, 519 pp.
The definitive work on early Buddhist philosophy by a famous Sinhalese scholar who studied at Cambridge under renowned

analytic philosophers (including Wittgenstein) and who adds considerable analytic acumen to his linguistic expertise.

331   Jayatilleke, K.N. *The Message of the Buddha*. London: George Allen and Unwin, 1975, 3 + 262 pp.
"The purpose of these talks is to present the basic tenets of Theravāda Buddhism as a self-consistent and rational system based throughout on empirical evidence." (Edward Conze)

332   Jha, Ganganatha. *Pūrva-Mīmāṃsā in Its Sources*. Benares: Benares Hindu University, 1942, 386 + xvii pp.
Jha's work studies major topics of Mīmāṃsā as found in Śabara, Prabhākara, and Kumārila. Both philosophical concepts and concepts having to do with the theory of sacrifice are examined. This work, the most important single source in English on Mīmāṃsā, belongs in every collection. Mishra's critical Bibliography of Mīmāṃsā, included as an appendix (81 pp.), identifies all Mīmāṃsakas known to us through their works or references to them.

333   Jha, Ganganatha. "A Synopsis of the Cardinal Doctrines of the Sāṃkhya Philosophy." In *Vācaspati Miśra's Tattvakaumudī on the Sāṃkhya-Kārikās*, translated by Ganganatha Jha. Poona Oriental Series, no. 10. Poona: Oriental Book Agency, 1934, pp. 30-45.
A useful, condensed account of the Sāṃkhya categories, the gist of the *Sāṃkhyakārikās*.

334   Jha, Mitra Nandan. *Modern Indian Political Thought: Ram Mohan Roy to Present Day*. Meerut: Meenakshi Prakashan, 1975, xx + 348 pp.
Short treatments of many modern thinkers and perspectives, whose philosophies are seen as expressions of a spiritualist view of life.

335   Johannson, Rune E.A. *The Dynamic Psychology of Early Buddhism*. Scandinavian Institute of Asian Studies Monograph Series, no. 37. London: Curzon Press, 1979, 236 pp.
An exhaustive attempt to understand the chain of dependent origination (*pratītyasamutpāda*). Johansson's style is engagingly challenging.

336   Johnston, E.H. *Early Sāṃkhya*. London: Royal Asiatic Society, 1937, 91 pp.
An essay on the historical development of Sāṃkhya. One of the best works of historical scholarship.

337   Johnston, E.H. "Some Sāṃkhya and Yoga Conceptions of the Śvetāśvatara Upaniṣad." *Journal of the Royal Asiatic Society of Great Britain and Ireland* (1930):855-78.
Traces origins of these systems in the Upaniṣads.

338 Joshi, K.S. "The Concept of Liberation in Yoga Philosophy." Journal of the University of Saugar 16 (1965-67):78-94.
Argues that liberation in Yoga is all mental.

339 Joshi, N.V. Indian Philosophy from the Ontological Point of View. Bombay: Somaiya Publications Private, 1977, xiii + 290 pp.
The "ontological point of view" contrasts with the "logical" point of view, which is claimed to come subsequently and to have obscured man's insight into the world. This approach attempts to avoid logic and to concentrate on ontology in a selection from the main systems.

340 Joshi, Shanti. The Message of Śaṃkara. Allahabad: Lokbharti, 1968, 196 pp.
Contents include: theories of self, theories of appearance (khyātivāda), and Śaṃkara and the contemporary context. The last section compares Saṃkara with existentialists, logical positivists, phenomenologists, Aurobindo, R.D. Ranade, K.C. Bhattacharya, and Radhakrishnan.

341 Kabir, Humayun. Education in New India. 2d ed. London: Allen and Unwin, 1959, ix + 235 pp.
Essays on a number of facets and problems by a leader in Indian education in the period after independence.

342 Kabir, Humayun. Indian Philosophy of Education. Bombay: Asia Publishing House, 1961, 256 pp.
Many of the essays are convocation addresses; the last four articulate various aspects of the philosophy of education--traditional and modern--in India.

343 Kajiyama, Yuichi. "Bhāvaviveka and the Prāsaṅgika School." Nava-Nalanda-Mahāvihāra Research Publications 1 (1957):291-331.
A fine account of the method of this most interesting Buddhist philosopher.

344 Kalghatgi, T.G. Jaina View of Life. Sholapur: Jaina Samskriti Samraksaka Sangha, 1969, xii + 200 pp.
A standard introduction to Jain philosophy.

345 Kalupahana, David J. Buddhist Philosophy: A Historical Analysis. Honolulu: University of Hawaii Press, 1976, xxi + 189 pp.
A philosopher looks at Buddhist thought, both Theravāda and Mahāyāna, both early and late.

346 Kalupahana, David J. Causality: The Central Philosophy of Buddhism. Honolulu: University of Hawaii Press, 1975, 320 pp.
Historical study of the concept as treated in early Buddhism. Comparisons and contrasts with Western doctrines.

347 Kalupahana, David J. "The Early Buddhist Notion of the Middle Path." *Eastern Buddhist* 12, no. 1 (1979):30-48.

"In the present paper I propose to show that early Buddhism is radically different from all these schools (such as Sarvāstivāda, Sautrāntika, Mādhyamika, Yogācāra, etc.), at least as far as their philosophical content is concerned." Specifically, it is argued here that Buddhism originally taught a "straightforward empiricist theory of causation."

348 Kalupahana, David J. "The Philosophy of Relations in Buddhism." *University of Ceylon Review* 20 (1962):19-54, 188-208.

Terms (*hetu*, *pratyāya*, *adhipati*, etc.) for causal factors are explained. Also discussed are: how the theory of *pratyāyas* supplements *pratītyasamutpāda*, and its relevance to basic problems of philosophy and ethics.

349 Kanakura, Yensho. *Hindu-Buddhist Thought in India*. Translated by Shotaro Iida and Neal Donner. Edited by Takao Maruyama and Thomas Quinn. Yokohama: Hokke Journal, 1980, xix + 286 pp.

A reasonably brief, clear account of Hindu and Buddhist philosophy, taken in systematic historical perspective. As may be expected from a scholar of Buddhism, Kanakura's comments on Buddhist materials is especially helpful.

350 Kandaswamy, S.N. *Buddhism as Expounded in Manimekhalai*. Annamalainagar: Annamalai University, 1978, iii + 410 pp.

Kandaswamy gives extensive argumentation to fix the date of the *Manimekhalai*'s author, Cattanar, as 450-550 A.D. A similarly exhaustive effort goes into the review of the work's treatment of Buddhism, unique as the work is in Tamil. The result is an especially instructive and unusual view of philosophy at work in south India.

351 Kane, P.V. *History of Dharmaśāstra*. Vol. 5, pt. 2. Poona: Bhandarkar Oriental Research Institute, 1962, xxxiv + 992 + xxii + 269 pp.

Chapters 28-35 deal with Mīmāmsā and Sāṃkhya in their relation to *dharmaśāstra*. Chapter 35, on karma and transmigration, provides an interesting bibliography of Indian and Western works on these topics.

352 Kaplan, Stephen. "Mind, *Māyā*, and Holography: A Phenomenology of Projection." *Philosophy East and West* 33 (1983):367-78.

Appeals to holographic theory to explain how something can appear, not exist where it appears, and yet not be part of "the mind" either. Our perceptions are images experienced but without existence.

353 Karmarkar, Raghunath Damodar. *Śaṃkara's Advaita*. Dharwar: Karnatak University, 1966, 111 pp.

Contains chapters on fundamental concepts in Śaṃkara's Advaita, Brahman and the world, Brahman and the jīva, and mokṣa--the highest goal. Appendixes include (1) role of analogy in Advaita (sixty-seven similes in Brahmasūtrabhāṣya), (2) Śaṃkara's date, life, and works, and (3) Śaṃkara as a philosopher.

354 Karunadasa, Y. Buddhist Analysis of Matter. Colombo: Department of Cultural Affairs, 1967, xviii + 186 pp.
An analysis of matter as expressed in Theravāda, especially Abhidharma, Buddhism. Scholarly, important study.

355 Karve, Irawati. Hindu Society: An Interpretation. Poona: Deccan College, 1961, xi + 171 pp.
A distinguished anthropologist who is sensitive to philosophical dimensions of her work includes a chapter on "Indian Philosophy and Caste" in this probing study. (Many other anthropological studies are also pertinent to the consideration of social philosophy in India.)

356 Katsura, Shoryu. "Dharmakīrti's Theory of Truth." Journal of Indian Philosophy 12 (1984):215-35.
Dharmakīrti holds two different views of truth, one pragmatic, the other purely epistemological. The clearest account of Dharmakīrti's puzzling epistemological theory available.

357 Kattackal, Jacob. Religion and Ethics in Advaita. Freiburg im Breisgau: Verlag Herder, 1980, iv + 280 pp.
Somewhat technical, this is the most thorough study to date of Advaita ethics. The author's coverage ranges from the Upaniṣads through Śaṃkara and his pupils, Vidyāraṇya, Madhusūdana, and others; and concludes with Rāmakṛṣṇa and Vivekānanda.

358 Katz, Nathan, ed. Buddhist and Western Philosophy. New Delhi: Sterling Publishers Private, 1981, xxviii + 491 pp.
A collection of papers (only eight are published elsewhere) on Buddhism. Some are explicitly comparative; almost all are provocative and/or helpful. The contributors range around the world.

359 Katz, Nathan. "Does the 'Cessation of the World' Entail the Cessation of Emotions? The Psychology of the Arahant." Pali Buddhist Review 4, no. 3 (1979):53-65.
The answer to the question is: yes and no, some emotions do cease (grasping, worry), others do not (loving-kindness, compassion), and still others, like the desire to become an arahant, are or are not, depending on the context.

360 Kaul, H.K. Sri Aurobindo: A Descriptive Bibliography. New Delhi: Munshiram Manoharlal, 1972, xxvii + 222 pp.

Section A (pp. 1-26), "Social and Political Thought of Sri Aurobindo," lists 267 items by and about Aurobindo, but provides very little annotation.

361 Kauṇḍa Bhaṭṭa. The Sphoṭanirṇaya of Kauṇḍa Bhaṭṭa. Edited and translated by S.D. Joshi. Publications of the Centre of Advanced Study in Sanskrit, Class C, no. 2. Poona: University of Poona, 1967, v + 244 pp.

Translation of a chapter of a seventeenth-century grammatical work expounding the sphoṭa theory. Valuable introduction and notes by Joshi.

362 Kauṭilya. Arthaśāstra. Translated by Rudrapatna Shamasastry. 5th ed. Mysore: Sri Raghuveer Printing, 1956, xlii + 484 pp.

From this most prominent of ancient texts on the arts of statecraft, one may deduce ingredients of social and political philosophy.

363 Kaviraj, Gopinath. Gleanings from the History and Bibliography of the Nyāya-Vaiśeṣika Literature. Edited by Gaurinath Sastri. Varanasī: Sarasvati Bhavana Library, 1982, 3 + iii + 215 pp. (Originally published serially in Princess of Wales Saraswati Bhavana Studies 3-7, 1924-27, 85 pp.)

A survey, by a famous Indian scholar, of important figures in the history of Nyāya, from Bhāsarvajña onwards. It is mostly concerned with the works and lives of those studied, containing little on philosophy itself.

364 Kaw, R.K. The Doctrine of Recognition. Hoshiarpur: Vishveshvaranand Vedic Research Institute, 1967, xix + 398 pp.

One of the best books on Kashmir Saivism. Pays special attention to Somānanda and Utpāladeva, their works and thought.

365 Keenan, John P. "Original Purity and the Focus of Early Yogācāra." Journal of the International Association of Buddhist Studies 5, no. 1 (1982):7-18.

This helpful article presents a plausible account of the lines of development of Yogācāra thought in four fundamental texts, the Mahāyānasūtrālaṃkāra, Saṃdhinirmocanasūtra, Mahāyānābhidharmasūtra and Madhyāntavibhāga, all of which Keenan argues predate Asaṅga and Vasubandhu. He concludes that tathāgatagarbha comes from the same source as the other Yogācāra texts.

366 Keith, Arthur Berriedale. Buddhist Philosophy in India and Ceylon. Oxford: Clarendon Press, 1923, 339 pp.

Now a bit out of date, this is nevertheless an outstanding work, mixing generalities with specific details in just the right amount.

367 Keith, Arthur Berriedale. Indian Logic and Atomism. Oxford: Clarendon Press, 1921, 291 + 1 pp.

An exposition of the Nyāya and Vaiśeṣika systems by a well-known scholar.

368 Keith, Arthur Berriedale. The Karma-Mīmāṃsā. London and New York: Oxford; Calcutta: Association Press, 1921, 1 + 112 pp.
Deals with Pūrvamīmāṃsā philosophy.

369 Keith, Arthur Berriedale. The Religion and Philosophy of the Vedas and the Upaniṣads. 2 vols. Harvard Oriental Series, nos. 31, 32. Cambridge: Harvard University Press, 1925, 683 pp.
"It is the object of this work to present . . . a comprehensive but concise account of the whole of the religion and philosophy of the Vedic period in India."

370 Keith, Arthur Berriedale. The Sāṃkhya System. Calcutta: YMCA Publishing House, 1949, 128 pp. (Orig. pub. London: Oxford, 1918.)
A history of Sāṃkhya philosophy that discusses the origins of Sāṃkhya; its relation to Buddhism, Yoga, and Greek philosophy; the Ṣaṣṭitantra and the Sāṃkhyakārikās; and later Sāṃkhya. An important study; it is now somewhat out of date, but still useful.

371 Kennedy, Melville T. The Chaitanya Movement. Calcutta: YMCA Association Press; New York: Oxford, 1925, x + 270 pp.
Chapter 6 outlines the teaching of the sect. Other chapters discuss the history, literature, and orders of the sects and Caitanya's life.

372 Kent, Stephan A. "A Sectarian Interpretation of the Rise of Mahāyāna." Religion 12 (1982):311-32.
Basing his account on the Ratnaguṇasaṃcaya, the Aṣṭasāhasrikā and the Saddharmapuṇḍarīkā, Kent rehearses the evidence of social change accompanying the development of Mahāyāna within Hīnayāna monasteries.

373 Keyes, Charles F., and E. Valentine Daniel, eds. Karma: An Anthropological Inquiry. Berkeley and Los Angeles: University of California Press, 1983, 313 pp.
Though not primarily in the field of philosophy, this volume supplements those by O'Flaherty and Neufeldt by covering the way karma is treated in modern Hinduism and Buddhism in South and Southeast Asia. Though some papers analyze karma as it appears in written material, most of them are by anthropologists and are based on verbal documentation.

374 Kiyota, Minoru. Mahāyāna Buddhist Meditation: Theory and Practice. Honolulu: University of Hawaii Press, 1978, xv + 313 pp.
A collection of important papers by major contemporary scholars, including Elvin Jones, Geshe Sopa, Gadjin Nagao, Stefan

Anacker, Yuichi Kajiyama, Charlene McDermott, Francis Cook, Leon Hurvitz, and the editor.

375 Kloetzli, Randy. Buddhist Cosmology. Delhi: Motilal Banarsidass, 1983, xi + 195 pp.

One finds in Buddhist texts occasional cosmological accounts which speak of astonishing numbers of worlds. They are by no means always the same. This work collects, classifies, rationalizes, and analyzes these speculations, paying closest attention to the Abhidharmakośa and Mahāprajñāpāramitāsūtra. The approach emphasizes the basic agnosticism which is served by these vast metaphysical displays.

376 Klostermaier, Klaus. "Some Aspects of the Social Philosophy of Dr. Sarvepalli Radhakrishnan." Religion and Society 14 (1967):31-49.

A summary and analysis of Radhakrishnan's attention to problems of modern society.

377 Kocmarek, Ivan. Language and Release: Sarvajñātman's Pañcaprakriyā. Delhi: Motilal Banarsidass, 1985, ix + 147 pp.

A relatively brief but important work. Kocmarek provides a faithful translation and reviews the reasoning placing Sarvajñātman's work at the end of the 10th to the beginning of the 11th centuries.

378 Koelman, Gaspar M. Pātañjala Yoga. Poona: Papal Athenaeum, 1970, 280 pp.

Scholarly study of Yoga notions by a Jesuit Sanskritist, utilizing basic primary and secondary sources.

379 Koller, John M., et al. "Dharma and Li (A Symposium)." Philosophy East and West 22 (1972):131-68.

The papers on dharma (by John M. Koller, Gerald J. Larson, and Austin B. Creel) explore the philosophical dimensions and social ramifications of this central concept.

380 Koller, John M. The Indian Way. New York: Macmillan Co., 1982, vii + 406 pp.

An approach to Indian thought practically devoid of Sanskrit jargon, operating at a general level requiring no effort to understand the abstractions and distinctions so beloved of a good many authors of expositions of Indian thought.

381 Koller, John M. Oriental Philosophies. New York: Charles Scribner's Sons, 1970, xiii + 303 pp.

Chapter 4 ("Society and Philosophy") of part 1 ("The Hindu Systems") provides a short philosophical examination of social ideas (pp. 33-51); such a conceptualization is subject to some amendment in a fuller account by historians and social scientists of the relation of daily life to ultimate goals.

382 Koller, John M. "Types of Society: The Social Thought of Sri Aurobindo." International Philosophical Quarterly 12 (1972):220-33.

Aurobindo's analysis of forms and stages of society is examined with particular attention to the social concomitants of individual freedom. (The preceding article, by Grace Cairns, in this Aurobindo Symposium, considers the "types of society" in the framework of the philosophy of history.)

383 Kothari, Rajni. Politics in India. Boston: Little, Brown & Co., 1970, xvi + 461 pp.

A knowledgeable reviewer calls this "by far the most sophisticated general study of Indian politics that has yet been written," also saying "this is too sophisticated a book to be recommended as an introduction to Indian politics," since it is "more analytic than descriptive." Modern issues of development are stressed.

384 Krishna, Daya. "Democracy and Traditional Indian Values." In Contemporary India, edited by Baidya Nath Varma. Bombay: Asia Publishing House, 1964, pp. 119-29.

A philosopher examines the issues involved in the interaction of democratic institutions and traditional values.

385 Krishna, Daya. Social Philosophy (Past and Future). Simla: Indian Institute of Advanced Study, 1969, viii + 82 pp.

Essays on social philosophy, distinguishing sociocentric and Ātmancentric perspectives and predicaments; treats approaches to action and freedom in relation to society (from an urban vantage point).

386 Krishna, Raj. "Vedānta and Social Reform--A Contemporary Challenge." In Human Person, Society, and State, edited by P.D. Devanandan and M.M. Thomas. Bangalore: Committee for Literature on Social Concerns, 1957, pp. 1-13.

An economist explores issues of social ethics in modern Hinduism, particularly the relation of the metaphysical and ethical planes and the function of determined social norms. A much more commonly expressed perspective is provided in the paper by P. Sankaranarayanan in the same collection, "Human Person, Society and State--The Classical Hindu Approach," pp. 56-76.

387 Krishnamurti, J. On Education. New Delhi: Orient Longman, 1974, 106 pp.

Reflections on the educational process by a religious leader of modern India, given in talks at the two schools run by the Krishnamurti Foundation, India.

388 Krishna Warrier, A.G. The Concept of Mukti in Advaita Vedānta. Madras University Philosophical Series, no. 9. Madras: University of Madras, 1961, 564 pp.

This valuable resource is likely to be the most complete survey of Indian schools' views concerning liberation.

389 Krishna Warrier, A.G. God in Advaita. Simla: Indian Institute of Advanced Study, 1977, viii + 234 pp.

Thorough study of the account of God in the Upaniṣads and in Śaṃkara's philosophy. The author, who is knowledgeable about and critical of other views, reassesses the philosophy of Advaita by examining it from the standpoint of saguṇa Brahman (God), a perspective he believes to have been relatively neglected in current accounts of Advaita.

390 Kumar, Shiv. Upamāna in Indian Philosophy. Delhi: Eastern Book Linkers, 1980, xiv + 167 pp.

The last word on this topic.

391 Kumarappa, Bharatan. The Hindu Conception of the Deity as Culminating in Rāmānuja. London: Luzac, 1934, xv + 356 pp.

Traces theism in India from the Upaniṣads through the Gītā, Pañcarātra, Purāṇas, the Ālvārs to Rāmānuja. Second part of the work is devoted to Rāmānuja's philosophy of religion.

392 Kundakunda. Kundakunda, Aṣṭaprābhṛta. Translated by Jagat Prasad. Delhi, 1942.

Consists of eight works called "pahudas," viz.: Darśana-, Caritra-, Bhava-, Sūtra-, Bodha- and Mokṣa- (together called Ṣaṭprābhṛta), Liṅga-, and Śīla-pahuda. A Jain work.

393 Kundakunda. Kundakunda, Pañcāstikāyasāra. Translated by A. Chakravarti. Jñāna-Pītha Mūrtidevī Jaina Granthamālā English Series, no. 4. Varanaśi: Bharatiya Jnanapitha Publications, 1975, lxvii + 210 pp.

Important Jain treatise.

394 Kundakunda. Kundakunda's Pravacanasāra with Amṛtacandra Sūri's Tattvapradīpikā. Edited, with an introduction by F.W. Thomas, and translated by Barend Faddegon. Cambridge: Cambridge University Press, 1935, xxiv + 227 pp.

Another of Kundakunda's fundamental Jain treatises.

395 Kundakunda. Kundakunda, Samayasāra, with Amṛtacandra's Ātmakhyāti. Translated by A. Chakravarti. Varanasi: Bharatiya Jnanapitha, 1950, 240 pp.

A Jain work on the nature of the self, translated with extensive notes and a long introduction placing Jain philosophy in its proper place in world thought.

396 Kunhan Raja, C. "Cārvāka System." Philosophical Quarterly 36 (1963):15-32.

Cārvāka is the original Vedic system of thought!

397 Kunhan Raja, C. "In Defence of Mīmāṃsā." Adyar Library Bulletin 16 (1952):115-38, 168-93.

A rather enthusiastic but interesting work which emphasizes the harmony between the Mīmāṃsā and Vedānta and minimizes later technical developments. Has a section on "Mīmāṃsā as the planning of a national life!"

398 Kunhan Raja, C. Some Fundamental Problems in Indian Philosophy. Delhi: Motilal Banarsidass, 1960, v + 425 pp.

One of the better attempts to throw Indian philosophical questions into a form which will appeal to the Western-trained philosopher. Part 1, "The Modes of Knowing," covers the pramāṇas. Part 2, "The World: What, Why and How," reviews Vedic, Sāṃkhya, Nyāya, Vedānta, and Mīmāṃsā views. Part 3, "Man and His Destiny," covers karma, transmigration, and liberation.

399 Kunjunni Raja, K. Indian Theories of Meaning. Madras: Adyar Library and Research Center, 1963, 360 pp.

Probably the best overall account of Indian philosophy of language. Manages to deal with almost all of the central notions--meaning, sphoṭa, conditions of knowing the meaning of a sentence, secondary meaning as in metaphor, dhvani theory.

400 Kuppuswami Sastri, S. A Primer of Indian Logic According to Annambhaṭṭa's Tarkasaṃgraha. 2d ed. Mylapore and Madras: Kuppuswami Sastri Research Institute, 1951, 282 pp.

The translator's copious notes to this familiar handbook of Nyāya provide an excellent opening wedge for understanding the system, although the book suffers from not having Annambhaṭṭa's own commentary (Dīpikā).

401 Kuppuswamy, B. "The Quintessence of Yogavāsishtha." Brahmavādin 12 (1977):66, 130, 194; 13 (1978):2.

A helpful running analysis of this mammoth work, clearly written. The final section attempts to gauge the work's relevance to contemporary life.

402 Lad, A.K. A Comparative Study of the Concept of Liberation in Indian Philosophy. Burhanpur: Girdharlal Keshandas, 1967, 208 pp.

The usual dissertation, exhaustive, dull, but helpful for those working on the topic. This topic, needless to say, is one which students of Indian philosophy can hardly help working on.

403 Lal, P., trans. The Mahābhārata: Translated from the Sanskrit of Vyāsa. 83 vols. Calcutta: Writers' Workshop, 1968-74.

The most available translation of the great epic.

404 Lamotte, Étienne. "The Assessment of Textual Authenticity in Buddhism." Buddhist Studies Review 1, no. 1 (1983-84):4-15; 2, nos. 1-2 (1985):4-24.

How do Buddhists decide which are, and which are not, authoritative Buddhist works? Lamotte reviews answers to this problem found in Buddhist works. The articles first appeared in French in 1949.

405 Lang, Karen Christine. "Via negativa in Mahāyāna Buddhism and Gnosticism." Eastern Buddhist 14, no. 1 (1981):43-60.

Edward Conze suggested over twenty years ago connections between the thought of Buddhism and gnosticism. Since then the tractates discovered at Nag Hammadi have been edited and translated, and it is possible now to explore the comparison. This Lang has done here, demonstrating a number of similarities.

406 Lannoy, Richard. The Speaking Tree: A Study of Indian Culture and Society. London: Oxford University Press, 1971, xxvii + 466 pp.

Many of the interpretations in this provocative book are subject to challenge. One unusual feature is its linkage of aesthetic and social concerns in the exploration of the dominant currents in Indian culture.

407 Larrabee, M.J. "The One and the Many: Yogācāra Buddhism and Husserl." Philosophy East and West 31 (1981):3-15.

Uses Husserl's theory of inner time-consciousness to shed light on Yogācāra's idea of the ālayavijñāna.

408 Larson, Gerald James. Classical Sāṃkhya: An Interpretation of Its History and Meaning. Delhi: Motilal Banarsidass, 1969, 312 pp.

Larson reviews the history of the interpretations of Sāṃkhya by famous European scholars, and then offers his own. He also provides the text and translation of the Sāṃkhyakārikās. This is the most recent and exhaustive summation of our understanding of this difficult-to-assess system.

409 Larson, Gerald James. "An Eccentric Ghost in the Machine: Formal and Quantitative Aspects of Sāṃkhya-Yoga Dualism." Philosophy East and West 33 (1983):219-34.

Sāṃkhya "is a classic case of a philosophy that wants to have its idealist/realist/materialist cake and eat it too!" The "ghost" is consciousness (puruṣa). A lively, friendly approach to Sāṃkhya.

410 Law, Bimala Churn. Buddhaghoṣa. Bombay Branch Royal Asiatic Society Monograph, no. 1. Bombay: Royal Asiatic Society, Bombay Branch, 1946, viii + 147 pp.

Mainly historical study, but contains chapters characterizing Buddhaghoṣa's philosophy.

411 Lazarus, F.K. Rāmānuja and Bowne. Bombay: Chetana, 1962, 332 pp.

A dissertation in comparative philosophy.

412 Lele, Jayant, ed. *Tradition and Modernity in Bhakti Movements*. International Studies in Sociology and Social Anthropology, no. 31. Leiden: E.J. Brill, 1981, 160 pp.

A group of mostly Western scholars examines many of the most important bhakti movements of present-day India as well as those of the past. Lele's introduction is a model of the genre.

413 Lester, Robert C. *Rāmānuja and the Yoga*. Adyar: Adyar Library and Research Centre, 1976, xix + 185 pp.

"The question is, 'Can a theist practise Yoga without compromising his theistic world-view?'" Lester explains how Rāmanuja can and does.

414 Lindtner, Christian. "Atīśa's Introduction to the Two Truths and Its Sources." *Journal of Indian Philosophy* 9 (1981):169-214.

Besides the Tibetan text and English translation of this brief work, Atīśa's *Satyadvayāvatāra*, Lindtner gives us his characteristic overflowing collection of helpful supplements, including a translation of a relevant portion of Atīśa's *Bodhipāthapradīpa*, translations of passages on the two truths from works of Nāgārjuna, and an introduction that reviews the history of the topic throughout Buddhist philosophy.

415 Lindtner, Christian. "Buddhapālita on Emptiness." *Indo-Iranian Journal* 23 (1981):187-217.

Translation of Buddhapālita's *Vṛtti* on Chapter 18 of Nāgārjuna's *Mādhyamikakārikās*, which Lindtner rates the most important section of Buddhapālita's work.

416 Lindtner, Christian. *Nagarjuniana: Studies in the Writings and Philosophy of Nāgārjuna*. Indiske studier, no. 4. Copenhagen: Akademisk Förlag, 1982, 327 pp.

The definitive account of scholarship on Nāgārjuna's works to date. Contains first English translations of *Śūnyatāsaptati*, *Vyavahārasiddhi*, *Yuktiṣaṣṭikā*, some of the *stavas*, the *Bodhicittavivaraṇa* and *Bodhisaṃbhāra(ka)*, the last two believed controversially by Lindtner to be Nāgārjuna's works. The current state of scholarship on the rest of Nāgārjuna's works is reviewed; Lindtner offers his views on which are authentic, which spurious.

417 Lindtner, Christian, ed. "A Treatise on Buddhist Idealism: Kambala's *Ālokamālā*." In *Miscellanea Buddhica*. Indiske studier, no. 5. Copenhagen: Akademisk Förlag, 1985, pp. 109-221.

Kambala is a hitherto practically unknown Buddhist philosopher; this is the first work of his to receive translation. Lindtner places Kambala's writing toward the beginning of the sixth century A.D. Kambala's philosophy is in the Yogācāra tradition.

418 Lingat, Robert. The Classical Law of India. Translated by J. Duncan M. Derrett. Berkeley and Los Angeles: University of California Press, 1973, xvii + 305 pp.

An introduction to the development of Hindu law, with a very useful bibliography.

419 Lipner, Julius J. The Face of Truth: A Study of Meaning and Metaphysics in the Vedantic Theology of Rāmānuja. London: Macmillan & Co., 1986, xiii + 183 pp.

This beautifully written little book approaches Rāmānuja as a theologian and not just a philosopher. It concentrates on Rāmānuja's hermeneutics, the theological aspects of Rāmānuja's metaphysics, and the relationship between the two.

420 Lipsey, Roger, ed. Coomaraswamy. 3 vols. Princeton, N.J.: Princeton University Press, 1977, 1:xxxviii + 580 pp.; 2:xxvi + 470 pp.; 3:xvii + 312 pp.

Fifty-six of Coomaraswamy's essays have been selected for this collection. Those in the first volume, Selected Papers: Traditional Art and Symbolism, include several of intrinsic interest to artists and art historians. Volume 2, Metaphysics, contains entirely philosophical papers, not necessarily the best-known, which can be found elsewhere. Volume 3, His Life and Work, is Lipsey's own account of Coomaraswamy's life and contributions, a sympathetic yet sophisticated biography.

421 Lokacarya, Pillai. Śrīvacanabhūṣaṇa. Edited, with an English translation, by Robert C. Lester. Madras: Kuppuswamy Sastri Research Institute, 1979, xi + 124 pp.

The brief introduction is helpful, especially the short summary of the contents of the work.

422 Lott, Eric L. God and the Universe in the Vedānta Theology of Rāmānuja: A Study in His Use of the Self-Body Analogy. Madras: Rāmānuja Research Society, 1976, xxiv + 247 pp.

An attempt to elucidate Rāmānuja's "principal thesis that the whole universe relates to God as body to soul," examine the sources of this notion, analyse how Rāmānuja distinguishes his position from others current at the time, and discuss the wider significance of the theory.

423 Lott, Eric L. Vedantic Approaches to God. London: Macmillan & Co., 1980, xii + 214 pp.

"Personally I find Vedānta to be essentially a theological discipline."

424 Loy, David. "The Difference between Saṃsāra and Nirvāṇa." Philosophy East and West 33 (1983):355-65.

"Craving, conceptualizing, and causality work together to sustain a sense of 'self' in an objective world. . . . The thing-in-itself--tathatā--must be realized to be distinct from any craving for it, from any representation of it, and from whatever causal associations it may have for me. For only then can I realize that I am it."

425 Loy, David. "Enlightenment in Buddhism and Advaita Vedānta: Are Nirvāṇa and Moksha the Same?" International Philosophical Quarterly 22, no. 1 (March 1982):65-74. "The Paradox of Causality in Mādhyamaka." International Philosophical Quarterly 25, no. 1 (March 1985):63-72. "The Mahāyāna Deconstruction of Time." Philosophy East and West 26 (1986):13-24.

This series of articles argues that Advaita Vedānta and early Buddhism are "diametrically opposed positions: which "are phenomenologically equivalent," "mirror images of each other."

426 Mabbott, I.W. "Nāgārjuna and Zeno on Motion." Philosophy East and West 34 (1984):401-20.

This delightfully written paper explores, and eventually rejects, the popular comparison drawn between the point of Zeno's paradoxes and of Nāgārjuna's arguments in the second chapter of Mūlamādhyamakakārikās. The author concludes that Zeno rejects motion "because it never starts," Nāgārjuna "because it has eternally ended." An illuminating comparative analysis.

427 Macnicol, Nicol. Indian Theism. London: Oxford University Press, 1915, xv + [1] + 292 pp.

Part 3, a critical consideration of karma, theism, liberation, and the tension between intellectualism and emotionalism in Indian theology, raises interesting philosophical questions.

428 MacQueen, Graeme. "Inspired Speech in Early Mahāyāna Buddhism." Religion 11 (1981):303-19.

Explores Hīnayāna and Mahāyāna understandings of the notions of the Buddha's words (buddhavacana) and "inspired speech" (pratibhāna) as involving the opening of Buddhist tradition to truths not necessarily revealed in the Buddha's own words.

429 Mādhava. Mādhava, Sarvadarśanasaṃgraha. Translated by E.B. Cowell and A.E. Gough. Delhi: Motilal Banarsidass, 1961, xi + 281 pp. (Orig. pub. London, 1892).

This is the best known and most studied of those classical works which survey all the systems known to the author at the time. It is a treasured resource for introductory sketches of all the classical systems of Hindu thought, and a unique source for the understanding of Cārvāka, or materialist thought.

430 Madhva. "Pramāṇalakṣaṇa." Edited and translated, with Jayatīrtha's Ṭīkā, by H.G. Narahari and Krishnamacharya. Adyar Library Bulletin 17 (1953):1-16.

A small treatise on the pramāṇas by the great Dvaita Vedāntin.

431 Madhva. Madhva, Tattvasaṃkhyāna. Translated by S. Subba Rau. Tirupati, 1923.

One of the most important of Madhva's prakaraṇa works, in which he provides an extended discussion of the relation of Brahman to the world and the selves, and develops characteristically Dvaita views on difference (bheda).

432 Mahadevan, T.M.P. Gauḍapāda: A Study in Early Advaita. Madras: University of Madras, 1952, xi + 292 pp.

An exhaustive survey of Gauḍapādakārikās and the problems surrounding them. It reviews critical literature and refutes charges of "crypto-Buddhism" directed against Advaita.

433 Mahadevan, T.M.P. "Indian Ethics and Social Practice." In Philosophy and Culture East and West: East-West Philosophy in Practical Perspective, edited by Charles A. Moore. Honolulu: University of Hawaii Press, 1962, pp. 476-93.

A leading modern Indian philosopher outlines the philosophical context of dharma.

434 Mahadevan, T.M.P. "The Social Philosophy of Sarvodaya." Indian Yearbook of International Affairs, 1960-61, 1961, pp. 291-300.

A leading modern philosopher interprets the Gandhian perspective on the oneness of all, expressed in the concept (and movement) of sarvodaya.

435 Mahadevan, T.M.P. Superimposition in Advaita Vedānta. New Delhi: Sterling Publishers Private, 1985, 80 pp.

A series of important questions concerning the proper understanding of Advaita philosophy is posed in this small but trenchant study. Mahadevan is well aware of the variety of differing interpretations found among modern Vedāntists.

436 Mahadevan, T.M.P. Time and the Timeless. Madras: Upanishad Vihar, 1953, viii + 88 pp.

Two lectures expounding a metaphysic of time by a contemporary Advaitin. Relevant to the philosophy of history although that is only indirectly examined.

437 Mahadevan, T.M.P., and G.V. Saroja. Contemporary Indian Philosophy. New Delhi: Sterling Publishers Private, 1981, 282 pp.

Systematically sums up the philosophical contributions of Tilak, Tagore, Vivekananda, Aurobindo, K.C. Bhattacharya, Ramana Maharshi, and Sarvepalli Radhakrishnan. Mahadevan supplies a helpful introduction.

438 Mainkar, T.G. A Comparative Study of the Commentaries on the Bhagavadgītā. 2d ed. Delhi: Motilal Banarsidass, 1969, 65 + ii pp.

Analysis of passages on bhakti, brahman, jñāna, karma, mokṣa, saṃnyāsa, etc.

439 Maitra, Susil Kumar. The Ethics of Hindus. 2d ed. Calcutta: Calcutta University Press, 1956, 295 pp. (Orig. pub. Calcutta: University of Calcutta, 1925.)

An influential work which contrasts (and relates) social ethics with individual or subjective ethics and transcendental or absolute ethics.

440 Maitra, Susil Kumar. Fundamental Questions of Indian Metaphysics and Logic. Calcutta: the author, 1956, 252 pp.

Part 1 covers metaphysical questions, with extended attention to Buddhism, Nyāya, Sāṃkhya, less to Vedānta. Part 2, on logic, discusses the pramāṇas in general and inference in particular, with brief accounts of a number of the most important technical problems of Indian thought.

441 Maitra, Susil Kumar. The Main Problems of Philosophy: An Advaita Approach. 2 vols. Calcutta: Progressive Publishers, 1 (1957):vi + 158 + ii pp.; 2 (1962):109 pp.

The procedure is to identify a philosophical problem, develop it as it is found in Western thought and then to indicate the Advaita attitude toward it. Some fifteen problems are treated in this fashion.

442 Maitra, Susil Kumar. "Mukti and Bhakti as Highest Values." Journal of the Indian Academy of Philosophy 2 (1963):14-28.

Probes the central challenge of the bhakti movement as philosophy.

443 Maitra, Susil Kumar. "The Philosophy of Śuddhādvaita." In B.C. Law Volumes, edited by D.R. Bhandarkar, et al. Vol. 1. Calcutta: Indian Research Institute, 1945, pp. 559-69. Reprinted in Studies in Philosophy and Religion, 2d ed. (Calcutta: 1956), pp. 288-309.

A brief account of the history and philosophy of Vallabha's version of Vedānta.

444 Majumdar, A.K. "The Doctrine of Evolution in the Sāṃkhya Philosophy." Philosophical Review 34 (1925):51-69.

There are also follow-up articles in the same journal dealing with bondage and release and the personalistic conception of nature as expounded in Sāṃkhya.

445 Majumdar, J.L. "Philosophy of Gauḍapāda (Ālāta-Śānti-Prakaraṇam)." Journal of the Gaṅganatha Jha Research Institute 8 (1950-51):115-29, 233-49, 335-71; 9 (1951-52):11-25.

Majumdar argues that Gauḍapāda got his ajātivāda from the Laṅkāvatāra Sūtra and that Śaṃkara misunderstands Gauḍapāda's purpose because he knew only Nāgārjuna, not the Laṅkāvatāra.

446 Malhotra, Shadi Lal. "The Social and Political Orientations of Neo-Vedantism." Philosophy East and West 16 (1966):67-80.

A useful survey of positions of major modern figures; brevity is accomplished by generalizations, but one finds a survey of key problems.

447 Malkani, G.R. "The Rationale of Law of Karma." Philosophical Quarterly 37 (1964):257-66.

Malkani's reply to W.E. Steinkraus's "Some Problems in Karma" (Philosophical Quarterly 38 [1965]:145-54). The whole discussion is instructive.

448 Mandal, Kumar Kishore. A Comparative Study of the Concepts of Space and Time in Indian Thought. Varanasi: Chowkhamba Sanskrit Series Office, 1968, xii + 223 pp.

Not very satisfactory as writing, but worthy as the only work of its kind, and important as a reference book. Mandal surveys the literature, picks out all theories on space and time he can find, and summarizes them.

449 Maṇḍana Miśra. Brahmasiddhi. Edited, with Śaṅkhāpāṇi's Commentary, and with introduction, appendixes and indexes, by S. Kuppuswami Sastri. Madras Government Oriental Series, no. 4. Madras: Government Oriental Manuscripts Library, 1937, xxvi + 159 + 78 + 300 + 10 pp.

The introduction discusses Maṇḍana's place in the history of Indian philosophy, and provides a rather good analysis of several aspects of his thought in the process of distinguishing Maṇḍana from Sureśvara, with whom he is thought by some to be identical.

450 Maṇḍana Miśra. Sphoṭasiddhi. Translated by K.A. Subramania Iyer. Poona: Deccan College Postgraduate and Research Institute, 1966, 30 + 95 pp.

Working through this compact, penetrating text can provide one with a thorough understanding of the Grammarians' contributions to theory of meaning as well as that of their rivals in this subject, the Mīmāṃsakas and Naiyāyikas.

451 Mandelbaum, David G. Society in India. 2 vols. Berkeley and Los Angeles: University of California Press, 1970, 1:xi + 1-323 + 37 + 14 pp.; 2:ix + 327-665 + 37 + 14 pp.

Delineation of social patterns essential for understanding philosophy.

452 Marathe, M.P. "An Analysis of 'Syāt' in Syādvāda." Indian Philosophical Quarterly 5 (1978):409-21.

The Jain logic of sevenfold predication (saptabhaṅgī) features the expression syāt--"it may be that. . . ." Marathe inquires as to which sort of possibility this expression designates, and to which sorts it doesn't.

453 Marcus, John T. "East and West Phenomenologies of the Self and the Existential Bases of Knowledge." International Philosophical Quarterly 11 (1971):5-48.

Part 1 covers "Forms of Consciousness," and Part 2 "Self-Identity and the Modes of Unity and Individuality." Contains wide-ranging, presumably controversial comparisons.

454 Marcus, John T. "History and the Indian World View." In Contemporary India, edited by Baidya Nath Varma. Bombay: Asia Publishing House, 1964, pp. 1-23.

Utilizing Western approaches for comparative purposes, Indian attitudes toward historical existence are examined. Modern perspectives are seen as revising ancient emphases.

455 Marfatia, Mrudula I. The Philosophy of Vallabhācārya. Delhi: Munshiram Manoharlal, 1967, xvi + 343 pp.

Gives a general account of Vallabha's thought, followed by summaries of each of his many works and the most important works of his followers.

456 Mathew, E.V. Role of Law in a Revolutionary Age. Bangalore: Christian Institute for the Study of Religion and Society, 1965, 43 pp.

An examination of the nature of law and legal issues in modern India by a distinguished Christian lawyer.

457 Matilal, Bimal Krishna. "Awareness and Meaning in Navya-Nyāya." In Analytical Philosophy in Comparative Perspective, edited by B.K. Matilal and J.L. Shaw. Dordrecht, Holland: D. Reidel, 1985, pp. 373-91.

Matilal elegantly brings out some of the more tantalizing principles underlying Nyāya theory of knowledge. Analyses of difficult material in a disarmingly readable manner.

458 Matilal, Bimal Krishna. Central Philosophy of Jainism (Anekānta-vāda). L.D. Series, no. 79. Ahmedabad: L.D. Institute of Indology, 1981, 72 pp.

Matilal combines skilful use of symbolic logic with a clear understanding of the Sanskrit texts to provide this illuminating study.

459 Matilal, Bimal Krishna. Epistemology, Logic, and Grammar in Indian Philosophical Analysis. The Hague: Mouton, 1971, 183 pp.

Explorations in philosophical analysis applied to Indian thought. There are five chapters, dealing with perception and language, individuals, universals and perception, early Grammarians on philosophical semantics, empty subject terms in logic, negation and the Mādhyamika dialectic. These are mainly confined to Nyāya, Buddhist logicians of Dignāga's school, and the Grammarians, except in the last chapter on Mādhyamika. Recommended for use in more advanced courses.

460 Matilal, Bimal Krishna. "Knowing that One Knows." Journal of Indian Council of Philosophical Research 2, no. 1 (Autumn 1984):19-48.

If I know that p does it follow that I know that I know that p? Matilal argues that Nyāya (as against, e.g., Jakko Hintikka) answers in the negative. A highly illuminating review of a serious technical problem of contemporary concern.

461 Matilal, Bimal Krishna. Logic, Language, and Reality: An Introduction to Indian Philosophical Studies. Delhi: Motilal Banarsidass, 1985, xii + 447 pp.

This approach to Indian philosophy is meant for Western philosophers--students and scholars--and its subject matter is deliberately chosen with such an audience in mind. Sections on logic, epistemology, ontology, and grammatical philosophy comprise it.

462 Matilal, Bimal Krishna. Logical and Ethical Issues of Religious Belief. Calcutta: University of Calcutta, 1982, xii + 187 pp.

Matilal here explores a number of central topics in philosophy that bear on religious belief, such as duḥkha, the problem of evil, skepticism, ineffability, and necessity. Of contemporary authors, Matilal is probably the one who has most insisted on relating traditional issues in Indian philosophy to current approaches in analytic philosophy.

463 Matilal, Bimal Krishna. The Navya-Nyāya Doctrine of Negation. Harvard Oriental Series, no. 46. Cambridge: Harvard University Press, 1968, 208 pp.

Following the lead established by Ingalls (in entry 315), Matilal provides extensive analyses of notions involved in understanding two short Navya-Nyāya texts. He poses a number of problems and puzzles, and tries to solve them using methods of symbolic logic and philosophical analysis.

464 Matilal, Bimal Krishna. Perception: An Essay on Classical Indian Theories of Knowledge. Oxford: Clarendon Press, 1986, xv + 438 pp.

Matilal's work, of which this book is the most impressive example to date, is unusual because of his ability to relate Indian problems and arguments to parallels in contemporary analytical philosophy in England and America. Here he ranges through Western and Indian philosophical analysis. A glance at the bibliography shows the nature of the work; the author is sophisticatedly aware of the developments in the philosophical journals and convincingly establishes their relation to Indian traditonal works, both genres being constantly enriched thereby.

465 Matthews, Bruce. Craving and Salvation: A Study in Buddhist Soteriology. SR Supplements, no. 13. Waterloo, Ontario, 1983, 135 pp.

What did the Buddha mean when he said that experience was to "burn with thirst"? This illuminating analysis of the Buddhist notion of trṣṇā (Pāli tanha, "craving" or "thirst") examines one key notion in Buddhism, going "beyond the formal textual data" and touching "upon the spiritual aspect of this teaching."

466 McDermott, A.C. Senape. An Eleventh-Century Buddhist Logic of "Exists." Dordrecht, Holland: D. Reidel, 1969, 88 pp.
Translation of half of Ratnakīrti's Kṣaṇabhaṅgasiddhi, which concerns logical problems arising from the Buddhist's attempts to prove that everything is momentary.

467 McDermott, James Paul. Development in the Early Buddhist Concept of Kamma/Karma. New Delhi: Munshiram Manoharlal, 1984, xvi + 195 pp.
Careful studies of the treatment of karma in the Pāli canon, the Kathāvatthu, the Milindapañha and the Abhidharmakośa. This book reworks material originally published in various books and journals, and shows how the idea of karma changed over the centuries covered by the works studied.

468 McEvilley, Thomas. "Early Greek Philosophy and Mādhyamika." Philosophy East and West 31 (1981):141-64.
Quoting W.T.K. Guthrie's authority at the outset that Indian and Greek philosophy are so "utterly different . . . that there is little profit in the comparison." McEvilley convincingly demonstrates that the parallels are extraordinary, so much so as to suggest--though not to prove--that there are historical links.

469 McEvilley, Thomas. "Pyrrhonism and Mādhyamika." Philosophy East and West 32 (1982):3-35.
Was there historical connection between Greeks such as Sextus Empiricus and Mādhyamika? A careful review of the evidence, with cautious conclusions.

470 McGovern, William Montgomery. Manual of Buddhist Philosophy. Vol. 1, Cosmology. London: Kegan Paul, Trench, Trubner, 1923, 205 pp.
A standard survey of Buddhism.

471 McKenzie, John. Hindu Ethics: A Historical and Critical Essay. London: H. Milford, 1922, xii + 267 pp.
Surveys the subject, with a particularly good discussion on karma and transmigration. The book is full of critical assessments--essentially unfriendly, but judicious.

472 Mees, Gualtherus Hendrik. Dharma and Society: A Comparative Study of the Theory and Ideal of Varṇa ("Natural Class") and the Phenomena of Caste and Class. The Hague: N.V. Servire, 1935, 206 pp.

An early study by a Western scholar of philosophical concepts basic to Hindu social organization, from the viewpoint of the universality of class categories, in which a number of comparisons to Western thought are advanced. Much information on social philosophy is given, but many readers will find a pervasive artificiality in Mees's approach.

473 Meghanādārisūri. Nayadyumaṇi. Critically edited, with introduction and notes, by V. Krishnamacharya and T. Viraraghavacharya. Madras Government Oriental Series, no. 141. Madras: Government Oriental Manuscripts Library, 1956, 283 pp.

Krishnamacharya's introduction traces the history of Vedānta schools by identifying three groups of Upaniṣadic passages emphasized by each of the three major Vedāntic schools. He outlines the history of Viśiṣṭādvaita and summarizes Nayadyumaṇi in eleven pages, indicating the author's special contributions to the system.

474 Mehta, Mahesh. "Kuṇḍalinī in the Light of Vedānta and Yoga." Indica 16 (1979):127-42.

A well-written, detailed account of kuṇḍalinī, which functions in Śāktism as jīva or jīvātman does in Advaita. The accounts of it in Haṭhayoga as well as in Patañjali's yoga are reviewed.

475 Mehta, Mohan Lal. Jaina Philosophy. Varanasi: P.V. Research Institute, 1971, ii + ii + 234 pp.

This is a revised and enlarged version of the author's Outlines of Jaina Philosophy. Describes works of major Jain authors and gives a general survey of Jain philosophy.

476 Mehta, P.D. Early Indian Religious Thought. London: Luzac, 1956, 532 pp.

A section of part 2, dealing with karma, contains an interesting discussion of whether karma is an ethical law or a process.

477 Menon, Y. Keshava, and Richard F. Allen. The Pure Principle: An Introduction to the Philosophy of Shankara. East Lansing: Michigan State University Press, 1960, 127 pp.

A brief, well-written, but not very incisive introduction.

478 Michael, Aloysius. Radhakrishnan on Hindu Moral Life and Action. Delhi: Concept Publishing Co., 1979, xiv + 226 pp.

The author pulls together Radhakrishnan's thoughts on morality and provides an impartial, though sympathetic, hearing while not refraining from analysis and criticism.

479 Minor, Robert N., ed. Modern Indian Interpreters of the Bhagavadgītā. Albany: State University of New York Press, 1986, 273 pp.

A group of mostly American scholars have a look at what recent Indians have made of the Bhagavadgītā. Those studied range from Aurobindo and Gandhi to Sivananda and Bhaktivedanta.

480 Minor, Robert N. "Sarvepalli Radhakrishnan on the Nature of 'Hindu' Tolerance." Journal of the American Academy of Religion 50 (1982):275-90.

This sober argument shows that while talking of "tolerance" Radhakrishnan indeed adopts a thoroughly intolerant position toward anyone who "challenges the basic dogma of tat tvam asi and its corollaries."

481 Minor, Robert N. Sri Aurobindo: The Perfect and the Good. Calcutta: Minerva & Associates, 1978, 191 pp.

The author applies the religious-historical method to Aurobindo's thought, basing his analysis on Aurobindo's complete works, and provides a serious and sober summation.

482 Mishra, Ganeswar. Analytical Studies in Indian Philosophical Problems. Bhubaneshwar: Utkal University, 1971, 116 pp.

A provocative series of journal articles collected mostly around a common theme, which involves a unique view of Śaṃkara's contribution to Indian philosophy. Mishra believes that Śaṃkara was more a philosopher of language than an epistemologist.

483 Mishra, Ganeswar. "Vidyāraṇya on Method, Object, and Limit of Philosophical Investigation." Indian Philosophical Quarterly 11 (1983):343-63.

"Authority absolutely has no place in Vedānta philosophy. . . . Māyā or avidyā is not the magical display of a transcendental Lord. . . . The Ātman which constitutes the ultimate nature of all intelligible beings is not . . . a spiritual entity . . . it is indescribable and incomprehensible. . . . Mokṣa is not liberation of the mystical soul from the shackles of the body. It is cognitive liberation from the illusion created by knowing the concrete by means of the abstract." Surprising and provocative claims, argued persuasively.

484 Mishra, G.S.P. "Beliefs Underlying the Ancient Indian Conception of History." Journal of Indian History 57 (1979):1-12.

Thoughts on the Indians' alleged lack of a sense of history.

485 Mishra, G.S.P. Development of Buddhist Ethics. New Delhi: Munshiram Manoharlala, 1984, xii + 184 pp.

A fairly straightforward review of Buddhist ethical theory.

486 Mishra, Kamalakar. Significance of the Tantric Tradition. Varanasi: Arddhanarisvara Publications, 1981, x + 200 pp.

Tantra literature is relatively unexplored in Western languages, except perhaps Abhinavagupta's work. Though not pretending to be exhaustive, this book presents an authoritative, if somewhat disorganized, account of some tantric conceptions.

487 Mishra, N. "Conception of Saṃskāra in the Yogasūtra." Journal of the Bihar and Orissa Research Society 37 (1951):48-65.

"Impression" is too static a translation of saṃskāra. The article contains insightful comparisons with McDougall and Freud.

488 Mishra, Umesh. "The Annihilation of Karman." Proceedings of the All-India Oriental Congress 7 (1935):467-80.

Karma and liberation as expounded in Padmapāda's Vijñānadīpikā.

489 Mishra, Umesh. Conception of Matter according to Nyāya-Vaiśeṣika. Allahabad: the author, 1936, 428 pp.

The most thorough account available of Vaiśeṣika ontology, this work draws from texts and commentaries of both the old and new schools. It also has a chapter on the conception of self (ātman) in Vaiśeṣika.

490 Mishra, Umesh. "Dream Theory in Indian Thought." Allahabad University Studies 5 (1929):269-321.

Thorough survey of views on dreams of several classical Indian philosophers--Advaitins, Naiyāyikas and Mīmāṃsakas.

491 Mishra, Umesh. History of Indian Philosophy. 2 vols. Allahabad: Tirabhukti Publications, 1 (1957):xxxv + 562 pp.; 2 (1966):xxix + 658 pp.

A complete summation of a famous scholar's knowledge of some of the schools: he did not live to complete all the volumes planned. Mishra's history is outstanding for its wealth of detail on texts and their authors. His analyses of philosophical positions are probably sounder than Dasgupta's (see entry 181), though not as easy for a Westerner to read. Volume 1 covers the philosophy of the Vedas and Upaniṣads, the Bhagavadgītā, materialism, Jainism, and Buddhism, while volume 2 is entirely devoted to Nyāya.

492 Mishra, Umesh. "Nimbārka School of Vedānta." Allahabad University Studies: Arts Section (1940):1-105. Reprint. Allahabad: Tirabhukti, 1966, 125 pp.

A thorough review of the history and philosophy of the Dvaitādvaita tradition. It is neither as long nor as easy to read as that of Roma Bose (see entry 552).

493 Mishra, Umesh. "Physical Theory of Sound and Its Origin in Indian Thought." Allahabad University Studies 2 (1926):239-91.

Exhaustive account of views on sound in various systems.

494 Mishra, Umesh. "Place of Yoga Among the Various Schools of Indian Thought." Allahabad University Studies 9 (1933):189-205.

Surveys classical schools, including Grammarians, Śākta and Kashmir Saivism.

495 Mishra, Umesh. "Synthetic Gradation in Indian Thought." Allahabad University Studies: Arts Section 1 (1925):77-97.

The several systems of Indian philosophy were viewed as aspects of a single truth by this veteran Indian scholar. Here he reviews different lists of the "six systems."

496 Mohanty, Jitendranath. Gaṅgeśa's Theory of Truth. Santiniketan: Visva-Bharati Centre of Advanced Study in Philosophy, 1966, 232 pp.

The introductory material to this translation is exceptionally fine, shedding great and much-needed light on the notion of truth (prāmāṇya), a notion expounded innumerable times elsewhere but never with the kind of insight this author brings to the task. Possibly the best writing on Indian epistemology available anywhere.

497 Mohanty, Jitendranath. "Nyāya Theory of Doubt." Vishwa-bharati Journal of Philosophy 3 (1966):15-35. Reprinted in Phenomenology and Ontology (The Hague: M. Nijhoff, 1970), pp. 198-219.

This technical but very sound essay examines the definition of doubt found in Viśvanātha's Siddhāntamuktāvalī.

498 Mohanty, Jitendranath. "Phenomenology and Existentialism: Encounter with Indian Philosophy." International Philosophy Quarterly 12 (1972):487-511.

Mohanty is an expert scholar in both Indian thought and phenomenology (has a book on Husserl to his credit), and is especially capable of speaking to the comparison.

499 Mohanty, Jitendranath. "Reflection on the Indian Theory of Avayavipratyaksa." Journal of the Indian Academy of Philosophy 1 (1961-62):30-41. Reprinted in Phenomenology and Ontology (The Hague: M. Nijhoff, 1970), pp. 184-97.

Studies the Nyāya theory that one can perceive wholes as well as parts, and finds the theory defective.

500 Monier-Williams, Monier. "On Buddhism in Its Relation to Brahmanism." Journal of the Royal Asiatic Society of Great Britain and Ireland 18 (1886):127-56.

The Buddha was a Hindu. A long, chatty, but incisive, account of the relation of Buddhism to Hinduism.

501 Mookerjee, Satkari. "The Absolutist's Standpoint in Logic." Nava-Nalanda-Mahāvihāra Research Publications 1 (1957):1-175.

Chapter 1: Summary of Nāgārjuna's Vigrahavyāvartanī section by section. Chapter 2: Running summary of chapter 1 of Candrakīrti's Prasannapadā. Chapter 3: Discussion of Srīharṣa's exposition of the Mādhyamika position. Chapter 4: The Buddhist and Vedāntic standpoints compared. It is an interesting attack on a fundamental problem of Indian philosophy.

502 Mookerjee, Satkari. The Buddhist Philosophy of Universal Flux. Calcutta: University of Calcutta, 1935, 448 pp.

An important work. It covers all aspects of technical Buddhist philosophy, together with arguments directed at Buddhists from other schools. Mookerjee gets deeper into the problems of Buddhist philosophy than just about any other writer.

503 Mookerjee, Satkari. "Impediments to Universalhood." Sarūp-Bhāratī: The Homage of Indology. Dr. Lakshman Sarup Memorial Volume. Hoshiarpur: Vishveshvaranand Institute Publications, 1951, pp. 153-61.

An excellent summary of Udayana's six conditions which must be satisfied by a "proper" universal.

504 Mookerjee, Satkari. The Jaina Philosophy of Non-Absolutism. Calcutta: Bharata Jaina Parisat, 1944, 323 pp.

A remarkable and undeservedly neglected study of Jain epistemology and metaphysics by one of the truly great philosopher-scholars of modern India. Unlike most other works on Jainism, or on Indian philosophy for that matter, Mookerji's writings raise significant philosophical problems rather than merely summarizing arguments and doctrines found in the texts. There are chapters on nonabsolutism (anekāntavāda), numerical difference and absolute nonexistence, absolute negativism and absolute particularism, the inexpressible or the indefinite, the dialectic of sevenfold predication, relations, the Nyāya conception of universals, and the Jain conception of universals.

505 Moore, Charles A. "Philosophy as Distinct from Religion in India." Philosophy East and West 11 (1961):3-26.

Presents the case for identifying philosophy with religion in India, and its refutation. A useful general introduction to the subject.

506 Morehouse, Ward. Science and the Human Condition in India and Pakistan. New York: Rockefeller University Press, 1968, xvii + 230 pp.

A volume of twenty-seven papers presented at an International Symposium on Science in India and Pakistan held at Rockefeller University in May 1966. Although none of the papers are by professional philosophers, most of them raise or address philosophical issues.

507 Motwani, Kewal. Manu Dharma Śāstra: A Sociological and Historical Study. Madras: Ganesh, 1958, xviii + 384 pp.

A sociologist, who views Manu's teachings to be of continuing relevance, undertakes to articulate the "principle of social life of man applicable at all times and in all climes," with the greatest philosophical import of the work being in the chapter on "Ideological Foundations."

508 Muhar, P.S. "Synthesists or Culturalists: A Study of Indian Political Thought." In Studies in Political Science, edited by J.S. Bains. Bombay: Asia Publishing House, 1961, pp. 207-47.

Examines three modern figures (Bipin Chandra Pal, Aurobindo, Tagore) who sought to synthesize Indian and Western thought.

509 Mukerji, Krishna Prasanna. The State. Madras: Theosophical Publishing House, 1952, xxii + 382 pp.

Seeks synthetic political philosophy, integrating, inter alia, ethics, metaphysics, and politics. This study in political philosophy is not limited to the Indian context, but is "inspired" by the tradition of dharma, "integrating ethical demands with a spiritual philosophy of transcendental metaphysics" (p. 287). Norman Palmer calls this "probably the most important contribution by an Indian political scientist in recent years to the field of political theory."

510 Mukherjee, Himangshu Bhushan. Education for Fullness: A Study of the Educational Thought and Experiment of Rabindranath Tagore. New York: Asia Publishing House, 1962, xvi + 495 pp.

This study of Tagore's educational philosophy and programs also encompasses a biographical dimension.

511 Mukherji, Santi Lal. The Philosophy of Man-Making: A Study in Social and Political Ideas of Swami Vivekananda. Calcutta: New Central Book Agency, 1971, viii + 468 pp.

Treats many phases of Vivekananda's biography and writings, with a corresponding limitation in the depth of the analysis of political thought.

512 Mukhopadhyaya, Pradyot Kumar. Indian Realism: A Rigorous Descriptive Metaphysics. Calcutta: K.P. Bagchi & Co., 1984, xxiii + 380 pp.

Despite an overly complex and very Indian linguistic style this work shows originality of a sort badly needed in studies of Indian logic, epistemology, and metaphysics. The topic here is the problem of universals, and the approach brings depth of knowledge of texts together with philosophical analysis of a modern Western sort to raise many new questions and provide new insights.

513 Mulla, Dinshah Fardunji. Principles of Hindu Law. Edited by Sunderlal T. Desai. 12th ed. Bombay: N.M. Tripathi, 1959, ix + 1203 pp. (Orig. pub. 1912.)

The introduction (pp. 1-73) provides a general orientation to Hindu law; this and several similar works help to acquaint one with the character of the Indian legal tradition.

514 Muller, F. Max. Six Systems of Indian Philosophy. Chowkhamba Sanskrit Series, no. 16. Varanasi: Chowkhamba Sanskrit Series Office, 1963, xxxii + 478 pp. (Orig. pub. London: Longmans, 1903.)

The basic work by the famous German Indologist who played an important role in the discovery of Indian thought by Continental and American thinkers.

515 Murti, T.R.V. The Central Philosophy of Buddhism. London: Allen and Unwin, 1955, 372 pp.

A definitive treatise which studies the Mādhyamika system in detail. Part 1, "The Two Traditions in Indian Philosophy," is a historical survey. Part 2, "The Dialectic as System of Philosophy," assesses the method of Mādhyamika and its applications (how the method relates to liberation and the general thrust of Mahāyāna thought). Part 3, "The Mādhyamika and Allied Systems," compares Mādhyamika with other Indian schools as well as with Western philosophers--Kant, Hegel, and Bradley.

516 Murti, T.R.V. "Rise of the Philosophical Schools." In The Cultural Heritage of India. Vol. 3, The Philosophical Systems. Rev. ed. Calcutta: Ramakrishna Mission Institute of Culture, 1953, pp. 27-40.

This is excellent as an introduction to the study of the systems. A basic distinction is drawn between those schools that affirm the existence of a self and those that deny it. Contains materials explaining stages in development of schools, dating, etc.

517 Murti, T.R.V. "Types of Indian Realism." Philosophical Quarterly 11 (1935):274-85; 12 (1936):141-55; 13 (1937):211-22.

An outstanding Indian scholar's important paper setting forth his criticism of the various realistic systems found in Indian thought.

518 Murti, T.R.V. "Rational Basis of Advaitism." Philosophical Quarterly 6 (1930):57-81.

How to establish Advaita without appeal to scripture. The study is excellent, but not simple.

519 Murti, T.R.V., G.R. Malkani, and R. Das. Ajñāna. Calcutta Oriental Series, no. 26. London: Luzac, 1933, 226 + iii pp.

Three interesting, extensive papers by leading figures of academic philosophy during the second and third quarters of the twentieth century, dealing with the pivotal concept of Advaita philosophy.

520 Murty, K. Satchidananda. "Ethics and Politics in Hindu Culture." In The Ethic of Power: The Interplay of Religion, Philosophy, and Politics, edited by Harold D. Lasswell and Harland Cleveland. New York: Conference on Science, Philosophy, and Religion, in Their Relation to the Democratic Way of Life, 1962, pp. 85-100.

An attempt to marshal traditional refrains to address contemporary moral and political issues.

521 Murty, K. Satchidananda. "History, Historical Consciousness, and Freedom." In Religious Pluralism and World Community, edited by Edward J. Jurji. Leiden: E.J. Brill, 1969, pp. 35-42.

A brief treatment of the ambiguous character of history, in relation to the transcendent.

522 Murty, K. Satchidananda. The Indian Spirit. Waltair: Andhra University Press, 1965, 296 pp.

A collection of essays, some of them dealing with Indian philosophy, notably those on the Greek image of Indian philosophy; philosophical thought in India; and experience, reason, and "transcendental materialism" in Indian philosophy. The latter contains critiques of several modern writers on Indian thought. Murty's style is somewhat disorganized, but his comments are usually quite interesting.

523 Murty, K. Satchidananda. Nāgārjuna. New Delhi: National Book Trust, 1971, 111 pp.

Murty collects what we know about Nāgārjuna's life, works, and teachings, also comparing Nāgārjuna with Śaṃkara and exploring his possible contributions to tantra and science. He concludes with selections from Ratnāvalī and the Mādhyamakakārikās.

524 Murty, K. Satchidananda, ed. Readings in Indian History, Politics, and Philosophy. London: Allen and Unwin, 1967, 392 pp.

Readings from the works of modern writers dealing with both ancient and contemporary political issues.

525 Murty, K. Satchidananda. Revelation and Reason in Advaita Vedānta. Waltair: Andhra University Press, 1959, 365 pp.

The author terms this "a fairly exhaustive study and criticism of the problem of scriptural authority (śruti, prāmānya vicāra) in the Advaita Vedānta." Readers will find it a tour de force of scholarship ranging widely over the whole extent of Indian thought but consistently attentive to the announced topic, of which this is surely the most complete treatment in English by far.

526 Muttarayan, K. Loganatha. "Arunanti's Theory of Moral Behaviour." Saiva Siddhanta 16 (1981):63-76.

As yet we have few helpful accounts of Indian ethics, especially any relating to Saiva Siddhānta thought. This piece shows that Arunanti recognizes no criteria of right and wrong; he does recognize "a universal concern for self-development," i.e., liberation, which serves as the basis for moral evaluations.

527 Naess, Arne. Gandhi and Group Conflict: An Exploration of Satyagraha. Theoretical Background. Oslo: Universitetsforleget, 1974, 172 pp.

A study supporting Gandhi's methods, analyzing the assumptions behind them, and comparing them with others past and contemporary.

528 Naga Raja Sarma, R. Reign of Realism in Indian Philosophy. Madras: National Press, 1937, 695 pp.

A vast, opinionated survey of Dvaita philosophy, which is especially helpful for extended summary-analyses of each of Madhva's ten prakaraṇa treatises. The final chapter, a reply to Madhva's critic is outspokenly enthusiastic, but raises many questions of real interest.

529 Nāgārjuna. Mūlamādhyamakakārikās. Translated, with an introductory essay, by Kenneth K. Inada. Tokyo: Hokuseido Press, 1970, x + 204 pp.

The fundamental text of the Mādhyamika school of Buddhist philosophy.

530 Nāgārjuna. "Sūtrasamuccaya." Translated by Bhikkhu Pasadika. Journal of Religious Studies 7, no. 1 (1979):19-44. Continued in Journal of Indian and Buddhist Studies 5, no. 2 (1982):101-9.

This Buddhist work is lost in Sanskrit, and is translated here for the first time from the Tibetan version. It appears to be largely a collection of passages from various Buddhist sūtras, and does not resemble Nāgārjuna's philosophical works. Pasadika leaves the questions of date and authorship open.

531 Nāgārjuna. "Vigrahavyāvarttanī." Translated by Kamalesh war Bhattacharya. Journal of Indian Philosophy 1 (1971):217-61.

An important work by the great Buddhist, with its autocommentary. This translation strives to improve on previous attempts.

532 Nagatomi, Masatoshi. "Mānasa-Pratyakṣa: A Conundrum in the Buddhist Pramāṇa System." In Sanskṛt and Indian Studies. Essays in Honour of Daniel H.H. Ingalls, edited by M. Nagatomi, et al. Dordrecht, Holland: D. Reidel, 1980, pp. 243-60.

What is the "mental perception" that we find spoken of by Dignāga and Dharmakīrti? Examples are sexual passion or compassion for others. These are neither sense-perceptions nor inferences, but otherwise no problem arises in this connection, except that Dharmakīrti failed to explain Dignāga's elliptical writing.

533 Nakamura, Hajime. "The Indian and Buddhist Concept of Law." In Religious Pluralism and World Community, edited by Edward J. Jurji. Leiden: E.J. Brill, 1969, pp. 131-74.

An excellent essay comparing Hindu and Buddhist approaches to law with some aspects of law in other traditions (e.g., Christian, Confucian).

534 Nakamura, Hajime. Ways of Thinking of Eastern Peoples. Edited by Philip P. Wiener. Rev. trans. Honolulu: East-West Center Press, 1964, 712 pp.

First published in 1960, this unusual work is an attempt to understand the ways of thinking of India, China, Tibet, and Japan by analyzing the language of each and its underlying logic. The results involve interesting generalizations from very particular verbal and conceptual evidence, generalizations which may or may not appeal to the reader and are at any rate easy enough to reject, given the nature of the reasoning which leads to them. Pages 39 through 172 deal with India, for the most part with Indian philosophy.

535 Nanajivaka, Bhikkhu. "Buddhism and Modern Philosophies of Existence." In Buddhist and Western Philosophy, edited by Nathan Katz. New Delhi: Sterling Publishers Private, 1981, pp. 328-78.

In useful contrast with the many comparisons of Buddhism with analytical traditions, this work seeks out its relations with such existentialists as Eckhart, Kierkegaard, Schopenhauer, Nietzsche, Heidegger, Sartre, Jaspers, and (in appendixes) others.

536 Nandimath, S.C. Handbook of Vīraśaivism. Dharwar: Literary Committee, Lingayat Educational Association, 1942, xv + 269 pp.

The most extensive treatment of Vīraśaiva (i.e., Lingayat) philosophy available, this treats the subject both historically and analytically.

537 Nandy, Ashis. "The Culture of Indian Politics: A Stock Taking." Journal of Asian Studies 30 (1970):57-79.

An analysis of contemporary politics that includes attention to the role of philosophical and religious ideas and ideals.

538 Nandy, Ashis. "The Making and Unmaking of Political Cultures in India." Daedalus 102 (1973):115-37.

A probe of the interaction of various facets of culture in the political milieu, with reference to major works on Indian politics (that are noted in the references). Such analyses of the political process are of great importance for the student of Indian political philosophy.

539 Narahari, H.G. Ātman in Pre-Upaniṣadic Vedic Literature. Adyar Library Series, no. 47. Adyar: Theosophical Society, 1944, xxxiv + 278 pp.

The notion of self as found in the Vedas.

540 Narahari, H.G. "The Yogavāsiṣṭha and the Doctrine of Free Will." Adyar Library Bulletin 10 (1946):36-50.

What is "the problem of free will"? Paraphrases the Yogavāsiṣṭha, the "most powerful advocate of human freedom ever met with in Indian literature." Sanskrit quotations, but generally helpful.

541 Narain, K. Critique of Mādhva Refutation of the Śaṃkara School of Vedānta. Allahabad: Udayana, 1964, vi + 392 pp.

Most of this is based on the famous controversy found in Vyāsarāya's Nyāyāmṛta and Madhusūdana Sarasvatī's Advaitasiddhi. Since these are excellent, difficult, and untranslated works the analysis is particularly helpful.

542 Narain, K. An Outline of Mādhva Philosophy. Allahabad: Udayana, 1962, 231 pp.

The book reviews in detail Madhva's school's views on the criterion and nature of reality, theory of knowledge, the defense of difference, causation, ontology, the conception of God, world and creation, the conception of individual soul, and ethics.

543 Na-Rangsi, Sunthorn. The Buddhist Concepts of Karma and Rebirth. Bangkok: Mahamakut Rajavidyalaya Press, 1976, xix + 301 pp.

Somewhat misleadingly titled, since it is confined to Theravāda concepts solely, this book is the more valuable for this limitation. The author has explored the Pāli canon and Abhidharma literature to provide an exhaustive summation of its views on karma theory.

544 Narasimhachari, M. Contribution of Yāmuna to Viśiṣṭādvaita. Madras: Prof. M. Rangacharya Memorial Trust, 1971, xxviii + 340 pp.

A doctoral dissertation on one of the early figures in Viśiṣṭādvaita; gathers much information, summarizes each text attributed to Yāmuna, and expounds Yāmuna's thought in general.

545 Naulakha, R.S. Shānkara's Brahmavāda. Kanpur: Kitab Ghar, 1964, 5 + iv + 431 + viii pp.

A fairly standard dissertation on Śaṃkara's thought.

546 Nayak, G.C., ed. Analytical Studies in Buddhist Philosophy. Bhubaneshwar: P.G. Department of Philosophy, Utkal University, x + 175 pp.

A collection of consistently interesting papers by a broad spectrum of professional scholars of Indian philosophy. Notable contributions by A.K. Chatterjee, Ganeswar Mishra, R.C. Pradhan, and N.H. Samtani, with concluding comments by Professor Nayak.

547 Nayak, G.C. Evil, Karma, and Reincarnation. Santiniketan: Centre of Advanced Study in Philosophy, 1973, viii + 176 pp.

A lively defense of the solution to the problem of evil by what is called here "the retributive hypothesis," that is, the classical Indian theory of karma and rebirth.

548 Neevel, Walter C., Jr. "Rāmānuja on Bhakti and Prapatti." Journal of Religious Studies 3 (1971):103-21.

One of the most recent contributions in a steady stream of essays trying to gauge the extent to which Rāmānuja espouses the characteristic Śrīvaiṣṇava notions.

549 Neufeldt, Ronald W., ed. Karma and Rebirth: Post-Classical Developments. Albany, N.Y.: State University of New York Press, 1986, 357 pp.

Supplements the volumes edited by O'Flaherty (see entry 558) and Keyes/Daniel (see entry 373) by considering karma and rebirth in contemporary Hindu and Buddhist thinking as well as the development of thought on them in the West.

550 Nikam, N.A., ed. Human Relation and International Obligations. Mysore: Indian Philosophical Congress, 1956.

In this international symposium, several of the papers by Indian philosophers examine moral dimensions of international relations.

551 Nikam, N.A. "Philosophy of Indian Culture: A Metaphysic of the Idea of History." In Philosophy, History, and the Image of Man. Bombay: Somaiya Publications Private, 1973, pp. 107-19.

Some preliminary clarification of significant components in the philosophy of history in Indian culture, with focus on the idea of time and the facets of timelessness.

552 Nimbārka. Vedāntapārijātasaurabha. Translated, with Śrīnivāsa's Vedāntakaustubha, by Roma Bose. 3 vols. Bibliotheca Indica, no. 259. Calcutta: Royal Asiatic Society of Bengal, 1940-43, 884 pp.

Nimbārka's commentary on the Brahmasūtras, here translated with commentary, is the fundamental work for the Dvaitādvaita system of Vedānta. Volume 3 of this massive work is Bose's doctoral dissertation entitled "Doctrines of Nimbārka and His Followers." It includes the life of Nimbārka, Nimbārka's philosophy, and a historical survey.

553 Norman, K.R. A History of Indian Literature. Vol. 7, fasc. 2, Pāli Literature. Wiesbaden: Otto Harrassowitz, 1983, ix + 210 pp.

The definitive account to date of what is known about Theravāda literature.

554 Northrop, F.S.C. The Meeting of East and West. New York: Macmillan Co., 1946, xxii + 531 pp.

A notorious work; the author tries to discover the essential genius of "Eastern" traditions, contrasting it with what is Western. It cannot be recommended except as an object lesson in the pitfalls of unwary comparisons on too broad a level.

555 Nyanaponika Thera. Abhidhamma Studies: Researches in Buddhist Psychology. Kandy: Buddhist Publication Society, 1949, 126 pp.

The difficulties of making sense of Abhidharma philosophy are handled here about as well as possible. Based closely on the Dhammasaṅganī, probably the oldest Theravāda philosophical work extant, and its authoritative commentary, Buddhaghoṣa's Aṭṭhasālinī, Nyanaponika carefully reviews the many groups of dharmas which make up the complex collection of Abhidharma categories. One of the very most informative works on a difficult topic.

556 Nyāyavijaya. Nyāyakusumāñjali. Translated into English and Gujarati by Hiralal Rasikdas Kapadia. Baroda: Luhana Mitra Steam P. Press, 1922, 11 + 351 + 3 pp.

Translation of a book by a twentieth-century Jain author. An examination of the contents, analyzed in a few pages, indicates that the work treats many of the central Jain tenets.

557 Obermiller, E. "Nirvāṇa according to the Tibetan Tradition." Indian Historical Quarterly 10 (1934):251-57.

Obermiller adduces evidence to support Stcherbatsky's Conception of Buddhist Nirvāṇa (see entry 781). The work is technical, but very important for students of Buddhism.

558 O'Flaherty, Wendy Doniger, ed. Karma and Rebirth in Classical Indian Traditions. Berkeley and Los Angeles: University of California Press, 1980, 342 pp.

A group of scholars consider the karma theory in classical Hinduism, Buddhism, and Jainism. The first of several recent volumes concentrating on this topic (see e.g., Keyes/Daniel [entry 373] and Neufeldt [entry 549]), the articles in this volume provide a pretty thorough understanding of how karma was understood in ancient times. The articles manage to generate some worthwhile critical considerations as well, examining karma as it appears not only in classical philosophical and religious works but also in epics, dharmaśāstras, medical texts, Buddhist tantras, and Tamil literature.

559 Olivelle, Patrick. Renunciation in Hinduism: A Medieval Debate. Vol. 1, The Debate and the Advaita Argument. Publications of the De Nobili Research Library, no. 13. Vienna: University of Vienna, 1986, 156 pp.

Discussion of "the dispute over the status and insignia of a renouncer" between Advaita and Viśiṣṭādvaita (this first volume covers the Advaita), which bears on their diverging views on the means to liberation. Passages from Śaṃkara, Ānandānubhava, and Mādhava are translated in this section.

560 Organ, Troy W. The Self in Indian Philosophy. The Hague: Mouton, 1964, 184 pp.

Despite many howlers of Sanskrit spelling, some inaccuracies, and perhaps precisely because of a certain naïveté about Indian thought, this little book is a rather attractive introduction to a fundamental notion in all Indian thought. It covers the Vedic, Upaniṣadic, Sāṃkhya-Yoga, Nyāya-Vaiśeṣika, Advaita, and Viśiṣṭādvaita theories of the self.

561 Ostergaard, Geoffrey Nielson, and Melville Currell. The Gentle Anarchists: A Study of the Leaders of the Sarvodaya Movement for Non-Violent Revolution in India. Oxford: Clarendon Press, 1971, x + 421 pp.

A study of diverse facets of the movement, including consideration of its "ideology." An excellent bibliography.

562 Padmapāda. Vijñānadīpikā. Translated by Umesh Mishra. Allahabad University Publications, Sanskrit Series, vol. 1. Allahabad: Senate House, 1940, 7 + 47.

Though this work, is most likely not by the famous Padmapāda, student of Śaṃkara, it seems, on the basis of Umesh Mishra's English summary, to be an especially instructive review of the details of karma and rebirth as found in some stage of Advaita Vedānta.

563 Padmarajiah, Y.J. A Comparative Study of the Jaina Theories of Reality and Knowledge. Bombay: Jain Sahitya Vikas Mandal, 1963, 423 pp.

A major work of this promising author, prematurely deceased. It resembles Mookerjee (see entry 504) in its philosophical acuteness, but deals in large part with ontology.

564 Palmer, Norman D. "Indian and Western Political Thought: Coalescence and Clash." American Political Science Review 49 (1955):747-61.

A short introduction to Indian political thought and to aspects of comparative studies of politics.

565 Pande, Susmita. Birth of Bhakti in Indian Religion and Art. New Delhi: Books & Books, 1982, x + 224 pp.

Neatly surveys devotion in Vedas and Upaniṣads, epics and

purāṇas, as well as in Buddhism, art, and various kinds of medieval literature.

566 Pandey, Kanti Chandra. Abhinavagupta: An Historical and Philosophical Study. Chowkhamba Sanskrit Series Studies, no. 1. Varanasi: Chowkhamba Sanskrit Series Office, 1936, 2 + 10 + ix + 427 pp. (Rev. ed. 1963, iii + 1014 pp.)

A life of Abhinavagupta, the prime figure in Kashmir Śaivism, with a summary in a few paragraphs or pages of each of his works. Also covers the historical background of his thought, his importance and influence, and his philosophy of ābhāsavāda, the basis of the Trika system.

567 Pandey, Kanti Chandra. Bhāskarī. Vol. 3, An English Translation of the Īśvara Pratyabhijñā Vimarśinī in the Light of the Bhāskarī with An Outline of History of Śaiva Philosophy. Princess of Wales Saraswati Bhavan Texts, no. 84. Lucknow: Chowkhambe Sanskrit Series Office, 1954, 331 pp.

The 206-page "Outline of the History of Saiva Philosophy" sheds welcome light on the distinctions among the various strands of Saivism: Pāśupata, Saiva Siddhānta, Lakulīśa Pāśupata, Saiva Viśiṣṭādvaita of Srīkaṇṭha, Vīra Saivism, Nandikeśvara Saivism, Raseśvara Saivism, and Kashmir Saivism. The philosophical positions of each of these eight schools is explained.

568 Pandey, Sangam Lal. Pre-Śaṃkara Advaita Philosophy. Allahabad: Darshan Peeth, 1974, xvi + 475 pp.

Comprehensive summary of evidence and theories concerning the development of Advaita between the time of the early Upaniṣads and Saṃkara.

569 Pandeya, Ram Chandra. "Jīvan-mukti and Social Concern." Indian Philosophical Annual 2 (1966):119-24.

A questioning of the view (argued in the chapter that follows) that the realized one in nondualistic systems maintains a "social concern."

570 Pandeya, Ram Chandra. The Problem of Meaning in Indian Philosophy. Varanasi: Motilal Banarsidass, 1963, 303 pp.

Approaches Indian grammatical philosophy from a viewpoint and with a style congenial to Western analytic philosophy. Not always as accurate, however, as Kunjunni Raja (see entry 399) or others on the same subject.

571 Panikkar, Kavalam Madhava. Indian Doctrines of Politics. Ahmedabad: Harold Laski Institute of Political Science, 1955, 15 pp.

A reflective statesman calls for recognition of a long and independent tradition of political thinking in India. Being brief, the lecture is introductory, articulating rather than expounding a point of view.

572 Panikkar, Raimundo. "The Law of Karman and the Historical Dimension of Man." Philosophy East and West 22 (1972):25-43.
An exploration of karma that seeks to fathom its relevance for cultural traditions other than the milieu of its origin, and relates this scrutiny to the understanding of historical existence.

573 Panikkar, Raimundo, et al. "Time and Temporality. (A Symposium)." Philosophy East and West 24 (1974):161-70.
In addition to papers by Panikkar and R. Puligandla, which are of greatest relevance, there are studies of Western and Buddhist views of time and temporality.

574 Paranjoti, Violet. Śaiva Siddhānta in the Meykanda Śāstra. London: Luzac, 1938, xii + 257 pp.
Studies the fourteen basic works of Śaiva Siddhānta, the so-called Meykanda Śāstra.

575 Paranjpe, A.C. "The Identity Theory of Prejudice: A Perspective from the Intellectual Tradition of India." Journal of Asian and African Studies 20 (1985):232-44.
Paranjpe suggests that "Vedānta methods, which are primarily aimed at self-realization, help an individual in transcending the ego's exclusive identification with a limited social sphere . . . and incidentally help rid oneself of all social prejudices." But, he warns, "one in a thousand . . . tries, and among those who try, a rare one succeeds."

576 Parrott, Rodney J. "The Experience Called 'Reason' in Classical Sāmkhya." Journal of Indian Philosophy 13 (1985):235-64.
"Thus, classical Sāmkhya is not a rationalistic system. The Sāmkhyas do not think their way to spiritual perfection. Charges of rationalism by scholars have been based on . . . the mistaken equation of reasoned proof and releasing wisdom, two drastically different sorts of knowing."

577 Patel, M.S. Educational Philosophy of Mahatma Gandhi. Ahmedabad: Navajivan Publishing House, 1953, xv + 288 pp.
A survey of the educational component in the whole of Gandhi's life and teaching, properly insisting that his educational perspective is far broader than the Wardha Scheme. The author champions Gandhi's views in a way that precludes searching criticism.

578 Pattammal, Kumari R., ed. and trans. "Śrī Totakācarya's Srutisārasamuddhāranam." Voice of Samkara 6 (1981-82):89, 190, 265, 359; 7 (1982-83):83, 215; 8 (1983-84):59.
This doctoral thesis provides text, the first translation of the work, and helpful scholarly supporting materials in the introduction.

579 Perrett, Roy W. "Dualistic and Nondualistic Problems of Immortality." Philosophy East and West 35 (1985):333-50.
How credible is the notion of disembodied existence? And if it is not credible, what happens to Indian philosophy? Perrett finds that Advaita, for one system, provides a radical but apparently coherent solution.

580 Perrett, Roy W. "The Problem of Induction in Indian Philosophy." Philosophy East and West 34 (1984):161-74.
Clear review of how the "justification of induction" problem was raised and discussed in India among Cārvākas, Naiyāyikas, Advaitins, and Buddhists. Perrett concludes that while the "problem of induction" is a pseudo-problem, discussion of it benefited philosophical inquiry in India substantially.

581 Perrett, Roy W. "Self-Refutation in Indian Philosophy." Journal of Indian Philosophy 12 (1984):237-63.
In this interesting piece a taxonomy of three distinct varieties of self-refutation--absolute, pragmatic, and operational--is posited, and examples are culled from Cārvāka, Nyāya, Nāgārjuna, and Srīharṣa.

582 Philips, C.H., ed. Politics and Society in India. Studies on Modern Asia and Africa, no. 1. New York: Praeger, 1962, 190 pp.
Most of the contributors do not offer philosophical approaches, but the volume contains a worthwhile sample of traditional and modern studies. Of special note are chapters by P. Hardy and W. Cantwell Smith on Islamic approaches.

583 Phillips, Stephen H. Aurobindo's Philosophy of Brahman. Leiden: E.J. Brill, 1986, xii + 200 pp.
A careful and insightful analysis and evaluation of Aurobindo's worldview.

584 Phillips, Stephen H. "The Conflict of Voluntarism and Dualism in the Yogasūtra (or How to Get Mukti from Metaphysics." Journal of Indian Philosophy 13 (1985):399-414.
A thorough review of previous scholarly interpretations of the Yogasūtras. Phillips argues that "the mystical reading" of the work "is misdirected"; the work "attempts, but fails, to integrate a voluntarist logic of its practices into an overriding metaphysics of dualism."

585 Phillips, Stephen H. "Is Sri Aurobindo's Philosophy Vedānta?" Adyar Library Bulletin 48 (1984):1-27.
Phillips develops an argument for the answer "no" to his question, even though he asks us to view his philosophy as Vedānta and many Vedāntins have been mystics, as Aurobindo believes himself to be.

586 Piatigorsky, A. "Some Remarks on 'Other Stream.'" In Buddhist Studies Ancient and Modern, edited by Philip Denwood and Alexander Piatigorsky. Collected Papers on South Asia, no. 4. London: Curzon Press, 1983, pp. 124-52.

A study of Dharmakīrti's Saṃtānāntarasiddhi, complete with charts and parallel European passages. The "other stream" (saṃtānāntara) refers to a stream of consciousness inferrable by yogis and known directly by buddhas.

587 Pind, O.H. "Emptiness--Towards a Semiotic Determination of Emptiness in Mādhyamika Discourse." In Contributions on Tibetan and Buddhist Religion and Philosophy, edited by Ernst Steinkellner and Helmut Tauscher. Wiener Studien zur Tibetologie und Buddhismuskunde, Vol. 11. Vienna: Arbeitskreis für Tibetische und Buddhistische Studien Universitat Wien, 1983, pp. 169-204.

A new departure among attempts to make sense of Nāgārjuna's catuṣkoṭi. The salient point is that virodha is construed by Pind as incompatibility and not contradiction; Nāgārjuna, it is argued, was talking about the illogicality of being itself, not just of the language we use to speak of it.

588 Plott, John C. A Philosophy of Devotion. Delhi: Motilal Banarsidass, 1974, xiii + 657 pp.

Study comparing Viśiṣṭādvaita with St. Bonaventura and Gabriel Marcel.

589 Ponniah, V. The Śaiva Siddhānta Theory of Knowledge. Annamalainagar: Annamalai University, 1952, 351 pp.

The definitive treatment of the topic, based on Sivajñāna Yogin's Bhāṣya, but compared instructively with other Indian systems. It also offers a concise survey of Saiva Siddhānta literature.

590 Potter, Karl H., ed. Advaita Vedānta up to Śaṃkara and His Pupils. Encyclopedia of Indian Philosophies, no. 3. Delhi: Motilal Banarsidass; Princeton, N.J.: Princeton University Press, 1981, x + 635 pp.

Summary, arranged in chronological order, of the early work of Advaita, mostly by Potter, but lengthy and important summaries of Maṇḍana Miśra's Brahmasiddhi by Allen W. Thrasher and of Bṛhadāraṇyakopaniṣadbhāṣyavārttika by S. Subrahmanya Sastri. The usual analytic introduction precedes the summaries.

591 Potter, Karl H., comp. Bibliography. Rev. ed. Encyclopedia of Indian Philosophies, no. 1. Delhi: Motilal Banarsidass; Princeton, N.J.: Princeton University Press, 1983, xxxix + 1023 pp.

An attempt to control the rapidly growing literature on classical Indian philosophy. With the coming of the computer age, it is hoped this effort can now be kept more or less up to date as the years pass by.

592 Potter, Karl H. "Does Indian Epistemology Concern Justified True Belief?" Journal of Indian Philosophy 12, no. 4 (1984):307-27.

Contemporary Western philosophy views knowledge as justified true belief. Potter argues that Indian epistemology has rather to do with workability, the tendency of a judgment to lead to satisfaction of purpose, and that Mohanty's claim that both the svataḥ and parataḥ theories of prāmāṇya can be correct misses the mark. The article is followed immediately by responses from Mohanty and K.K. Chakrabarti.

593 Potter, Karl H., ed. Indian Metaphysics and Epistemology: The Tradition of Nyāya-Vaiśeṣika up to Gaṅgeśa. Encyclopedia of Indian Philosophies, no. 2. Delhi: Motilal Banarsidass; Princeton, N.J.: Princeton University Press, 1977, xiii + 744 pp.

A group of scholars from around the world provides a series of summaries of texts of Nyāya-Vaiśeṣika from the sūtras up to the thirteenth century. Potter provides a lengthy introduction which may itself serve as an independent summation of the system during this period.

594 Potter, Karl H. "The Naturalistic Principle of Karma." Philosophy East and West 14 (1964):39-49.

The article counters the usual assumption that karma theory involves ethical nonnaturalism. The reader should compare Walhout, in Philosophy East and West 16 (1966):235-37, in rebuttal, and Potter's reply, in the same journal, 18 (1968):82-84.

595 Potter, Karl H. Presuppositions of India's Philosophies. New York: Greenwood Press, 1973, 276 pp. (Orig. pub. Englewood Cliffs, N.J.: Prentice-Hall, 1963.)

Intended as an introductory textbook for American college students, this work attempts to show the connection between technical problems of epistemology and metaphysics and the central Indian themes of transmigration and liberation. Contains a section on Indian logic, with exercises, and suggestions for teachers.

596 Potter, Karl H. "Śaṃkarācārya: The Myth and the Man." In Charisma and Sacred Biography, edited by Michael A. Williams. Chico, Calif.: Scholars Press, 1982, pp. 113-25.

Saṃkara's preference for the term parivrājya to saṃnyāsa in speaking of the stage of liberation is invoked in contrast to Vidyāraṇya's account of jīvanmukti. It is argued that Saṃkara, but not Vidyāraṇya, believed pravṛtti and nivṛtti to be absolutely incompatible, and that being the case, the Daśanāmin's bhakti interpretation of Saṃkara's Advaita as well as the hagiographies of his time and after seriously misrepresent Saṃkara's contribution.

597 Potter, Karl H. "A Speech-Act Model for Understanding Navya-Nyāya Epistemology." In Analytical Philosophy in Comparative Perspective, edited by Bimal Krishna Matilal and Jaysankar Lal Shaw. Dordrecht, Holland: D. Reidel, 1985, pp. 213-30.

Argues that contemporary speech-act analysis (as in Austin, Strawson, and Searle) provides a better basis for comparison with Navya-Nyāya than does analytic philosophy as practiced by Russell, Quine, et al.

598 Prabhavananda. Spiritual Heritage of India. New York: Doubleday, 1963, xxii + 449 pp.

Predictably, Vedānta gets the lion's share of attention in this survey of Indian thought by one of the foremost disciples of the Ramakrishna order.

599 Prabhu, Pandharinath H. Hindu Social Organization: A Study in Socio-Psychological and Ideological Foundations. 4th ed. Bombay: Popular Prakashan, 1963, xx + 389 pp.

A study of Hindu social forms and ideas from a psychological standpoint that presents many considerations relevant to a philosophical approach.

600 Prakāśānanda. Prakāśānanda, Vedāntasiddhāntamuktāvali. Edited and translated by Arthur Venis. Benares: E.J. Lazarus Co., 1890, 192 pp. Reprint. Motilal Banarsidass, 1975.

This work presents a solipsistic version of Advaita which is absolutely fascinatingly iconoclastic in its implications. A brief index also contains clarifications of technical neo-Nyāya terminology--svarūpasambandha, avacchedaka, etc.

601 Prakash, Buddha. "The Hindu Philosophy of History." Journal of the History of Ideas 16 (1955):494-505.

Attention to certain issues in philosophy of history and historiography, developed from the "organic view of nature," seen as expressed in the rhythm of states of activity, sleeping and awakening in India's history.

602 Prasad, Hari Shankar. "Time a Substantive Reality in Nyāya-Vaiśeṣika." Philosophy East and West 34 (1984):233-66.

A thorough review of the treatment given to this most difficult of topics in Nyāya.

603 Prebish, Charles S., ed. Buddhism: A Modern Perspective. University Park: Pennsylvania State University Press, 1975, xv + 330 pp.

A useful collection of brief summaries of aspects of Buddhism, prepared by a group of scholars. Many of the papers concern specific writings or distinct groupings of them.

604 Preceptors of Advaita. Secunderabad: Sri Kanchi Kamakoti Sankara Mandir, 1968, x + 570 pp.

A collection of essays on great Advaitins past and present. Some of the essays are of solid scholarly calibre, shedding light on historical and, occasionally, philosophical aspects of Advaita.

605 "Proceedings of the Seminar on the Concept of Progress." Indian Philosophical Annual 3 (1967):3-98.

Fourteen papers, plus introductory and concluding remarks by T.M.P. Mahadevan, exploring various facets of the concept of progress.

606 Radhakrishnan, Sarvepalli. The Brahma Sūtra. London: G. Allen and Unwin, 1960, 606 pp.

A translation of the work, with extensive summaries of the comments of the various Vedāntists, not only Saṃkara, Rāmānuja, and Madhva, but practically all others of any importance. The introduction discusses reason and revelation, reality, self, the way to perfection, and rebirth.

607 Radhakrishnan, Sarvepalli. "Hindu Dharma." International Journal of Ethics 33 (1922):1-22.

A modern explanation (and defense) of major aspects of Hindu society, structured around dharma.

608 Radhakrishnan, Sarvepalli. The Hindu View of Life. New York: Macmillan Co., 1927, 92 pp.

Besides its general stature as an interpretation of Hindu themes to the West, the two chapters on dharma outline ingredients of Radhakrishnan's social philosophy.

609 Radhakrishnan, Sarvepalli. "Indian Culture." Reflections on Our Age: Lectures Delivered at the Opening Session of UNESCO at the Sorbonne University, Paris. New York: Columbia University Press, 1949, pp. 115-33.

Social responsibility combined with spiritual freedom is advocated.

610 Radhakrishnan, Sarvepalli. Indian Philosophy. 2 vols. London: G. Allen and Unwin, 1923, 1:738 pp.; 2:807 pp.

Famous and influential exposition of Indian thought, in extensive detail, by India's most famous modern philosopher, recently president of India. The first volume deals with Vedic philosophy, materialism, Jainism, early Buddhism, the epics and Bhagavadgītā, Buddhism as a religion, and the schools of Buddhism. The second volume considers Nyāya, Vaiśeṣika, Sāṃkhya, Yoga, Pūrva Mīmāṃsā, the Vedāntasūtras, Advaita Vedānta of Śaṃkara, Rāmānuja's system, and Śaiva, Śākta, and later Vaiṣṇava theism. Radhakrishnan is a master stylist and his expositions are a pleasure to read, but one must beware of his Vedāntic bias.

611 Radhakrishnan, Sarvepalli. "The Individual and the Social Order in Hinduism." In The Individual in East and West,

edited by Ernest Richard Hughes. London: Oxford University Press, 1937, pp. 109-52. Reprinted in Eastern Religions and Western Thought (Oxford: Clarendon Press, 1939), pp. 349-85.
Major concepts pertaining to social life are interpreted in a contemporary perspective.

612 Radhakrishnan, Sarvepalli. Kalki or the Future of Civilization. London: Kegan Paul, Trench, Trubner & Co., 1929, 96 pp.
Radhakrishnan's advocacy of social responsibility, to counter individualistic trends, is related to a metaphysical position.

613 Radhakrishnan, Sarvepalli, trans. The Principal Upanishads. New York: Harper, 1953, 958 pp.
Has Sanskrit text in transliteration facing translation. Scholarly work by India's former president.

614 Radhakrishnan, Sarvepalli. Religion and Society. 2d ed. London: George Allen and Unwin, 1948, 242 pp.
The Kamala lectures express an important part of a modern philosophical leader's understanding of social issues.

615 Radhakrishnan, Sarvepalli. "The Vedāntic Approach to Reality." Monist 26 (1916):200-231.
An approach to Brahman through the sheaths (kośas). This may be the quintessential Radhakrishnan.

616 Radhakrishnan, Sarvepalli, and Charles A. Moore, eds. A Source Book in Indian Philosophy. Princeton, N.J.: Princeton University Press, 1957, 684 pp.
The best, and really the only, book of its kind, covering the whole gamut of Indian philosophy from the Vedas to modern times, Buddhism and Jainism as well as Hindu schools. Selections of sources are always interesting, occasionally brilliant, though sometimes the texts chosen (e.g., sūtras) are in need of commentary beyond what is provided. There are helpful brief introductions on each of the schools.

617 Raghavachar, S.S. "Place of Reason in Advaita." The Half-Yearly Journal of the Mysore University 19 (1959-60):29-48.
A good, succinct survey (see K.S. Murty, entry 525 for a more extensive one), which covers several important early Advaitins.

618 Raghavachar, S.S. Sri Rāmānuja on the Upanishads. Madras: Prof. M. Rangacharya Memorial Trust, 1972, xii + 146 pp.
Although Rāmānuja did not write commentaries on the Upaniṣads as the other great Vedāntins did, his writings are full of quotations, which are here identified and analyzed.

619 Raghavan, V.K.S.N. History of Viśiṣṭādvaita Literature. Delhi: Ajanta Publications, 1979, xx + 132 pp.
Mainly a list of extant works on Viśiṣṭādvaita philosophy, this work is nevertheless the most complete account of that literature. A useful and important tool.

620 Raghunātha Śiromaṇi. Raghunātha Śiromaṇi, Padārthatattvanirūpaṇa. Edited and translated by Karl H. Potter. Harvard Yenching Institute Studies, no. 17. Cambridge: Harvard University Press, 1957, 102 pp.
Raghunātha in this work substantially revises the classical Vaiśeṣika ontology. It is one of the more original works in Indian philosophy.

621 Raju, P.T. "Activism in Indian Thought." Annals of the Bhandarkar Oriental Research Institute 39 (1958):158-226.
An examination of Mīmāṃsā as the traditional philosophical approach to the regulation of life in the world, arguing against the view that social philosophy was totally absent in the past.

622 Raju, P.T. Idealistic Thought of India. London: G. Allen and Unwin, 1953, 454 pp.
One of the most enthusiastic works of the movement for comparative philosophy, pioneered by Radhakrishnan and Raju. Raju counts Advaita in particular and other Vedāntas to some extent, the Bhagavadgītā, and Mahāyāna Buddhism as "idealist." There is a lot of freewheeling speculation about relations between East and West in spiritual values.

623 Raju, P.T. "Identity in Difference in Some Vedāntic Systems." New Indian Antiquary 2 (1939):317-31.
Of Bhāskara, Rāmānuja, Nimbārka, Śrīkaṇṭha, and Śrīpati, who all use the concept of identity-in-difference (bhedābheda), only Nimbārka is consistent.

624 Raju, P.T. Indian Idealism and Modern Challenges. Chandigarh: Panjab University, 1961, 208 pp.
An expanded version of lectures delivered at Chandigarh in 1960. The first two parts deal historically with the development of Vedānta. Part 3, "Critical and Comparative," offers comparisons between Vedānta and every kind of Western philosophical movement, from which Vedānta emerges triumphant.

625 Raju, P.T. "Influence of Industrialization and Technology on the Philosophies of India." Prabuddha Bharata 62 (1957):298-303, 352-56.
A call for the development of social philosophy.

626 Raju, P.T. "Intuition as a Philosophical Method in India." Philosophy East and West 2 (1952):187-207.
This should be read in conjunction with Herbert Feigl's

rejoinder, in Philosophy East and West 8 (1958):1-16. The two articles constitute a challenging confrontation.

627 Raju, P.T. The Philosophical Traditions of India. Pittsburgh: University of Pittsburgh Press, 1972, 256 pp.
Usable as an introductory textbook for a course on Indian philosophy.

628 Raju, P.T. "Skepticism and Its Place in Śaṃkara's Philosophy." Philosophical Quarterly 13 (1937):46-57.
Descartes' method compared with Saṃkara's. The degree to which Saṃkara is a skeptic is different than, say, the skepticism of Mādhyamika.

629 Raju, P.T. Structural Depths of Indian Thought. Albany: State University of New York Press, 1985, xxxi + 599 pp.
This may be the best introductory textbook to Indian philosophy available in English. It avoids the temptation to trivialize the subject in order to obtain brevity. Yet it is genuinely philosophical (in a recognizably Western way) as well as being thoroughly documented. The result is a challenging review of Indian philosophy that gives its subject the kind of stature that, as Raju himself hopes, Windelband's account of Western philosophy provided his, while remaining accessible to the student of genuine interest.

630 Ramachandran, R.P. The Concept of the Vyāvahārika in Advaita Vedānta. Madras, 1969.
The vyāvahārika is the empirical or commonly considered "veridical" truth, which is contrasted in Advaita with the pāramārthika or supreme truth. Under this rubric the author considers the preparation of the Advaita adept; his intellectual and moral training; and the place of devotion in religion, aesthetics, theory of knowledge, ontology, and cosmology.

631 Ramachandran, T.P. The Indian Philosophy of Beauty. 2 vols. Madras: University of Madras, 1 (1979):xv + 104 pp.; 2 (1980):x + 152 pp.
A lucid scholarly study of Indian aesthetic theory. The first volume (Perspective) is more general philosophy, the second (Special Concepts) expounds many of the central concepts and terms of Sanskrit aesthetic theory.

632 Ramaiah, C. Problem of Change and Identity in Indian Philosophy. Tirupati: Sri Venkateswam University, 1978, vii + 107 + ix pp.
How do the most important systems treat change and persistence through time? This small book gives serious concern to Sāṃkhya-Yoga, Advaita, Buddhism, and Nyāya-Vaiśeṣika on the question.

633 Ramakrishna Rao, K.B. Theism of Pre-Classical Sāṃkhya. Mysore: Prasaranga, University of Mysore, 1966, xvi + 444 + iv + 24 pp.

A recent exploration of the puzzle about the status and nature of early Sāṃkhya. Work explores Upaniṣads, Mahābhārata, the lost Ṣaṣṭitantra, Pañcarātra, medical texts, etc.

634 Rāmānujācārya. Rāmānujācārya, Tantrarahasya: Critically Edited with Introduction and Appendices. Edited by K.S. Ramaswami Sastri. 2d ed. Gaekwad's Oriental Series, no. 24. Baroda: Oriental Institute, 1956, 167 pp.

Ramaswami Sastri's introduction discusses the development of the Prābhākara school of Mīmāṃsā and contrasts it with that of the Bhāṭṭa school as expounded in the Tantrarahasya, here summarized. Full of valuable information. (This Rāmānuja is a Mīmāṃsaka, not the famous Viśiṣṭādvaitin.)

635 Ramanujam, P.S. A Study of Vaiśeṣika Philosophy with Special Reference to Vyomaśivācārya. Mysore: University of Mysore, 1979, x + 226 pp.

Vyomaśiva has been overlooked among commentators on Praśastapāda. This study sets the record straight. It is shown that Vyomaśiva was a particularly fiery critic of Buddhist idealism.

636 Ramaswami Aiyar, C.P. "The Philosophical Basis of Indian Legal and Social Systems." In Essays in East-West Philosophy: An Attempt at World Philosophical Synthesis, edited by Charles A. Moore. Honolulu: University of Hawaii Press, 1962, pp. 336-52. Reprinted in The Indian Mind: Essentials of Indian Philosophy and Culture, ed. Charles A. Moore (Honolulu: University of Hawaii Press, 1967), pp. 248-66.

A general and largely uncritical survey of values and practices associated with the legal system.

637 Ranade, R.D. A Constructive Survey of Upaniṣadic Philosophy. Poona Oriental Series, no. 7. Poona: Oriental Book Agency, 1926, 438 pp.

Satisfying survey by one of India's most respected saintly scholars.

638 Ranade, R.D. Vedānta: The Culmination of Indian Thought. Bombay: Bharatiya Vidya Bhavan, 1970, ix + 234 pp.

A thorough review of many of the main problems of Indian philosophy by a scholar whom many revered as a saint. It is by no means confined to Vedānta.

639 Randle, Henry N. Indian Logic in the Early Schools. London: Oxford University Press, 1930, 404 pp.

This work studies the history of classical Nyāya logic and theory of knowledge in relation to Dignāga's school and other rivals. It sticks very closely to the texts.

640 Ranganathananda, Swami. "The Philosophy of Service." Prabuddha Bharata 73 (1968):328-41, 373-82, 415-19.
An address enunciating many themes of the approach to social ethics of the Ramakrishna Mission.

641 Rani, Vijaya. The Buddhist Philosophy as Presented in Mīmāṃsā-Śloka-Vārttika. Delhi: Parimal Publication, 1982, xxiii + 264 pp.
What does the Ślokavārttika tell us about Buddhist philosophy as it was known to Kumārila? This useful thesis explores that topic carefully and thoroughly.

642 Rao, M.A. Venkata. "An Indian Philosophy of History." Aryan Path 35 (1964):349-54.
Brief modern treatment of the theory of yugas, suggesting a reversal of moral decline, toward the goal of returning to the Kṛta age. It is suggested that Indian thought thus has a point of comparison with the perspective of Pierre Teilhard de Chardin.

643 Rao, P. Nagaraja. "The Epistemology of Dvaita Vedānta." Adyar Library Bulletin 22, no. 3-4 (1958):vii + 120 pp.
Based on Jayatīrtha's Pramāṇapaddhati, the veteran scholar of Dvaita here presents a straightforward review of Dvaita epistemology. It is the definitive account of the subject, and there are appendixes on Dvaita views on difference (bheda) and God. A useful work for those who are trying to place Madhva's philosophy among the other epistemological theories.

644 Rao, Srinivasa. Advaita: A Critical Investigation. Bangalore: Indian Philosophy Foundation, 1985, ii + 88 + vii pp.
Arranged and written in a manner reminiscent of Wittgenstein's Tractatus (from 1.1 to 16.8), this small work attempts a scathing critique of Advaita which deserves consideration by fair and philosophically minded students of that system.

645 Rao, Veluri Subba. The Philosophy of a Sentence and Its Parts. New Delhi: Munshiram Manoharlal, 1969, xviii + 258 pp.
Thorough account of grammatical theories--syntax and semantics of words and sentences studied in detail.

646 Rastogi, Navjivan. Introduction to Tantrāloka: A Study in Structure. Delhi: Motilal Banarsidass, 1987, xxx + 589 pp.
A thorough introduction to a forthcoming edition of this mammoth work, Rastogi provides copious information about Abhinavagupta, author of the Tantrāloka; Jayaratha, author of its Viveka; and the structure of the text. A variety of appendixes analyze the work in summary fashion.

647 Rastogi, Navjivan. The Krama Tantricism of Kashmir. Delhi: Motilal Banarsidass, 1979, xxix + 296 pp.

Since K.C. Pandey's work we have had little in the way of general studies of Kashmir Saivism. Rastogi's work is especially valuable, therefore, for directing a magnifying glass, as it were, on one of the several branches of Saivism, and bringing out in great detail the little-known names and contributions of many hitherto forgotten writers of bygone days. An important supplement to the history of Indian philosophy.

648 Rastogi, Navjivan. "Theory of Error According to Abhinavagupta." Journal of Indian Philosophy 14 (1986):1-33.

Within the classifications of theories of error standardly offered, where does Abhinavagupta's theory (which he calls "apūrṇakhyātivāda") lie? Rastogi argues that it is different from any others, but perhaps closer to the viparītakhyāti theory of Kumārila than any other.

649 Ratnayaka, Shanta. "The Bodhisattva Ideal of Theravāda." Journal of the International Association of Buddhist Studies 8, no. 2 (1985):85-110.

Despite popular belief to the contrary, Theravāda taught the doctrine of the bodhisattva. If "Hīnayāna" be a term to describe Buddhists who do not recognize bodhisattvas, Theravāda is not Hīnayāna. This paper corrects this and other related misunderstandings about Theravāda.

650 Ratnayaka, Shanta. Two Ways to Perfection: Buddhist and Christian. Colombo: Lake House Investment, 1978, xiv + 180 pp.

A comparative study of Buddhaghoṣa's Viśuddhimagga and John Wesley's writings.

651 Ray, Roma. "Gettier-Like Problem in Indian Philosophy." Indian Philosophical Quarterly 12, no. 4 (1985):381-402.

Besides finding a Gettier-like problem in Vidyāraṇya's Pañcadaśī, this paper concludes with a challenging analysis to show that Prābhākara Mīmāṃsā is committed to the view that awareness cannot be false.

652 Ray, Roma. "Is Pariṇāmavāda a Doctrine of Causality?" Journal of Indian Philosophy 10 (1982):377-96.

It is not just a causal doctrine, answers the author; furthermore it terminates when the five categories (pañcamahābhūta) appear and wasn't intended to be applied to everyday cases. In these cases the category of nimitta kāraṇa applies, but the Sāṃkhya metaphysical account ends prior to this point.

653 Ray, Santosh Kumar. The Political Thought of President Radhakrishnan. Calcutta: Firma K.L. Mukhopadhyaya, 1966, xii + 204 pp.

An introductory study, largely uncritical, with brief passages offering comparisons to Western political philosophers, modern Indian thinkers, and some American statesmen. Brings together material on political philosophy from Radhakrishnan's writings.

654 Rege, M.P. "The Indian Philosophical Tradition." Quest 44 (1965):9-24.

Thoughtful, well-written general piece comparing Western and Indian philosophy.

655 Rhys-Davids, T.W. "On Nirvāna, and on the Buddhist Doctrines of the 'Groups,' the Saṃskāras, Karma and the 'Paths.'" Contemporary Review 29 (1877):249-70.

Important, rather long explication of key concepts of Buddhism.

656 Richards, Glyn. The Philosophy of Gandhi. London: Curzon Press, 1982, ix + 178 pp.

"My contention is that the unity of Gandhi's thought and the interrelatedness of the various aspects of his teaching spring from firmly held metaphysical beliefs."

657 Riepe, Dale. Indian Philosophy since Independence. Calcutta: Research India Publications, 1979, iv + 360 + A-37.

The only work to attempt to consider the contributions to philosophy of academic philosophers recently and presently working in India. While Riepe has his biasses, the attention to this group and their work is important and unique.

658 Riepe, Dale. The Naturalistic Tradition in Indian Thought. Seattle: University of Washington, 1961, 308 pp.

"Naturalism"--defined here so as to include about every Indian school other than Vedānta--is particularly characteristic of early Vedic and other Hindu thought. For example, Nyāya-Vaiśeṣika is naturalistic in its nontheistic phases, but not later on. Riepe reviews the essentials of Cārvāka, Jainism, Hīnayāna Buddhism, Sāmkhya, and Vaiśeṣika, but his approach is hampered by dependence on secondary sources.

659 Riepe, Dale. "Recent Assessments and Misconceptions of Indian Philosophy." In Quest for Truth. A Felicitation Volume in Honour of Prof. S.P. Kanal, edited by Kewal Krishna Mittal. Delhi: Prof. S.P. Kanal Abhinanden Samiti, 1976, pp. 62-79.

Riepe is rightly concerned to set right the misconception that Indian philosophy is totally subjectivist, and has some trenchant points to make. While this sort of thing can easily be mismanaged, it is illuminating to have sacred oxen occasionally gored!

660 Robinson, Richard H. "The Classical Indian Axiomatic." Philosophy East and West 17 (1967):139-54.

Lays down a number of basic propositions characterizing Indian philosophy's approach to problems.

661 Robinson, Richard H. Early Mādhyamika in India and China. Madison: University of Wisconsin Press, 1967, 347 pp.
Part 1 contains an authoritative summation of Nāgārjuna and Mādhyamika philosophy. The book goes on to detail the transmission of Mādhyamika to China in the hands of Kumārajīva and others.

662 Robinson, Richard H. "Some Logical Aspects of Nāgārjuna's System." Philosophy East and West 6, no. 4 (1956):291-308.
An influential article which argues that Nāgārjuna does not flout any logical principles. Passages from Mādhyamikakārikās and catuṣkoṭi are rendered into symbols.

663 Roy, S.S. The Heritage of Śaṃkara. Allahabad: Udayana Publications, 1965, xiv + 230 pp.
An essay defending Advaita, especially against the charge of crypto-Buddhism. Spends a good deal of time on Gauḍapāda and Saṃkara; discusses Nāgārjuna, Candrakīrti, and Srīharṣa as well.

664 Rudolph, Susanne Hoeber. "Self-Control and Political Potency: Gandhi's Asceticism." American Scholar 35 (1965-66):79-97.
A study of the social relevance of asceticism, wherein traditional values are manifest in modern politics.

665 Ruegg, David Seyfort. A History of Indian Literature. Vol. 7, fasc. 1, The Literature of the Mādhyamaka School of Philosophy in India. Wiesbaden: Otto Harrassowitz, 1981, ix + 146 pp.
The definitive account to date of Mādhyamaka literature known to us at present, written by a famous scholar. Though largely concerned with identifying and reviewing the literature on texts, Ruegg is able to give brief summaries of their contents as well.

666 Ruegg, David Seyfort. "On the Term Buddhaviparināma and the Problem of Illusory Change." Indo-Iranian Journal 2 (1958):271-83.
Traces features in grammatical theory which may have influenced development of vivartavāda. Also touches on Triṃśikā's theory of vijñānapariṇāma, and Maṇḍanamiśra's Brahmasiddhi on the nature of words, which provides a link with the Mahābhāṣya. Important article, rather technical.

667 Śabarasvāmin. Śabarasvāmi, Śabara Bhāṣya. Translated by Ganganatha Jha. 2d ed. Gaekwad's Oriental Series, nos. 65, 70, 73. Baroda: Oriental Institute, 65 (1973):xv + 1-705; 70 (1973):xx + 706-1416; 73 (1974):xxviii + 1417-2429.
Remarkable effort by one of India's greatest scholars. Śabara's Bhāṣya is the basic commentary on Jaimini's Mīmāṃsā-sūtras. It is a vast resource for understanding not only Mīmāṃsā exegetics and early thought, but also for the light it sheds on affairs of its time.

668 Sadānanda. Sadānanda, Vedāntasāra. Edited and translated by Mysore Hiriyanna. Poona: Oriental Book Agency, 1929, 97 pp.
Probably the best of several translations of this relatively easy introduction to Advaita Vedānta. Hiriyanna's introduction covers the preliminary training of a seeker after liberation, the teaching of the Vedānta, the discipline necessary for its realization, and jīvanmukti.

669 Sadāśiva, Brahmendra Sarasvatī. "Ātmānuṣaṃdhāna." Edited and translated by N. Gangadharan. Voice of Saṃkara 5 (1980-81):348-64.
Sadāśiva (seventeenth century) "was the 57th pontiff of the Kamakotipitha." This is a short, enthusiastic expression of Vedāntic sentiment.

670 Saha, Sukharanjan. Advaita Theory of Illusion. Calcutta: Progressive Publishers, 1982, v + 138 pp.
A close study of the Advaita theory known as anirvacanīyakhyāti, contrasted with its rivals, the theories of illusion of sat- and asat-khyāti attributed traditionally to the other major schools of classical Indian philosophy. The author provides his own acute critical evaluation.

671 Saiyidain, K.G. The Humanist Tradition in Modern Indian Educational Thought. Madison: Dembar Educational Research Services, 1967, 239 pp.
Review of the contributions of Tagore, Gandhi, Iqbal, Azad, Radhakrishnan, and Husain, with prefatory and concluding chapters analyzing the contemporary situation regarding education in India.

672 Saksena, S.K. Nature of Consciousness in Hindu Philosophy. Banaras: Nand Kishore & Bros., 1944, 223 + v pp.
Doctoral dissertation by this always original and provocative author. Mainly concerns the issues of svataḥ vs. parataḥ-prakāśatva and prāmāṇya--i.e., whether knowledge illumines itself and/or provides its own validation, or whether these contentions are not correct.

673 Saletore, Bhasker Anand. Ancient Indian Political Thought and Institutions. Bombay: Asia Publishing House, 1963, 695 pp.
A comprehensive and comparative study which makes frequent reference to the positions of modern scholars, thus bewildering to a beginner. Its somewhat encyclopedic character has its compensating virtues, and the footnotes are a mine of citations of scholarly studies on a wide variety of topics (there is no bibliography). Somewhat historical, but political thought is treated. Greatest usefulness would be for specialists.

674 Samartha, S.J. The Hindu View of History: Classical and Modern. Bangalore: Christian Institute for the Study of Religion and Society, 1959, 36 pp.

Two lectures (based on a doctoral dissertation) in which a greater disparity between traditional and contemporary views is discerned than in the interpretations of some other writers. A helpful introductory review of pertinent issues.

675 Śaṃkarasvāmin. Nyāyapraveśa. Translated by Musashi Tachikawa. Journal of Indian Philosophy 1 (1970-71):111-45.
Once thought to be by Dignāga, this small treatise provides a succinct summary of Dignāga's views on inference.

676 Sangharaksita. A Survey of Buddhism. 2d ed. Bangalore: Indian Institute of World Culture, 1959, vii + 527 pp.
Standard survey.

677 Sanghvi, Sukhlalji. Advanced Studies in Indian Logic and Metaphysics. Calcutta: Indian Studies Past and Present, 1961, vi + 122 pp. (Orig. pub. in Indian Studies Past and Present 2 [1960-61]:189-201, 387-494.)
Based on Hemacandra's Pramāṇamīmāṃsā, this study consists of notes on a variety of epistemological matters developing numerous technical notions.

678 Śāntideva. Śikṣāsamuccaya. Translated by C. Bendall and W. Rouse. London: J. Murray, 1922, vii + 328 pp.
A Buddhist work dwelling on the ethical side of things rather than epistemology or metaphysics. It is useful for getting the feel of the Buddhist monk's point of view.

679 Sarasvati, Hariharananda. "The Ego and the Self." Translated by A. Danielou. Adyar Library Bulletin 19 (1955):241-312.
An unusual and useful thing, a contemporary work expounding classical themes in an original manner, and made available in English.

680 Sarkar, Anil Kumar. Changing Phases of Buddhist Thought. Patna: Bharati Bhawan, 1968, 147 pp.
Revised versions of articles the author has published previously are here combined to touch on the highlights of Buddhist philosophy: Aśvaghoṣa, Nāgārjuna, Dignāga, Candrakīrti, and Gauḍapāda. There is a chapter on the affinity of existentialism with Buddhist thought.

681 Saroja, G.V. Tilak and Śaṃkara on the Gītā. New Delhi: Sterling Publishers Pvt., 1985, xviii + 200 pp.
A lively critique of Lokamanya B.G. Tilak's interpretation of the Bhagavadgītā; Tilak's explication is contrasted with Śaṃkara's to the former's disadvantage.

682 Sarvajñātman. Saṃkṣepaśarīraka. Critically edited and translated by N. Veezhinathan. Madras University Philosophical Studies, no. 18. Madras: Centre for Advanced Study in Philosophy, University of Madras, 1972, vii + 150 + 544 pp.

A famous and important work on Advaita philosophy, generally following Sureśvara's line of thought, here made available in an excellent translation.

683 Scharfe, Hartmut. A History of Indian Literature. Vol. 5, Grammatical Literature. Wiesbaden: Otto Harrassowitz, 1977, 216 pp.

An exceedingly helpful guide to materials in Sanskrit grammar and grammatical philosophy, from Pāṇini and Yāska to modern times.

684 Schayer, Stanislaw. Contributions to the Problem of Time in Indian Philosophy. Krakow: Polska Akademia Umiejetnosci, 1938, 76 pp.

A remarkable monograph, in which Vaiśeṣika and Mīmāmsā arguments for time as substance, older Buddhist views of time as phases of dharmas, and the Sautrāntika critique of time are illuminated by translations of key textual passages drawn from little-studied sources. Technical but highly authoritative.

685 Schilpp, Paul Arthur, ed. The Philosophy of Sarvepalli Radhakrishnan. New York: Tudor Publishing Co., 1952, xviii + 883 pp.

Three papers, by Humayun Kabir, B.K. Mallik, and A.R. Wadia, focus on Radhakrishnan's social and political thought. Some sections of Radhakrishnan's introductory essay and the concluding reply to critics also outline aspects of his social philosophy.

686 Schmithausen, Lambert. "On the Problem of the Relation of Spiritual Practice and Philosophical Theory in Buddhism." In German Scholars on India. Vol. 2. Bombay: Nachiketa Publishing, 1976, pp. 235-50.

Through a close examination of the Yogācārabhūmi, Saṃdhinirmocanasūtra, and other texts, Schmithausen shows that idealism made its "first appearance in connection with reflections on objects of visionary meditation" in Mahāyāna.

687 Schopen, Gregory. "The Generalization of an Old Yogic Attainment in Medieval Mahāyāna Sūtra Literature: Some Notes on Jātismara." Journal of the International Association of Buddhist Studies 6, no. 1 (1983):109-47.

Jātismara means "the ability to recollect or remember one's former births." Schopen shows how the idea grew to mean "a radical restructuring of behavior and attitude . . . and . . . the release from, or avoidance of, rebirth in the hells and other unfortunate destinies."

688 Schubring, Walther. The Doctrine of the Jains Described after the Old Sources. Delhi: Motilal Banarsidass, 1962, 335 pp.

Reprint of classic work on Jain thought. Includes but goes well beyond technical philosophy.

689 Schweitzer, Albert. Indian Thought and Its Development. London: A. and C. Black, 1936, xii + 279 pp.

A controversial, not very trustworthy, account of early Indian thought by the famous doctor, who was out of his element here.

690 Scott, Roland W. Social Ethics in Modern Hinduism. Calcutta: YMCA Publishing House, 1953, 243 pp.

A survey of religious responses to and implications of modern social, political, and economic developments, providing an essential orientation to contemporary philosophy.

691 Sen, Debabrata. The Concept of Knowledge: Indian Theories. Calcutta: K.P. Bagchi & Co., 1984, xii + 296 pp.

Considers three issues: whether consciousness is objectful (saviṣaya) or objectless, formless (nirākāra) or form-filled, self-manifesting (svaprakāśa) or other-manifesting. The author's treatment is both clear and deep.

692 Sen, Prabal Kumar. "Vaṃśadhara's Works and His Textual Criticism of the Nyāyasūtras." Journal of Indian Philosophy 8 (1980):99-133.

Vaṃśadhara was a disciple of Gokulanātha Upādhyāya and must have lived in the mid-eighteenth century. His work is only available in manuscripts and has so far remained unknown. Sen shows the importance and relevance of the most important passages from two of his works, one a commentary on the Nyāyasūtras, the other on Raghunātha's Dīdhiti.

693 Sen, Sachin. The Political Thought of Tagore. Calcutta: General Printers and Publishers, 1947, iii + 360 pp.

A general and largely uncritical survey of Tagore's views on social themes, such as politics, nationalism, and education.

694 Sen, Saileswar. "The Nyāya-Vaiśeṣika Theory of Salvation." In Cultural Heritage of India. Vol. 3, The Philosophical Systems. 1st ed. Calcutta: Ramakrishna Mission Institute of Culture, 1937, pp. 449-58.

Relates to Gaṅgeśa's Muktivāda. A tough but solid analysis.

695 Sen, Sanat Kumar. "Indian Philosophy and Social Ethics." Journal of the Indian Academy of Philosophy 6 (1967):63-74.

Discusses "the nature and value of social ethics in Indian philosophy in general," reviewing major concepts and assessing the prospects for various Hindu systems overcoming traditional individualism. Notes the dichotomy between temporal goods and the eternal goal, concluding that "social values have, in some way or other, to be incorporated in our conception of ultimate value."

696 Sen, Sushanta. "Is Buddhism a Radical Departure from Upanishadic Hinduism?" Visvabharati Quarterly 47, nos. 1-2 (1981):48-72.

Answers "yes" as against Mrs. Rhys-Davids, Sarvepalli Radhakrishnan, et al.

697 Sen, Sushanta. A Study of Universals with Special Reference to Indian Philosophy. Santiniketan: Visva-Bharati Research Publications Committee, 1978, iv + 168 pp.

Argues that a category of "inexact resemblances" in addition to qualitative identity is commonly taken by the realist to be required ontologically by the fact that things resemble each other. On the way to this conclusion the author subjects all schools of Indian thought to a lively criticism that is extremely illuminating.

698 Sengupta, Anima. Classical Sāṃkhya: A Critical Study. Lucknow: Manoranjan Sen, 1969, vii + 178 + 18 pp.

Just what the title implies.

699 Sengupta, Anima. A Critical Study of the Philosophy of Rāmānuja. Chowkhamba Sanskrit Series Studies, no. 55. Varanasi: Chowkhamba Sanskrit Series, 1967, 263 pp.

Covers epistemology, metaphysics, ethics, and theology of the great medieval Vedāntin.

700 Sengupta, Bratindra Kumar. A Critique on the Vivaraṇa School. Calcutta: S.N. Sengupta, 1959, 278 pp.

A detailed review of the literature of the main post-Śaṃkara school of Advaita. Chapters 2-4 have especially interesting sections. The work is full of hard analysis but also full of untranslated Sanskrit terms.

701 Seth, Kirti Dev. "The Educational Philosophy of Swami Vivekananda." Prabuddha Bharata 66 (1961):465-75.

Exploration of themes of Vivekananda, and his "religious" approach to education.

702 Seth, Kirti Dev. Idealistic Trends in Indian Philosophies of Education. Allahabad: Education Department, 1966, xv + 510 pp.

This doctoral thesis (1953) offers a general survey of ancient and modern thought as it pertains to education, within the framework of idealism.

703 Shah, Jethalal G. Shrī Vallabhāchārya: His Philosophy and Religion. Nadiad: Pushtimargiya Pustakalaya, 1969, xi + 501 pp.

This work follows the same pattern as Marfatia (see entry 455), except that the summaries are less extensive and a different set (and more) of Vallabha's followers' works are chosen for discussion.

704 Shah, Nagin J. Akalaṅka's Criticism of Dharmakīrti's Philosophy. Lalpat Dalpatbhai Series, no. 11. Ahmedabad: L.D. Institute of Indology, 1967, 316 pp.

At present the best work in English on Dharmakīrti's thought as found in the Pramāṇavārttika, it is also unusually interesting as an in-depth analysis of a work of Jain logic. The book follows the texts very closely, yet manages to get to the bottom of epistemological problems of great importance. An especially useful dissertation.

705 Shah, Nagin J. "Jaina Conception of Space and Time." Sambodhi 6, nos. 3-4 (1977-78):12-31.

Distinguishes two views about the number of material elements within Jainism. According to one there are five, for the other only four, since sound is not a quality and requires no substratum. Similar clear and cogent analyses of Jain conceptions of time.

706 Shah, Sukharanjan. "A Study in Gaṅgeśa's Theory of Viśeṣaṇa." In Logical Form, Predication, and Ontology, edited by Pranab Kumar Sen. Jadavpur Studies in Philosophy, no. 4. Delhi: Macmillan, 1982, pp. 109-65.

Another attempt to solve the puzzle posed in understanding Gaṅgeśa's Tattvacintāmaṇi. Not a translation, but more of a running explanation of the several definitions that constitute this chapter.

707 Shanbhag, Dayanand N. Some Problems in Dvaita Philosophy. Dharwad: Shri Rama Prakashana, 1982, xv + 207 pp.

The author has selected a dozen important topics from Vyāsatīrtha's Nyāyāmṛta and discussed them in detail.

708 Sharma, Arvind. The Hindu Gītā: Ancient and Classical Interpretations of the Bhagavadgītā. London: Gerald Duckworth & Co., 1986, xxx + 269 pp.

Unusual in books about the Gītā. Sharma offers chapters on the Aṇugītā, usually ignored, and on Bhāskara and Madhva as well as Saṃkara and Rāmānuja. The author is very much aware of current scholarship and offers many provoking remarks plus a helpful bibliography of mostly recent publications.

709 Sharma, B.N. Krishnamurti. The Brahmasūtras and Their Principal Commentaries. 3 vols. Bombay: Bharatiya Vidya Bhavan, 1 (1971):xxviii + 428 pp.; 2 (1975):xxviii + 464 pp.; 3 (1978):xlviii + 835 pp.

These volumes are comparable to Radhakrishnan (see entry 606), but Sharma covers many more commentators.

710 Sharma, B.N. Krishnamurti. A History of the Dvaita School of Vedānta and Its Literature. Vol. 1, From the Earliest Beginnings to the Age of Jayatīrtha (c. 1400 A.D.) (1960),

370 pp. Vol. 2, <u>From the 15th Century to Our Own Time</u> (1961), 420 pp. Bombay: Booksellers.

The definitive survey of Dvaita Vedānta, covering every known author and work of that school. Sharma won national honors with this work, certainly one of the most exhaustive studies of a philosophical school ever undertaken.

711 Sharma, B.N. Krishnamurti. <u>Madhva's Teaching in His Own Words</u>. Bombay: Bharatiya Vidya Bhavan, 1961, 180 pp.

One of a series of small books in which important philosophers' writings are selected and rearranged. Sharma is known for several definitive works on Dvaita: this one maintains his high standards of scholarship and style.

712 Sharma, B.N. Krishnamurti. <u>Philosophy of Śrī Madhvācārya</u>. Bombay: Bharatiya Vidya Bhavan, 1962, 375 pp.

Sharma claims this work is "the first complete critical and comparative exposition of Śrī Madhvācārya's Philosophy in English." It is probably the best single introduction to Dvaita thought, although the author uses Sanskrit quotations in Devanāgari to illustrate his analyses.

713 Sharma, Brij Lal. "Authority and Obedience in Vedānta." <u>International Journal of Ethics</u> 46 (1936):350-63.

Explores the relation of individuals to institutions; the context is contemporary and the approach is systematic or constructive rather than historical or analytic.

714 Sharma, Chandradhar. <u>A Critical Survey of Indian Philosophy</u>. New York: Barnes and Noble, 1962, 405 pp. (Orig. pub. as <u>Indian Philosophy</u> [Banaras: Nand Kishore, 1952].)

Perhaps the most successful of the numerous introductions to Indian philosophy written by Indian academicians. The virtue of Sharma's book is that he does not remain content merely to report the doctrines of each system, but is willing to subject them to searching questions. Furthermore, Sharma is willing and able to name the names of specific Indian thinkers rather than merely presenting each system as a monolithic production.

715 Sharma, Dhirendra. <u>The Differentiation Theory of Meaning in Indian Logic</u>. The Hague: Mouton, 1969, 129 pp.

Translation of Ratnakīrti's <u>Apohasiddhi</u>, dealing with Buddhist logic's theory of meaning. Translation is not always easy to follow.

716 Sharma, Dhirendra. <u>The Negative Dialectics of India</u>. Leiden: E.J. Brill, 1970, 155 pp.

Revised version of a Ph.D. thesis. Deals especially with Pūrva-Mīmāṃsā, Nyāya, and Buddhist logic on negation. Very difficult to follow for the non-Sanskritist.

717 Sharma, Ishwar Chandra. Ethical Philosophies of India. Jullundur: S. Nagin, 1964; Lincoln: University of Nebraska, 1965, v + iii + 275 + iv pp.

The most recent and probably the best work available on Indian moral philosophy.

718 Sharma, L.N. Kashmir Śaivism. Varanasi: Bharatiya Vidya Prakashan, 1972, ix + v + 373 pp.

T.R.V. Murti says in his foreword, "The most valuable feature of this book is its comparative and critical study of Kashmir Saivism with the Advaita Vedānta."

719 Sharma, Rakesa Ranjan. "The Yogācāra Theory of the External World." Proceedings of the All-India Oriental Conference 5 (1930):883-910.

A philosophically sophisticated, useful account of Yogācāra arguments against the existence of the external world.

720 Shastri, Arunchandra Devshankar. Purusottamaji: A Study. Surat: Chunilal Gandhi Vidyabhavan, 1966, ix + 450 pp.

Purusottama was one of the greatest philosophers of Vallabha's school, and he wrote many, many works, all of which are reviewed here. One of the very few studies of such depth devoted to philosophers who flourished as late as this one (end of the 17th century).

721 Shastri, Dakshina Ranjan. "The Chārvāka Philosophy." In The Cultural Heritage of India. Vol. 3, The Philosophical Systems. 1st ed. Calcutta: Ramakrishna Mission Institute of Culture, 1937, pp. 473-92. Reprinted as Chārvāka Philosophy (Calcutta: Purogami Prakashani, 1967), 52 pp.

Distinguishes four stages of Cārvāka.

722 Shastri, Dharmendra Nath. Critique of Indian Realism. Agra: Agra University, 1964, 562 pp.

Subtitled "A Study of the Conflict between the Nyāya-Vaiśeṣika and the Buddhist Dignāga School," this work is an impressively able survey of that conflict. The author tends to rely overly heavily on Stcherbatsky, but his worrying of arguments brings them alive as few treatments of this period have done. He covers all important topics in epistemology and metaphysics, probing with skill the fundamental doctrines which generate the opposing views. Highly informative and stimulating.

723 Shastri, Gaurinath. The Philosophy of Word and Meaning. Calcutta: Sanskrit College, 1959, 292 pp.

Mainly intended to expound the philosophy of Bhartṛhari, in the process this work provides a sound introduction to philosophy of language as found in all the systems. It is not, however, easy to read.

724 Shastri, N. Aiyasvami. Śaṃkarācārya on Buddhist Idealism." Journal of the Sri Venkateśvara Rao Institute 1 (1940):71-86.
Studies the section of Saṃkara's Brahmasūtrabhāṣya in which Vijñānavāda is refuted. It is important because of the widely held opinion that Saṃkara was much influenced by Buddhism.

725 Shastri, P.S. "Time and Philosophy of History," and "The Process of History." Prabuddha Bharata 60 (1955):420-24, and 440-42.
The first article (October) reviews general issues in historiography in relation to the ultimate focus of historical processes. The second (November) briefly touches on different types of philosophy of history, then questions, in the light of the view of the Brahman or Absolute Spirit beyond change, the fruitfulness of the attempt to make history intelligible.

726 Shastri, S.N. Ghoshal. Elements of Indian Aesthetics. Vol. 1, Aesthetic Beauty and Bliss in Indian Literature and Philosophy. Varanasi: Chaukhamba Orientalia, 1978, xxii + 242 pp.
A voluminous and thorough treatment.

727 Shaw, J.L. "Negation and the Buddhist Theory of Meaning." Journal of Indian Philosophy 6 (1978):59-77.
Clarifies and in some respects criticizes the earlier work of Staal, Kajiyama, Matilal, and Herzberger on double negation as it arises in the Buddhist theory of meaning. Concludes that the Buddhist theory (of meaning) can be brought into the mainstream of contemporary semantics.

728 Shaw, J.L. "Negation: Some Indian Theories." In Studies in Indian Philosophy: A Memorial Volume in Honour of Pandit Sukhlalji Sanghvi, edited by Nagin J. Shah. L.D. Series, 84. Ahmedabad: L.D. Institute of Indology, 1981, pp. 57-78.
Shaw makes several points, the most important of which is that the Nyāya concept of negation is neither term-, proposition-, nor even propositional-function negation.

729 Shaw, J.L. "The Nyāya on Cognition and Negation." Journal of Indian Philosophy 8, no. 3 (1980):279-302.
Complex but clear; Shaw argues here that the Nyāya theory of negation is neither term-negation, sentence-negation, nor the negation of a propositional function, and is thus an original contribution to epistemology, "a new type of animal in our zoo."

730 Shaw, J.L. "Proper Names: Contemporary Philosophy and the Nyāya." In Analytical Philosophy in Comparative Perspective, edited by B.K. Matilal and J.L. Shaw. Dordrecht, Holand: D. Reidel, 1985, pp. 327-72.
The views of proper names of Gottlob Frege, Bertrand Russell and Saul Kripke are here placed alongside those of Jayanta Bhaṭṭa, Jagadīśa and Raghunātha Siromaṇi. The conclusion

is that the Nyāya account incorporates the positive features of the views of Frege and Kripke.

731 Siddalingaiah, T.B. Origin and Development of Śaiva Siddhānta up to the 14th Century. Madurai: Nepolean Press, 1979, 187 + 18 pp.

Provides a much-needed summary account of the works of Meykāṇṭa, Aruṇanti, and Umāpati.

732 Siderits, Mark. "The Mādhyamika Critique of Epistemology." Journal of Indian Philosophy 8 (1980):307-36; 9 (1981):121-60.

Highly illuminating analysis and estimation of Nyāya's answer to Nāgārjuna's critique of realist epistemology. Siderits concludes that Nāgārjuna's kind of transcendental idealism is not satisfactorily refuted by Nyāya theory.

733 Siderits, Mark. "The Prābhākara Mīmāṃsā Theory of Related Designation." In Analytical Philosophy in Comparative Perspective, edited by B.K. Matilal and J.L. Shaw. Dordrecht, Holland: D. Riedel, 1985, pp. 253-97.

Besides giving a generous and elegant account of the anvitābhidhāna theory of meaning, Siderits argues that the Prābhākara theory represents an improvement on theories of Aristotle, Frege, or Quine as to how sentence meaning is constructed out of word meaning.

734 Siderits, Mark, and J. Devin O'Brien. "Zeno and Nāgārjuna on Motion." Philosophy East and West 26 (1976):281-99.

This carefully reasoned analysis finds that Zeno's and Nāgārjuna's "treatments of motion are remarkably similar, despite their great separation in time, place and culture. What differences there are . . . can largely be accounted for by the differing purposes of these accounts."

735 Singh, Amar. The Heart of Buddhist Philosophy--Diṅnāga and Dharmakīrti. New Delhi: Munshiram Manoharlal Publishers Pvt., 1984, xvi + 168 pp.

Scholars have had severe difficulty in finding sensible classifications of Buddhist schools. This book attempts to straighten out one aspect of the problem by bringing Dignāga and Dharmakīrti within the Sautrāntika tradition. A highly polemical criticism of many scholars is involved, and the reader cannot help but be informed by being challenged to form his own views on the problem.

736 Singh, Avtar. Ethics of the Sikhs. Patiala: Punjabi University, 1970, 288 pp.

A work in an area noted for the paucity of material. Chapter 6, "Social Ethics" (pp. 146-201) argues for the distinctive Sikh view of social values, especially the rejection of caste inequalities.

737 Singh, Balbir. Foundations of Indian Philosophy. New Delhi: Orient Longman, 1971, vii + 301 pp.

Singh argues that Indian philosophy not only has ethics, but is fundamentally moral philosophy, and that the social practices taught are positive. This is a vigorous book on an interesting theme, though the author is a bit uncritical in his enthusiasm.

738 Singh, J. "The Concept of Duḥkha in Indian Philosophy." Journal of the Ganganatha Jha Research Institute 2 (1945):357-69.

Duḥkha means (a) unrest, commotion, (b) disharmony, and (c) finitude, insufficiency. A needed exegesis, though a bit long, of this critical concept, usually inadequately translated as "pain."

739 Singh, Jaideva, trans. Vijñānabhairava or Divine Consciousness. Delhi: Motilal Banarsidass, 1979, xxx + 173 pp.

The first English translation of one of the Śaiva tantras. The subject matter concerns yoga.

740 Singh, Ramjee. The Concept of Omniscience in Ancient Hindu Thought. New Delhi: Oriental Publishers & Distributors, 1979, xiv + 336 pp.

This doctoral dissertation carefully surveys the concept of omniscience (sarvajñatva) in all the Indian philosophical systems as well as in the Vedas, Upaniṣads, epics, and Purāṇas.

741 Singh, Ram Pratap. The Vedānta of Śaṃkara: A Metaphysics of Value. Jaipur: Bharat, 1949, 426 pp.

"Saṃkara binds together the different strands of thought present in his writings with the help of the unique point of view, . . . the standpoint of Value. . . . I believe its discovery and adoption have enabled me to clear up some of the major tangles left by the previous interpreters. . . ."

742 Singh, Satyavrata. Vedānta Deśika: His Life, Works, and Philosophy. Chowkhamba Sanskrit Series Studies, no. 5. Varanasi: Chowkhamba Sanskrit Series Office, 1958, 503 pp.

Part 1 reviews Vedānta Deśika's life, works, and place in Indian religion and philosophy. Part 2 expounds his philosophy; part 3 concerns bhakti, prapatti, ethics, and ritual; part 4 studies him as poet.

743 Singh, Sheo Kumar. History of Philosophy of Buddhism Based Mainly on Pāli Canonical and Exegetical Literature. Patna: Associated Book Agency, 1982, ix + 434 pp.

A handy summation of the development of Buddhism from its beginnings to its disappearance from India.

744 Singh, Yogendra. Modernization of Indian Tradition. Delhi: Thomson Press, 1973, xi + 267 pp.

This is an important treatment of modernization from a sociological perspective. The literature on the subject is noted and analyzed as part of the author's process of coming to understand modernization of the Indian tradition. The first chapter, "Social Change in India: An Approach" (pp. 1-27) deals with methodological issues, comparing different concepts of and approaches to social change in India. Chapter 2 (pp. 28-59) deals with orthogenetic changes in cultural traditions. Chapter 3 deals with Islam and modernization; chapter 4 with Western impact on modernization; chapter 5 with macrostructural changes; chapter 6 with microstructural changes. Chapter 7 is a summary and analysis of the Indian tradition in the context of modernization. Although Singh is a sociologist, this work will be of interest to philosophers of technology concerned with India.

745 Sinha, Ajit Kumar. "Śaṃkara's Doctrine of Nescience in the Context of Present-Day Science." Rtam, Journal of Akhila Bharatiya Sanskrit Parishad 1 (1970):55-68.

Interprets Saṃkara's views on māyā and avidyā as explanations of the inevitability of errors in empirical knowledge due to limitations of the knower. This is seen as anticipating the epistemological implications of Heisenberg's Uncertainty Principle. Over half the essay is concerned with explorations of modern physics.

746 Sinha, Braj M. Time and Temporality in Sāṃkhya-Yoga and Abhidharma Buddhism. New Delhi: Munshiram Manoharlal Publishers Pvt., 1983, xiv + 215 pp.

Argues that the Sāmkhya and Abhidharma agree in holding that "in the mode of beiṅg of subjectivity, the mutual otherness of the subject and object . . . is constantly and steadily overcome, . . . is subject to systematic disappearance. This is what is implied by becoming aware of something."

747 Sinha, Debabrata. The Idealist Standpoint: A Study in the Vedānta Metaphysics of Experience. Santiniketan: Visva-Bharati Centre of Advanced Study in Philosophy, 1965, xii + 184 pp.

An interpretive study of the central Advaita thesis of cit and related issues.

748 Sinha, Jadunath. History of Indian Philosophy. 2 vols. Calcutta: Central Book Agency, 1 (1956):xv + 912 pp.; 2 (1962):762 pp.

This is written in a style which is essentially unintelligible for the casual reader but probably excellent for the Indian student who needs to memorize for his exams. Volume 1 covers the philosophy of the Upaniṣads, epics, Purāṇas, Gītā, Cārvākas, Vaiśeṣika, Nyāya, Mīmāṃsā, and Grammarians. Volume 2 deals with Sāṃkhya, Yoga, Jainism, Buddhism, Advaita,

Viśistādvaita, Dvaita, Dvaitādvaita (Nimbārka), Śuddhādvaita (Vallabha), Acintyabhedābheda (Caitanya), Śaivism, and Śāktism. A worthwhile reference resource.

749 Sinha, Jadunath. Indian Epistemology of Perception. Calcutta: Sinha Publishing House, 1969, 11 + 224 + 2 pp.
In this author's usual encyclopedic fashion every line in the literature on each subject is set forth succinctly. Sinha's books are of tremendous utility for the student exploring a topic for a term paper or a thesis.

750 Sinha, Jadunath. Indian Psychology: Cognition. Calcutta: Sinha Publishing House, 1958, 512 pp.
Contains chapters on memory, imagination, thought, and language, as well as a thorough review of theories on perception. Of inestimable value as a reference resource, it guides the reader to practically every locus of primary materials relating to each topic and subtopic covered.

751 Sinha, Jadunath. Indian Psychology: Emotion and Will. Calcutta: Sinha Publishing House, 1961, xi + 568 pp.
Companion volume to the preceding entry, the work is divided into five parts--the psychology of feeling and emotions, aesthetic sentiments, sex, religion and conation. A guide to passages bearing on these topics; an indispensable reference work for teachers and scholars.

752 Sinha, Jadunath. Indian Realism. London: Kegan Paul, Trench, Trubner & Co., 1938, 287 pp.
The title is misleading; the book is really a review of Vijñānavāda Buddhist arguments for subjective idealism and the critical arguments directed against them by Sāṃkhya, Jainism, Mīmāṃsakas, Nyāya-Vaiśesika and Advaita. An excellent resource for those arguments, which are summarized in standard Indian fashion, although Sinha's way with this sort of thing is superior to some other writers in that he takes pains to provide frequent comparisons with Western literature (although the Western philosophers he knows are no longer known to most readers!).

753 Sinha, Jadunath. "The Modified Nominalism of the Jains." Philosophical Quarterly 6 (1931):249-61.
A useful presentation of arguments of Jains vs. Buddhists on universals in Parīkṣāmukha and Prameyakamalamārtaṇḍa.

754 Sinha, Jadunath. Problems of Post-Śaṃkara Advaita Vedānta. Calcutta: Sinha Publishing House, 1971, 232 + 19 pp.
All the important problems of medieval Advaita are rehearsed with this author's usual thoroughness, though his prose style does not make this bedtime reading--rather, Sinha's books should be viewed as valuable reference works.

755 Sircar, M.L. "The Philosophy of Bhāskara." Philosophical Quarterly 3 (1927):107-39.
Bhāskara's critique of Śaṃkara's thought examined and criticized.

756 Sircar, M.N. Comparative Studies in Vedantism. Bombay: Oxford University Press, 1927, 4 + xii + 311 pp.
One of the few books to explore the later literature of the various Vedāntic systems, Sircar's comprises theory of knowledge, metaphysics, the creative order, realization, and discipline.

757 Smart, Ninian. Concept and Empathy: Essays in the Study of Religion. Edited by Donald Wiebe. London: Macmillan & Co., 1986, xi + 246 pp.
A number of the papers in this collection relate to Indian philosophy and/or religion, and provide a variety of interesting approaches to the subject.

758 Smart, Ninian. Doctrine and Argument in Indian Philosophy. London: George Allen and Unwin, 1964, 255 pp.
This excellent introductory survey, by an outstanding contemporary scholar of religious philosophy, is especially praiseworthy in its insistence on discovering and assessing arguments for each of the schools' theories. The writing is unfailingly intelligent.

759 Smith, Donald E. India as a Secular State. Princeton, N.J.: Princeton University Press, 1963, xix + 518 pp.
A review of the history of the theory and the embodiment of the secular state.

760 Smith, Donald E. Nehru and Democracy: The Political Thought of an Asian Democrat. Bombay: Orient Longmans, 1958, xiv + 194 pp.
Nehru's philosophical stance surveyed with attention both to theoretical positions and to issues faced in his career.

761 Smith, Donald E., ed. South Asian Politics and Religion. Princeton, N.J.: Princeton University Press, 1966, xii + 563 pp.
Most of the papers survey contemporary movements; but there are a number of ideological, if not also philosophical elements, especially in the editor's introductory chapter and in "The Concept of Change in Hindu, Socialist, and Neo-Gandhian Thought," by Joan V. Bondurant and Margaret W. Fisher (pp. 235-48). Part 3 deals with "Pakistan: The Politics of Islamic Identity."

762 Sogani, Kamal Chand. Ethical Doctrines in Jainism. Jivaraj Jaina Granthamala, no. 19. Sholapur: Lalchand Hirachand Doshi, 1967, 302 pp.
A thorough review of Jain ethics, with comparisons with other Indian and Western views.

763 Solomon, Esther A. Avidyā--A Problem of Truth and Reality. Ahmedabad: Gujarat University, 1969, xxviii + 572 pp.

Thesis by widely respected scholar ranges over all the Indian systems' contributions on this crucial topic.

764 Solomon, Esther A. Indian Dialectics: Methods of Philosophical Discussion. 2 vols. Sheth Bholabhai Jeshingbhai Institute of Learning and Research Series, nos. 70, 74. Ahmedabad: Gujarat Vidya Sabha, 70 (1976):1-518 + 14; 74 (1978):8 + 519-950.

These two volumes explore a wide range of topics in Indian logic. The approach is not at all technical, however, and the work serves as an excellent resource provided one knows how to find what he is looking for. Part 1 treats dialectics in Indian literature, medicine, and law as well as giving the standard accounts of verbal fallacies and debate theory. Part 2 explores central epistemological topics--pramāṇas, knowledge, and truth. Part 3 widens the approach and looks at methodology of dialectics in Navya-Nyāya, Buddhism, Jainism, the literature on ethics and grammar, and on into the methods of debate wherever they occur. Contains an appended translation of a significant section on intrinsic vs. extrinsic validity in Abhayadeva's Sanmatitarkatattvabodhavidhāyinī.

765 Spellman, John W. Political Theory of Ancient India: A Study of Kingship from the Earliest Times to Circa A.D. 300. Oxford: Clarendon Press, 1964, xxiv + 288 pp.

A recognized work, typical in approach, in this much-discussed area.

766 Sponberg, Alan. "Dynamic Liberation in Yogācāra Buddhism." Journal of the International Association of Buddhist Studies 2, no. 1 (1979):44-64.

A clear presentation of the close relationship between Yogācāra and Mādhyamika Buddhism. Yogācāra is "the old Abhidharmic enterprise carried on in the light of Mādhyamika critical epistemology."

767 Sprung, Mervyn. "Non-Cognitive Language in Mādhyamika Buddhism." In Buddhist Thought and Asian Civilization, edited by Leslie S. Kawamura and Keith Scott. Emeryville, Calif.: Dharma Publishing, 1977, pp. 241-53.

Sprung argues that from the Mādhyamika viewpoint "at no level and at no point does language in fact name anything," and he explores the implications of that. What, for example, does it mean to speak of truth and falsehood under such conditions?

768 Sprung, Mervyn, ed. The Problem of Two Truths in Buddhism and Vedānta. Dordrecht, Holland: D. Reidel, 1973, 125 pp.

A collection of papers on a specific topic by a number of famous authorities, including T.R.V. Murti, Frederick Streng,

B.K. Matilal, A.K. Warder, Shotaro Iida and Herbert Guenther. The problem is of central philosophic importance.

769 Srinivasachari, P.N. "The Ethics of Kant and the Gītā." Philosophical Quarterly 7 (1931-32):315-23.
Gives the advantages of the Gītā over Kant.

770 Srinivasachari, P.N. The Philosophy of Viśiṣṭādvaita. Adyar: Adyar Library, 1943, 640 pp.
Probably the most complete survey of Viśiṣṭādvaita philosophy in print in English, though the writing style leaves something to be desired.

771 Srinivasachari, S.M., Advaita and Viśiṣṭādvaita: A Study Based on Vedānta Deśika's Śatadūṣaṇī. New York: Asia Publishing House, 1961, 204 pp.
This is not a translation, but a running account of the Viśiṣṭādvaita critique of Advaita Vedānta views arranged under eight topics, epistemological, metaphysical, and eschatological.

772 Srinivasan, G. The Existentialist Concepts and the Hindu Philosophical Systems. Allahabad: Udayana Publications, 1967, xi + 285 pp.
Probably the most extensive piece of work developing this comparison. It discusses being-in-the-world, dread, death, and nothingness in Indian thought.

773 Srinivasiengar, K.R. "Fate or Free Will: The Indian Solution." Philosophical Quarterly 5 (1929-30):106-25.
A discussion accurately described by the title.

774 Śrīpati. The Śrīkara Bhāṣya. Edited by C. Hayavadana Rao. Vol. 1. Bangalore: Bangalore Press, 1936, lvi + 888 pp.
The introduction compares and contrasts the philosophical standpoint of this fifteenth century Vedāntin, who continues the bhedābheda philosophy, with the views of various other schools of Vedānta.

775 Staal, J. Frits. Advaita and Neoplatonism: A Critical Study in Comparative Philosophy. Madras: University of Madras, 1961, xii + 262 pp.
A Ph.D. thesis by a noted contemporary philosopher-scholar, the bulk of whose work deals with logic and language, but who has done interesting research as well in aspects of Indian religion.

776 Staal, J. Frits. "Correlations between Language and Logic in Indian Thought." Bulletin of the School of Oriental and African Studies, University of London 23 (1960):109-22.
Studies Navya-Nyāya definitions of pervasion (vyāpti) using symbolic techniques, diagrams.

777 Staal, J. Frits. "Negation and the Law of Contradiction in Indian Thought: A Comparative Study." Bulletin of the School of Oriental and African Studies, University of London 25 (1962):52-71.

Symbolizes distinction between paryudāsa and prasajya negation; explores Indian logic on double negation and term vs. sentence negation.

778 Staal, J. Frits, ed. A Reader on the Sanskrit Grammarians. Cambridge: MIT Press, 1972, xxiii + 557 pp.

Vast collection of materials, with an insightful introduction by the editor.

779 Stcherbatsky, Theodore. Buddhist Logic. 2 vols. Bibliotheca Buddhica, no. 26. Leningrad: Academy of Sciences of the USSR, 1 (1930):559 pp.; 2 (1932):468 pp.

A pioneering work, so influential that the subsequent history of scholarship on the Buddhist logicians has largely consisted of attempts to get beyond Stcherbatsky. The first volume is largely taken up with a Kantian exegesis of the philosophy of Dignāga's and Dharmakīrti's school, with generous comparisons to other systems. Volume 2 contains a complete translation of Dharmakīrti's Nyāyabindu with Dharmottara's Ṭikā thereon, together with a number of sections on other Buddhist and Nyāya works bearing on the topics of perception and inference taken up in Dharmakīrti's text. Stcherbatsky's translation of this work is probably the best known, most accessible rendition of Buddhist philosophy in the Western world. A scholarly masterpiece.

780 Stcherbatsky, Theodore. The Central Conception of Buddhism and the Meaning of the Word "Dharma." 2d ed. Royal Asiatic Society Prize Publication Fund, no. 7. Calcutta: Susil Gupta, 1956, 96 pp. (Orig. pub. Calcutta: Royal Asiatic Society, 1923, 1926.)

An indispensable summary of the basic notions of Abhidharma Buddhism, especially as found in the Abhidharmakośa. The tables at the end provide at a glance a helpful survey of the dharmas and their interrelationships.

781 Stcherbatsky, Theodore. The Conception of Buddhist Nirvāṇa. The Hague: Mouton, 1965, 246 pp.

The introduction attempts to trace the development of the notion of nirvāna in Buddhism. The sections on Buddhist yoga, Yogācāras, and positive aspects of Nāgārjuna's philosophy are especially good. The body of the work contains translations of two chapters of the Mādhyamikakārikās (Chs. 1 and 25) and Candrakīrti's Prasannapadā thereon.

782 Stcherbatsky, Theodore. "Dharmas of the Buddhists and Guṇas of the Sāmkhyas." Indian Historical Quarterly 10 (1934):737-60.

Criticizes Vidhusekhara Bhattacharya's Basic Conception of Buddhism (see entry 91). Traces history of scholarship favoring Sāmkhya influence on Buddhism (Jacobi, Oldenberg, Pischel, Garbe).

783 Streng, Frederick J. Emptiness: A Study in Religious Meaning. Nashville: Abingdon Press, 1965, 252 pp.

The book is "an investigation into the nature and dynamics of religious meaning found in the conceptual, or 'theoretical,' mode of expression." It proceeds through an analysis of the meaning of śūnyatā in Nāgārjuna's philosophy, and is particularly concerned with the symbolic meaning of Mādhyamika dialectics.

784 Śubhagupta. Bāhyārthasiddhikārikā. Edited in Tibetan and translated by N. Aiyaswami Sastri. Bulletin of Tibetology 4 (1967):1-96.

The work is by a Buddhist author who espouses a realist position in epistemology and is criticized vigorously by idealist Yogācārins.

785 Subrahmanian, N. The Hindu Tripod: An Essay on Hinduism and Western Values. Madras: Institute of Traditional Cultures, 1965, 65 pp.

A forceful presentation of the view that modern democratic social ideals are incompatible with the practices and the values embodied in traditional institutions. (The "tripod" refers to the caste system, the joint family, and the "twin and complementary ideas of karma and rebirth.")

786 Subramaniam, S.V., and R. Vijayalakshmi, eds. Philosophical Heritage of the Tamils. Madras: International Institute of Tamil Studies, 1983, xxiv + 400 pp.

Because Tamil literature on philosophy has not been extensively studied, this volume fills an important need, providing a spectrum of scholarly approaches to Saiva Siddhānta, southern Vaiṣṇavism, and Vīraśaivism.

787 Sukhtankar, V.S. "The Teachings of Vedānta according to Rāmānuja." Wiener Zeitschrift für die Kunde des Morgenlandes 22 (1908):121-53, 287-333.

The body of the monograph largely follows the Vedārthasaṃgraha and contains discussion of views of other scholars.

788 Sundaram, P.K. Advaita Epistemology with Special Reference to the Iṣṭasiddhi. Madras: University of Madras, 1968, xxi + 408 + iv + x pp.

Discusses the pramāṇas, truth and reality, difference and error, and the nature of release, as found in an early post-Śaṃkara Advaita text.

789 Sundaram, P.K. Advaita and Other Systems. Madras University Philosophical Series, no. 32. Madras: University of Madras, 1981, ii + 143 pp.

Each of Śaṃkara's arguments in the Brahmasūtrabhāṣya--arguments in which he refutes other schools--is briefly stated with a summary of Śaṃkara's refutation of it.

790 Sundaram, P.K. "Radhakrishnan and the Concept of Māyā." Indian Philosophical Annual 12 (1977-78):251-74.

A scholarly refutation of Radhakrishnan's attempt to distinguish between different senses of māyā in Gauḍapāda and Śaṃkara. Radhakrishnan hopes to convince us that Śaṃkara was not an illusionist. Sundaram suggests he is one.

791 Sureśvara. Bṛhadāraṇyakopaniṣadbhāṣyavārttika: Sambandha Section. Edited by T.M.P. Mahadevan. Madras: University of Madras, 1958, xxvi + 614 pp.

A section of the work by one of Śaṃkara's students. The introduction has a good summary of the issue between Mīmāṃsā and Advaita over the relation between the knowledge (jñāna) and action (karman) aspects of parts of the Vedic corpus.

792 Sureśvara. Naiṣkarmyasiddhi. Translated by A.J. Alston. London: Shanti Śadan, 1959, ii + v + 230 pp.

The introduction provides an excellent discussion of the controversy between Advaita and Pūrvamīmāṃsā on the efficacy of karma in getting liberation.

793 Sureśvara. Taittirīyopaniṣadbhāṣyavārttika. Edited and translated by R. Balasubramaniam. Madras: Centre for Advanced Study in Philosophy, University of Madras, 1974, viii + 209 + 559 pp.

A welcome addition to the body of Advaita translations, complete with a generous introduction and helpful explanations on each verse.

794 Suryanarayana Sastri, S. "Advaita, Causality, and Human Freedom." Indian Historical Quarterly 16 (1940):331-69. Reprinted in Collected Papers of Suryanarayana Sastri, ed. T.M.P. Mahadevan (Madras: University of Madras, 1961), pp. 201-32.

A critique of causality, determinism, and indeterminism.

795 Suryanarayana Sastri, S. "Omniscience." Indian Historical Quarterly 14 (1938):280-92. Reprinted in Collected Papers of Suryanarayana Sastri, ed. T.M.P. Mahadevan (Madras: University of Madras, 1961), pp. 77-86.

The Yoga inference to God's omniscience defended. Advaita's resort to śruti not helpful. Omniscience is not reconcilable with the demands of human freedom.

796 Suryanarayana Sastri, S. "On the Study of Indian Philosophy." Journal of the Madras University (Humanities) 1 (1928):135-52. Reprinted in Collected Papers of Suryanarayana Sastri, ed. T.M.P. Mahadevan (Madras: University of Madras, 1961), pp. 1-19.

Why should one study Indian philosophy? Objections to its study are considered. A good introductory piece.

797 Suryanarayana Sastri, S. "The Philosophy of Śaivism." The Cultural Heritage of India. Vol. 3, The Philosophical Systems. Calcutta: Ramakrishna Mission Institute of Culture, 1953, pp. 387-99. Reprinted in Collected Papers of Suryanarayana Sastri, ed. T.M.P. Mahadevan (Madras: University of Madras, 1961), pp. 423-36.

The author attempts to identify basic features of Śaivism common to both the Kashmir and Saiva Siddhānta systems.

798 Suryanarayana Sastri, S. "Truth in the Śaiva Siddhānta." Journal of the Madras University (Humanities) 2 (1929):111-27.

A good, hard analysis of a school on which any kind of critical study is largely lacking.

799 Suryanarayana Sastri, S., and T.M.P. Mahadevan. A Critique of Difference. Madras Department of Indian Philosophy Publication, no. 2. Madras: University of Madras, 1936, xiii + 52 pp.

Translation of Nṛsiṃhāśrama's Bhedadhikkāra, dealing with Advaita polemics in favor of nondifference. A difficult text that needs very careful study even in translation.

800 Suzuki, D.T. Outline of Mahāyāna Buddhism. London: Luzac, 1907, xii + 420 pp.

Suzuki's accounts and interpretation of Buddhism have always been found attractive by Western readers, though one probably should beware of depending overly on his scholarship.

801 Taber, John A. Transformative Philosophy: A Study of Śaṃkara, Fichte, and Heidegger. Honolulu: University of Hawaii Press, 1983, 191 pp.

A "transformative" philosopher is one "intent on effecting a total transformation of consciousness, the basic relationship between the knower and the things he knows." Taber considers the three philosophers whose thought is the topic of this book to be transformative philosophers, and argues tellingly for his opinion. There are few efforts to compare Indian philosophy with Continental thought as telling as this.

802 Tachikawa, Musashi. "The Structure of the World in Udayana's Realism: A Study of the Lakṣaṇāvalī and the Kiraṇāvalī." Studies of Classical India. Vol. 4. Dordrecht, Holland: D. Reidel, 1981, xiv + 180 pp.

Translations, carefully done, of two of Udayana's important works. The introduction, while not always clear, uses the methods and diagrams of symbolic logic to assist in the understanding of difficult notions.

803 Tahtinen, Unto. Indian Philosophy of Value. Annales Universitatis Turkuensis, Series B, Tom 106. Turku, Finland: Turun Yliopisto, 1968, 124 pp.

The puruṣārthas are studied closely as values. The unity of the several values involved is emphasized, the pursuit of one not negating that of the others.

804 Takakusu, Junjiro. The Essentials of Buddhist Philosophy. Honolulu: University of Hawaii Press, 1947, 221 pp.

Though essentially about Chinese and Japanese sects, each of those is traced back to its original inspiration in one or more Indian texts, and considerable information is conveyed about the Indian schools as well.

805 Talib, Gurbachan Singh, ed. Jainism. Patiala: Punjabi University, 1975, vi + 114 pp.

Six well-written, informative papers by some of the foremost contemporary Jain scholars, covering history, philosophy, ethics, religion, literature, and art.

806 Tanaka, Kenneth K. "Simultaneous Relation (Sahabhūhetu): A Study in Buddhist Theory of Causation." Journal of the International Association of Buddhist Studies 8, no. 1 (1985):91-111.

How can a causal condition be simultaneous with its effect? If this were the case, which would be cause and which effect? This paper straightens out confusions over such puzzles. Tanaka argues, quoting little-studied texts such as Mahāvibhāṣā and Nyāyānusāra, that the sahabhūhetu is not another kind of causal event but is a "unifying relationship between simultaneously-produced dharmas," specifically involving simultaneity, inseparability, and having a common effect.

807 Tandon, Vishwanath. The Social and Political Philosophy of Sarvodaya after Gandhiji. Varanasi: Sarva Seva Sangh Prakashan, 1965, xiv + 252 pp.

An analysis of the work and perspective of Gandhi's principal followers, providing a useful introductory survey.

808 Tatia, Nathmal. "Paticcasamuppāda: Causation in Pāli Buddhism." Nava-Nalanda-Mahavira Research Publications 1 (1957):179-239.

A clear account of this basic Buddhist theory which scholars and students find so difficult to interpret. This exposition is based on the Viśuddhimagga.

809 Tatia, Nathmal. Studies in Jaina Philosophy. Banaras: Jain Cultural Research Society, 1951, 327 pp.

In many ways the best single work on Jain philosophy, combining clear exposition with an appropriate level of detail and many helpful comparisons with other systems. It is highly recommended.

810 Thrasher, Allen Wright. "The Dates of Maṇḍana Miśra and Śaṃkara." Wiener Zeitschrift für die Kunde Südasiens 23 (1979):117-39.

Given the importance that the date of Śaṃkara implies for the history of Indian philosophy it is irritating to find opinions so varied about the matter. Though Thrasher's conclusions are not universally accepted, the arguments provide the most detailed and unbiased reasoning on the question to this point. Thrasher's conclusion is that Śaṃkara flourished around 700, Maṇḍana slightly later.

811 Tilak, Bal Gangadhar. The Hindu Philosophy of Life, Ethics, and Religion; Srīmad Bhagavadgītā Rahasya; or Karma-Yoga-Śāstra. Translated by Bhalchandra Sitaram Sukthankar. 2 vols. Poona: R.B. Tilak, 1 (1935):lxxx + 1-618 pp.; 2 (1936):lxviii + 621-1210 + 123 pp.

The commentary on the Gītā presents Tilak's immensely influential view that the Gītā teaches the superiority of the path of work, the implication of which is active service of India and defense of its historic ideals.

812 Tiwari, Kapil N. Dimensions of Renunciation in Advaita Vedānta. Delhi: Motilal Banarsidass, 1977, 156 pp.

This doctoral thesis explores the notion of saṃnyāsa (renunciation) in its metaphysical, ethical, personal, and social dimensions. The author concentrates on Advaita as a theory of social ethics primarily.

813 Tola, Fernando, and Carmen Dragonetti. "Anāditva or Beginninglessness in Indian Philosophy." Annals of the Bhandarkar Oriental Research Institute 61 (1980):1-20.

Not a new insight, this paper cites evidence that practically all Indian philosophers assumed the beginninglessness of the universe.

814 Tola, Fernando, and Carmen Dragonetti. "Āryabhavasaṃkrāntināmamahāyānasūtra: The Noble Sūtra on the Passage Through Existence." Buddhist Studies Review 3, no. 1 (1986):3-18.

This short sūtra deals with last thoughts before death and the mechanism of "transmigration" in Buddhism.

815 Tola, Fernando, and Carmen Dragonetti. "The Hastavālanāmaprakaraṇavṛtti." Journal of Religious Studies 8, no. 1 (1980):18-31.

The title of this work means "treatise named 'the hair on the hand.'" It has been attributed to either Dignāga or Āryadeva. There are six stanzas and brief commentaries on each.

816 Tola, Fernando, and Carmen Dragonetti. "Nāgārjuna's Catustava." Journal of Indian Philosophy 13 (1985):1-54.
The authors consider the four hymns to be the Lokātīta-, Niraupamya-, Acintya-, and Paramārtha-stavas. They also provide a translation of the Cittavajra, sometimes also counted in this group.

817 Tola, Fernando, and Carmen Dragonetti. "The Yuktiṣaṣṭikā of Nāgārjuna." Journal of the International Association of Buddhist Studies 6, no. 2 (1983):94-123.
Besides the Tibetan text and English translation the authors provide an exhaustive summation of previous scholarship on this work, as well as Uriutso Ryushin's Sanskrit reconstruction of the first twelve stanzas.

818 Tripathi, Chhote Lal. "The Idealistic Theory of Inference." Annals of the Bhandarkar Oriental Research Institute 51 (1970):175-88.
Presents views of Buddhist logicians--Dignāga, Dharmakīrti, and their followers--on inference, its nature, methods, and status as a pramāṇa.

819 Tripathi, Chhote Lal. The Problem of Knowledge in Yogācāra Buddhism. Varanasi: Bharat-Bharati, 1972, 396 pp.
An extremely thorough dissertation covering the epistemology of the Dignāga-Dharmakīrti school and criticisms of it contributed by Naiyāyikas.

820 Tripathi, Chhote Lal. "The Problem of Svalakṣaṇas in the Sautrāntika Epistemology." Journal of Oriental Research 20 (1970-71):216-25.
An important paper that clarifies the vexing technical term of Dignāga and Dharmakīrti. It concludes with a critique of Stcherbatsky's assimilation of Buddhism to Kant.

821 Tucci, Giuseppe. "Buddhist Logic before Diṅnāga." Journal of the Royal Asiatic Society of Great Britain and Ireland (1929):451-88.
Tucci studies Chinese translations of pre-Diṅnāga logical works (Upāyahṛdaya, Tarkaśāstra, Yogācārabhūmi, Vādavidhi, etc.). This is ground-breaking scholarship.

822 Tucci, Giuseppe. Pre-Diṅnāga Buddhist Texts on Logic. Gaekwad's Oriental Series, no. 49. Baroda: Oriental Institute, 1929, xxx + 40 + 32 + 77 + 89 + 91 + 6 pp.
Contains valuable materials for the study of Buddhism, notably translations of Nāgārjuna's Vigrahavyāvartanī and Āryadeva's Śataśāstra. The translation of the former, from

Chinese, provides not only the stanzas but the commentary on them, presumably also by Nāgārjuna, though Tucci's English (or perhaps it is the Chinese?) is sometimes so awkward the problem is to translate it, too.

823 Tucci, Giuseppe. The Theory and Practice of the Maṇḍala. Translated by A.H. Brodrick. London: Rider, 1961, ix + 146 pp.

Covers the doctrinal basis of the maṇḍala, the maṇḍala as a means of reintegration, symbolism of the maṇḍala and its various parts, the liturgy of the maṇḍala, and the maṇḍala in the human body--psycho-physics. The first and last chapters are especially good.

824 Udayana. Nyāyakusumāñjalikārikās. Edited and translated, with Haridāsa Nyāyālamkāra's Vyākhyā, by E.B. Cowell and Mahesa Candra Nyayaratna. Varanasi: Bharat-Bharati, 1980, xv + 65 + 85 pp. (Orig. pub. Calcutta, 1864.)

The only complete translation of even the stanzas of this famous work, which provides the definitive treatment of arguments for and against God's existence. Haridāsa's commentary is not as helpful as Udayana's own, which is unfortunately unavailable in complete translation.

825 Ul-Hak, Mahbub. The Poverty Curtain: Choices for the Third World. New York: Columbia University Press, 1976.

A critique of traditional strategies of growth and development, this book makes, raises, and clarifies basic social problems and issues that underlie norms of technology-induced social change for the sake of "development." Although primarily concerned with economic issues, philosophers of technology will find this work valuable.

826 Umāpati Devanayanar. Śivaprakāśam. Edited and translated by T.N. Ramachandran. Saiva Siddhānta 12 (1977):153-60; 13 (1978):44-53, 98-104; 14 (1979):103-10, 197-204.

Rather old fashioned translation. "Three streams of ichor flow from Vinaayaka. . . ."

827 Umāsvāti. Pt. Sukhlalji's Commentary on Tattvārtha Sūtra of Vācaka Umāsvāti. Translated by Krishna Kumar Dixit. L.D. Series, no. 44. Ahmedabad: Institute of Indology, 1974, 425 pp.

A fundamental Jain treatise expounded by one of its greatest modern teachers.

828 Upadhyayaya, Kashi Nath. Early Buddhism and the Bhagavadgītā. Delhi: Motilal Banarsidass, 1971, xix + 567 pp.

In this book the epistemological implications of the Bhagavadgītā have been brought out in detail and depth, and compared carefully with early Buddhist epistemologies. Contains also comprehensive comparative treatment of metaphysics and ethics.

829 Upadhyaya, Veermani Prasad. Lights on Vedānta. Chowkhambe Sanskrit Series Studies, no. 6. Varanasi: Chowkhambe Sanskrit Series Office, 1950, 261 pp.
Expounds Sureśvara's views on epistemology in great and useful detail. Somewhat jungly in style, with the interspersing of Devanāgarī in the text making the going difficult, but an important resource for the Advaita scholar.

830 Upadhye, A.N., ed. Siddhasena's Nyāyāvatāra and Other Works. Bombay: Jain Sahitya Vikasa Mandal, 1971, xxvii + 72 + 264 pp.
Contains a bibliographic essay on Siddhasena and his works by Upadhye; edition and translation by S.C. Vidyabhusana of Nyāyāvatāra; texts of Dvātriṃśikā and Sanmai-Suttam; edition and translation by M.D. Desai of Vinaya Vijaya's Nayakarṇikā.

831 Vādidevasūri. Pramāṇanayatattvālokalaṃkāra. Translated by Hari Satya Bhattacharya. Bombay: Jain Sahitya Vikas Mandal, 1967, viii + 30 + viii + 684 + iv pp.
Vādideva's is an extensive work on Jain ontology and epistemology.

832 Van Buitenen, J.A.B., ed. and trans. The Mahābhārata. 3 vols. Chicago: University of Chicago Press, 1 (1973):xlvii + 492 pp.; 2, n.p., n.d.; 3 (1978):x + 572 pp.
This translation, unfortunately unfinished by Van Buitenen, will be definitive when it is completed by other hands.

833 Varadachari, K.C. Aspects of Bhakti. Mysore: University of Mysore, 1956, 86 pp.
Treats philosophical bases of devotion, bhaktiyoga, sādhana, and historical development of bhakti.

834 Varadachari, K.C. Idea of God (The Foundations of Religious Consciousness). Tirupati: Tirumalai-Tirupati Devasthanam Press, 1950, 155 + ii pp.
Surveys the notions of deity in Vedas, Upaniṣads, the philosophical systems, Pañcarātra, and in Rāmānuja's thought especially.

835 Varadachari, K.C. The Living Teachings of Vedānta. Madras: Modern Book Mart, 1934, 48 pp.
A lecture attempting to show that Rāmānuja's and Madhva's versions of Vedānta are as relevant today as Saṃkara's.

836 Varadachari, K.C. Śrī Rāmānuja's Theory of Knowledge. Sri Venkatesvara Oriental Institute Studies, no. 1. Tirupati: Tirumalai-Tirupati Devasthanam Press, 1943, 239 pp.
A thorough analysis of all aspects of Viśiṣṭādvaita

epistemology. This is the definitive treatment of the subject. It contains an interesting appendix on dreams.

837 Varadachari, V. Yāmunāchārya. Madras: Prof. M. Rangacharya Memorial Trust, 1984, vii + 88 pp.

Helpful summaries of Yāmuna's main philosophical works constitute the heart of this volume.

838 Varma, Vishwanath Prasad. "The Element of Values in Ancient Hindu Political Thought." Journal of the Bihar Research Society 47 (1961):336-67.

An exploration of the form and content of attention to social values in traditional thought, and critical assessment of the stance, both theoretically and actually, of "transcendental thinking" regarding society and polity issues, suggesting a void that can mask an affinity for authoritarianism.

839 Varma, Vishwanath Prasad. "Indian Philosophic Idealism and the Reconstruction of the Aims of Education." Vedānta Kesarī 60 (1973):226-28.

A brief contrast of Indian and Western approaches and statement of ingredients in a contemporary Indian philosophy of education.

840 Varma, Vishwanath Prasad. "Introduction to a New Philosophy of History." Viśvabhāratī Quarterly 22 (1956):114-25.

After discussing briefly some emphases in philosophy of history in the West, Varma notes comparable ingredients in Indian thought. Notwithstanding, he asserts, "It is indeed very true that in India we do not find any systematic work on the philosophy of history."

841 Varma, Vishwanath Prasad. Modern Indian Political Thought. 4th ed., rev. and enl. Agra: Lakshmi Narain Agarwal, 1971, xiv + 640 pp.

Although some sections are primarily historical, this survey provides an orientation to many currents of contemporary political philosophy. The book is somewhat diffuse, detracting from the value of its comprehensiveness. Chapters 16 and 17 introduce Islamic political thought.

842 Varma, Vishwanath Prasad. "The Origins and Sociology of the Early Buddhist Philosophy of Moral Determinism." Philosophy East and West 13 (1963):25-47.

Karma and determinism traced in the Vedas from a sociological point of view. Important topic. Rather long.

843 Varma, Vishwanath Prasad. "Philosophical Foundations of Gandhi's Political Thought." Indian Political Science Review 4 (1969/70):7-16.

A general survey; among a group of related articles in a "Gandhi Centenary Issue."

844 Varma, Vishwanath Prasad. "Philosophy of History in the Bhagavadgītā." Philosophical Quarterly 30 (Amalner 1957):93-114. Reprinted in Studies in Hindu Political Thought and Its Metaphysical Foundations (Delhi: Motilal Banarsidass, 1959), pp. 298-323.

Delineates various refrains in the Gītā; noteworthy is the discussion of the "avatāra theory." Also discusses the role of the Gītā in shaping modern developments in the philosophy of history.

845 Varma, Vishwanath Prasad. The Political Philosophy of Mahatma Gandhi and Sarvodaya. Agra: Lakshmi Narain Agarwal, 1959, iii + 311 pp.

An appreciative (but not uncritical) review of major Gandhian themes, which appends a short study to the philosophy of the continuing Gandhi-inspired Sarvodaya movement.

846 Varma, Vishwanath Prasad. Political Philosophy of Sri Aurobindo. New York: Asia Publishing House, 1960, xxiii + 471 pp.

A wide ranging study, explaining and interpreting various aspects of Aurobindo's social and political philosophy.

847 Varma, Vishwanath Prasad. "Sri Aurobindo's Philosophy of History." Indian Journal of Political Science 18 (1957).

Views of the "Godsent leader," "Kali or Zeitgeist," and "divine determination in history" are the principal themes from Aurobindo elaborated. (Chapter 1 of Varma's Political Philosophy of Sri Aurobindo [see entry 846] also treats his philosophy of history.)

848 Varma, Vishwanath Prasad. "Sri Aurobindo's Philosophy of Political Vedantism." Indian Journal of Political Science 18 (1957):24-35.

A brief study of the contrast between early phases of Aurobindo's work when he preached "political Vedāntism" and later writings which deleted the political from spiritual considerations; the context is the relations of Vedānta teaching to social values.

849 Varma, Vishwanath Prasad. Studies in Hindu Political Thought and Its Metaphysical Foundations. 2d ed. Delhi: Motilal Banarsidass, 1959, iv + 332 + vii + ii pp.

The most significant book of a scholar who has given continual attention to matters of political philosophy. Originally a Ph.D. dissertation (University of Chicago, 1950), it was first published in serial form. Portions are historical in character, but approached by a philosopher. Varma's work has been criticized, since many of his views are unconventional, but no serious student should ignore his work.

850 Vasugupta. Spandakārikās: The Divine Creative Pulsation. Translated by Jaideva Singh. Delhi: Motilal Banarsidass, 1980, xxiii + 209 pp.

Besides the translation, the Sanskrit text is offered, together with a brief summary.

851 Vattanky, John. Gaṅgeśa's Philosophy of God. Madras: Adyar Library and Research Center, 1984, xiii + 422 pp.

This volume fills a real need, the first full translation of the section of Gaṅgeśa's masterpiece which deals with arguments concerning the nature and existence of God. Vattanky provides a great deal of help to the reader: besides the Sanskrit text and English translation, he has provided an extended commentary (which is just as well, since mere translation of this work, no matter how clear, is still hardly readable), and he has also given us an analysis of the work and a long introduction discussing more obscure writers of Gaṅgeśa's period. A very important part of Gaṅgeśa's puzzle is now in place.

852 Vedānta Deśika. Vedānta Deśika Rahasyatrayasāra. Translated by M.R. Ayyangar. Kumbakonam: Agnihothram Ramanuja Thathachariar, 1956, 589 pp.

This Tamil work deals authoritatively with liberation and the preparation and way to it, according to Viśiṣṭādvaita Vedānta. It has several chapters on prapatti, and is extremely useful for students of Indian philosophy of religion. Ayyangar's introduction surveys the history of the system, offering a brief summary of the teachings of the work.

853 Veezhinathan, N. "Liberation--Its Nature and Its Means in Advaita." Voice of Saṃkara 5 (1980):293-318.

Neat, clear account of Advaita's views on liberation and, in particular, how it refutes rival theories in which karma, whether in combination with or independently of knowledge, functions as means to liberation.

854 Veezhinathan, N., and T.P. Ramachandran. "The Social Concern of the Jīvanmukta." Indian Philosophical Annual 2 (1966):125-30.

A defense of the view that the realized one is positively related to society, rendering the "highest form of service to society."

855 Venkata Ramanan, K. Nāgārjuna's Philosophy as Presented in the Mahā-Prajñāpāramitā-Sāstra. Rutland and Tokyo: C.E. Tuttle, 1966, 409 pp.

It is a bit mysterious what this book actually represents. The first part is clear, an interesting account of the positive aspects of Nāgārjuna's philosophy, needed to fill out the negative side on which most scholars concentrate their attention. Starting with Chapter 2 the material appears to be translations of passages from the Mahā-Prajñāpāramitā-Sāstra with explanatory notes, but it is difficult to distinguish the translations from the notes. Regardless of the difficulty, the work is an important one for those wishing to understand Mādhyamika.

856 Vidyabhusana, Satischandra. A History of Indian Logic. Delhi: Motilal Banarsidass, 1971, 648 pp. + table.

Vast survey of Indian logic, incorporating his previously published work and going well beyond it, extensively reviewing Nyāya history and literature. Contains a 46 page summary of Gaṅgeśa's Tattvacintāmaṇi and many other briefer summaries. A gold mine of information, much of it now out-of-date or even shown to be inaccurate. Appendixes take up all manner of interesting side topics--the state of things at various Indian universities of ancient times, reminiscences of the author's visits to Tibet and Ceylon, etc. Impossible to summarize.

857 Vidyāraṇya. Vidyāraṇya, Jīvanmuktiviveka. Edited and translated by Sastri S. Subrahmanya and T.R.S. Ayyangar. Adyar: Theosophical Publishing House, 1935, 385 pp.

A thorough review of Hindu, especially Advaita, views about release-while-living (jīvanmukti). Quite readable; free from technicalities, the exposition proceeds through the review of stories from epics, Yogavāsiṣṭha, etc.

858 Vidyāraṇya. Vidyāraṇya, Pañcadaśī. Translated by Hari Prasad Shastri. London: Shanti Sadan, 1956, 257 pp.

Probably the most popular exposition of Advaita after Śaṃkara's own works, this work is widely read and enjoyed. Several translations have appeared, but this is one of the more recent and is relatively available.

859 Vidyarthi, P.B. Knowledge, Self, and God in Rāmānuja. New Delhi: Oriental Publishers & Distributors, 1978, xxiii + 327 pp.

Although primarily concerned with religion, this book is in fact a rather thorough analysis of Rāmānuja's epistemology, with emphasis on psychological topics.

860 Vimuktātman. Vimuktātman's Iṣṭasiddhi, with Extracts from the Vivaraṇa of Jñānottama. Edited by Hiriyanna Mysore. Gaekwad's Oriental Series, no. 65. Baroda: Oriental Institute, 1933.

The editor's introduction is one of the best brief accounts of the several theories of error (khyātivāda) available.

861 Vimuktātman. Iṣṭasiddhi of Vimuktātman. Translated by P.K. Sundaram. Madras: Swadharma Swarejya Saṃgha, 1980, ix + 480 pp. (Introduction published separately as Advaita Metaphysics, v + 111 pp.)

This translation is not easy to read, but it is the only one yet available.

862 Walker, Benjamin. The Hindu World: An Encyclopedic Survey of Hinduism. 2 vols. New York: Praeger, 1968, 1:xii + 609 pp.; 2:xi + 696 pp.

"Politics" (2:223-28) offers a brief sketch of the literature, basic ideas, and practices of politics. "Law" (1:587-92) gives a helpful overview of legal texts and issues in the Hindu tradition.

863 Warder, A.K. Indian Buddhism. Delhi: Motilal Banarsidass, 1970, 622 pp. + 2 maps.

"A historical survey of Buddhism as it developed and spread in the land of its origin." Invaluable guide to the literature on Buddhist philosophy, summarizing many of the most important works. Extensive bibliography.

864 Warder, A.K. Outline of Indian Philosophy. Delhi: Motilal Banarsidass, 1971, 262 pp.

Endeavoring to limit itself to "philosophy" as distinct from "religion," and to stay close to the original texts, this book presents a peculiarly truncated version by comparison with standard introductions, ignoring Vedānta altogether and halting its survey of the other Hindu schools (except Navya-Nyāya) and Buddhism about the time of Dignāga. Constant textual references interfere with easy comprehension. Not really satisfactory as an introduction, but may well be of considerable interest to the practising philosopher.

865 Watanabe, Fumimaro. Philosophy and Its Development in the Nikāyas and Abhidhamma. Delhi: Motilal Banarsidass, 1983, xiii + 241 pp.

Argues that abhidhamma means "elementary philosophical study of dhammas," and he explores how the dhammas were arranged into mātikās, lists of topics. Watanabe then turns to the beginnings of logic in Buddhism, especially as found in Kathāvatthu and Vijñānakāya. His studies of portions of the latter are the first glimpse in English of the contents of that work.

866 Watts, Jeffrey D. "Necessity and Sufficiency in the Buddha's Causal Schema." Philosophy East and West 32, no. 4 (October 1982):407-23.

By distinguishing between normal and nonnormal causal processes, Watts is able to show how some of the members of the pratītyasamutpāda or "twelvefold chain of origination" are merely necessary, others both necessary and sufficient, for bondage. In this way he sheds much light on this fundamental Buddhist doctrine.

867 Wayman, Alex. "Buddhism." In Historia Religionum, edited by C. Jouce Bleeker and Geo Widengren. Vol. 2, Religions of the Present. Leiden: E.J. Brill, 1971, pp. 372-464.

While Wayman's view of Buddhism will not be everyone's, it is of constant interest. He also supplies an extensive history of the study of Buddhism, complete with his own bibliography.

868 Wayman, Alex. Buddhist Insight. Edited, with an introduction by George Elder. Religions of Asia Series, no. 5. Delhi: Motilal Banarsidass, 1984, 470 pp.

Twenty-four of Wayman's essays are collected here, most of them on Buddhist studies, and all except one published elsewhere initially. They have been topically divided into sections dealing with Buddhist practice and doctrine, interpretive studies of Buddhism, texts of the Asaṅga school, and remaining Hindu and Buddhist studies.

869 Wayman, Alex. "Reflections on the Study of Buddhist Logic." Indologica Taurinensia 5 (1977):289-308.

Stcherbatsky distinguishes three types of commentaries on Dharmakīrti's Pramāṇavārttika, but Wayman suggests there are only two. Again, there are four kinds of Yogācāra--the schools of (1) Asaṅga's Yogācārabhūmi based on the Saṃdhinirmocanasūtra, (2) of Laṅkāvatārasūtra, (3) of Madhyāntavibhāga, (4) of Vasubandhu's Viṃśatikā and Triṃśikā. Several other important points are made.

870 Wayman, Alex. "Yogācāra and the Buddhist Logicians." Journal of the International Association of Buddhist Studies 2, no. 1 (1979):65-78.

Yogācāra (or Vijñānavāda) Buddhism is regularly characterized as presenting epistemological subjective idealism. Wayman argues that no such position can be found in Yogācāra at least until after Dharmakīrti. He examines the writings of Vasubandhu and Dignāga, as well as the Saṃdhinirmocanasūtra, Asañga's Madhyāntavibhāga, and the Laṅkāvatārasūtra, showing that none of them deny an ālambana, though some recommend disregarding it. Wayman's view is that though the school is nominalistic, it is not idealistic.

871 Weber, Max. The Religion of India: The Sociology of Hinduism and Buddhism. Translated and edited by Hans H. Gerth and Don Martindale. Glencoe: Free Press, 1958, vii + 392 pp.

This classical study of the Hindu social system requires amendment in the light of study since it appeared in 1921, but it has been influential in posing questions about the conceptualization of Hindu society.

872 Werner, Karel. "Bodhi and Arahattaphala from Early Buddhism to Early Mahāyāna." In Buddhist Studies Ancient and Modern. Collected Papers on South Asian Studies (of the School of Oriental and African Studies, University of London), no. 4. London: Curzon Press, 1982, pp. 167-81.

Proposes plausible explanation of how and why the title of the bodhisattva arose, and thus why we have both Mahāyāna and Hīnayāna.

873 Whaling, Frank. "Śamkara and Buddhism." Journal of Indian Philosophy 7 (1979):1-42.

Reviewing at the outset the variety of approaches in the literature to the question of Saṃkara's relationship to Buddhism, Whaling brings out all the important aspects of this question. His conclusions are judicious: Samkara did not bring about the demise of Buddhism in India, which had already begun by his time, but he played a part in it. He also incorporated some of its elements into Hindu thought and practice.

874 Williams, Paul M. "On the Abhidharma Ontology." Journal of Indian Philosophy 9 (1981):227-57.

The most important Sarvāstivādin philosopher is arguably Saṃghabhadra, who, in his Nyāyānusāra, attacked Vasubandhu's Abhidharmakośabhāṣya so forcefully. Saṃghabhadra's work is not yet available outside of Tibetan, except in a section translated by de La Vallée Poussin. This paper lucidly explains Saṃghabhadra's views as presented in that section.

875 Williams, Paul M. "Some Aspects of Language and Construction in the Mādhyamika." Journal of Indian Philosophy 8 (1980):1-45.

Hard to read, this complex paper nevertheless explores some important and not generally understood aspects of Mādhyamika. The first part, on the meaning of prajñaptisat, concludes that the "prajñapti is the referent of a term with no ultimate referent." Subsequently the author explores the meaning of the puzzling term saṃjñā in Abhidharma, and thence into Mādhyamika, where other words, such as vikalpa, are more common, but appear to refer to what is merely constructed from verbal conceptualization.

876 Williams, R. Jaina Yoga: A Survey of the Medieval Śrāvakacāras. London and New York: Oxford University Press, 1963, xxx + 296 pp.

Overview of the subject.

877 Wiltshire, Martin G. "The 'Suicide' Problem in the Pāli Canon." Journal of the International Association of Buddhist Studies 6, no. 2 (1983):124-40.

"Suicide need not necessarily be regarded as wrongful in Buddhism. . . . Buddhism therefore is not coterminous with stoical behavior, but recognizes that there are conditions and situations too oppressive to be endured."

878 Winthrop, Henry. "Indian Thought and Humanistic Psychology: Contrasts and Parallels between East and West." Philosophy East and West 13 (1963):137-54.

Gives some central concepts of Indian thought as a contrast to the Western way of life as well as some parallels and comparisons with Maslow and other recent psychologists.

879 Wood, Ernest. Yoga. Baltimore: Penguin Books, 1959, 272 pp.
Standard, handy introduction to Yoga. Chapters on the practice of Yoga--breathing, postures, Kuṇḍalinī-control, use of sounds, on the yogas in the Bhagavadgītā, and on the Pātañjala system.

880 Yamaguchi, Susumu. "Development of Mahāyāna Buddhist Beliefs." In The Path of the Buddha, edited by Kenneth W. Morgan. New York: Ronald Press, 1956, 153-81.
A veteran Japanese Buddhist scholar's survey of Mahāyāna concepts and literature.

881 Yamunacharya, M. Rāmānuja's Teachings in His Own Words. Bombay: Bharatiya Vidya Bhavan, 1963, 160 pp.
One of a series in which important philosophers' writings are excerpted and rearranged topically. Introductory materials include a synopsis of Rāmānuja's life and an outline of his philosophy and theology.

882 Yaśovijaya. Mahopādhyāya Yaśovijaya's Jaina Tarka Bhāṣā. Edited and translated by Dayanand Bhargava. Delhi: Motilal Banarsidass, 1973, xx + 30 + 173 pp.
Brief text on logic gives interesting view on epistemological problems from standpoint of a seventeenth century Jain.

883 Zimmer, Heinrich. Philosophies of India. Edited by Joseph Campbell. New York: Pantheon, 1951, 687 pp.
A highly unusual approach to Indian thought by a famous art historian and student of Indian mythology. Zimmer did not finish the book: Campbell fills the gaps in an appendix on the six systems. Zimmer's own material is divided into 1) "The Highest Good," 2) "The Philosophies of Time" (of success, pleasure, and duty), and 3) "The Philosophies of Eternity" (Jainism, Sāṃkhya and Yoga, Vedas, Upaniṣads, Gītā and Vedānta, Buddhism, and Tantra). Much Indian teaching is expounded through summaries of myths, and the author tends to make things more mysterious than perhaps they really are.

884 Zimmerman, R. "Truth and Its Criterion in Śaṃkara's Vedānta." Indian Philosophical Review 2 (1918-19):304-38.
Flowery, but right on. V.S. Iyer responded, to which Zimmerman replied in turn.

Name Index

Abhayadeva, 764
Abhidharmakośa (Vasubandhu), 282, 328, 375, 467, 780
Abhidharmakośabhāsya (Vasubandhu), 271, 874
Abhidharmapradīpa (with Vibhāsaprabhāvṛtti), 328
Abhidharmasamuccaya (Asaṅga), 328
Abhidharmasamuccayabhāsya, 271
Abhinavagupta, 486, 566, 646, 648
Acintyastava (Nāgārjuna), 816
Advaitasiddhi (Madhusūdana Sarasvatī), 61, 541
Āgamaśāstra (Gaudapāda). See Māṇḍūkyakārikās (Gauḍapāda)
Aghoraśiva, 225
Agrawal, Madan Mohan, 1, 2
Aitareya Upaniṣad, 311
Aitareyopaniṣadbhāṣya (Śaṃkara), 253
Akalaṅka Bhaṭṭa, 704
Akhilananda, Śwami, 3
Allen, Richard F., 477
Ālokamālā (Kambala), 417
Alper, Harvey P., 4
Ālvārs, 181, 391
Ames, William L., 5, 6
Amma Visweswari, 7
Amṛtacandra, 394, 395
Anacker, Stefan, 8, 9, 374
Anand, Kewal Krishna, 10
Ānandagiri, 299
Ānandānubhava, 559
Ānandapūrṇa Vidyāsāgara, 11
Anantakrishna Sastri, N.S., 11
Anantharangachara, N.S., 12
Anderson, Tyson, 13
Annambhaṭṭa, 14, 403
Anugītā, 708
Apohasiddhi (Ratnakīrti), 715
Appadorai, Angadipuram, 15
Archer, J.C., 16
Archer, William, 22
Aristotle, 733
Arnold, (Sir) Edwin, 232
Aronson, Harvey B., 17
Arora, V.K., 18
Arthaśāstra (Kauṭilya), 362
Aruṇanti, 526, 731
Āryadeva, 19, 815, 822
Asaṅga, 272, 365, 869, 870
Aṣṭaprābhṛta (Kundakunda), 392
Aśvaghoṣa, 680
Aṣṭasāhasrikaprajñāpāramitaśāstra, 372
Athalye, Y.V., 14
Atisa, 414
Ātmānusaṃdhāna (Sadāśiva), 669
Atthasālinī (Buddhaghosa), 555
Aurobindo, (Sri), 20, 21, 22, 60, 118, 120, 144, 254, 255, 340, 360, 382, 437, 479, 481, 508, 583, 585, 846, 847, 848
Austin, J.L., 597
Ayyangar, M.R., 852
Ayyangar, T.R.S., 857
Azad, 671

Bādarāyaṇa. See Brahmasūtras
Bagchi, Sitansusekhar, 23
Bāhyārthasiddhikārikā (Subhagupta), 784

Baijnath, Bahadur Lal, 24
Bains, J.S., 508
Bāladeva Vidyabhūsana, 181
Balasubramanian, R., 25, 793
Balslev, Anindita Niyogi, 26
Bandyopadhyay, Nandita, 27, 28, 29
Bandyopadhyaya, Jayantaniya, 30
Banerjee, Anukul Chandra, 32
Banerjee, Kali Krishna, 33, 34
Banerjee, Krishna Mohan, 31
Banerjee, Nikunja Bihari, 35
Barlingay, S.S., 36, 37
Basham, Arthur L., 38, 39
Bechert, Heinz, 40
Bedekar, D.K., 41
Bedekar, V.M., 42, 43
Behanan, Kovoor T., 44
Belvalkar, S.K., 45, 46
Bendall, C., 678
Bergson, Henri, 60
Betty, L. Stafford, 47
Bhaduri, Sadananda, 48
Bhāgavatapurāṇa, 181
Bhaktivedanta, Swami, 479
Bhandarkar, R.G., 49
Bharadwaja, V.K., 50, 51, 52
Bharati, Agehananda, 53
Bhargava, Dayananda, 882
Bhartiya, Mahesh Chandra, 54
Bhartṛhari, 55, 66, 157, 289, 319, 723
Bhartṛprapañca, 300, 303
Bhāsarvajña, 363
Bhāskara (the Bhedābhedavādin), 59, 181, 316, 623, 708, 755
Bhāskara (author of Īśvara-pratyabhijñāhṛdaya-Bhāskarī), 567
Bhatia, Baldeva, 56
Bhatia, Kamala, 56
Bhatt, G.H., 57
Bhatt, Govardhan P., 58
Bhattacharya, A., 59
Bhattacharya, A.C., 60
Bhattacharya, Asutosh, 61
Bhattacharya, B.P., 62
Bhattacharya, Candrodaya, 63
Bhattacharya, Dinesh Chandra, 64, 65
Bhattacharya, Gaurinath, 66
Bhattacharya, Gopikamohan, 67, 68
Bhattacharya, Hari Mohan, 69
Bhattacharya, Hari Satya, 70, 831
Bhattacharya, Janakivallabha, 71, 72
Bhattacharya, Kalidas, 73, 74, 75, 76, 77, 78, 79, 80, 119
Bhattacharya, Kamaleswar, 81
Bhattacharya, Karuna, 82
Bhattacharya, Krishna Chandra, 83, 84, 85, 183, 340, 437
Bhattacharya, Narendra Nath, 86, 87
Bhattacharya, Sibajiban, 249
Bhattacharya, Tarasamkar, 88
Bhattacharya, U.C., 89
Bhattacharya, Vidhusekhara, 90, 91, 92, 782
Bhavasaṃkrāntisūtra (Nāgārjuna?), 814
Bhāvaviveka, 230, 313, 343
Bhave, Vinobha, 93, 110
Bhedadhikkāra (Nṛsiṃhāśrama), 799
Biderman, Shlomo, 94
Bishop, Donald H., 95
Biswas, Sri Bijan, 96
Blackwood, R.T., 97
Bleeker, C. Jouce, 867
Bochenski, I.M., 98
Bodas, M.R., 14
Bodhi, Bhikkhu, 99
Bodhicittavivaraṇa (Nāgārjuna), 416
Bodhipāthapradīpa (Atīśa), 414
Bodhisaṃbhāra(ka) (Nāgārjuna), 416
Bodhisattvasaṃvāravimśikā (Candragomin), 123
Bonaventura, 588
Bond, George D., 100, 101
Bondurant, Joan V., 102, 103, 761
Bos, Mike, 104
Bowne, B.P., 411
Bradley, F.H., 515
Brahmachari, Mahanama Brata, 105
Brahmasiddhi (Maṇḍana Miśra), 287, 449, 590, 666

Brahmasiddhivyākhyā (Samkhāpani), 446
Brahmasūtras (Bādarāyana), 200, 606, 610, 709
Brahmasūtrabhāsya (Śamkara), 82, 104, 108, 200, 316, 353, 789
Brahmasūtrabhāsya (Śrīkantha), 151
Brhadāranyakopanisad, 311
Brhadāranyakopanisadbhāsya (Samkara), 25, 104, 316
Brhadāranyakopanisadbhāsyavārttika (Sureśvara), 25, 299, 590, 791
Bronkhorst, Johannes, 107, 108
Brooks, Richard, 109
Brown, D. Mackenzie, 110, 111, 112
Brown, W. Norman, 113
Bucknell, Rod, 114
Buddhaghosa, 17, 227, 272, 410, 555, 650
Buddhapālita, 5, 415
Buddhaśānti, 123
Budhananda, Swami, 115
Buhler, Georg, 116
Bulcke, Camille, S.J., 117

Cairns, Grace E., 118, 119, 120, 121, 122, 382
Caitanya, 105, 181, 191, 371
Campbell, Joseph, 883
Candragomin, 123
Candragomipranidhāna (Candragomin), 123
Candrakīrti, 6, 81, 126, 240, 312, 680, 781
Cardona, George, 124
Carman, John Bransted, 125
Casey, David F., 126
Cattanar, 350
Catuhśataka (Āryadeva), 19
Catuhstava (Nāgārjuna), 816
Chakrabarti, A., 127
Chakrabarti, Krishna Kumar, 592
Chakraborty, Nirod Baran, 128
Chakravarti, Appaswami, 129, 393
Chakravarti, P.C., 130, 131
Chakravarti, Pulinbihari, 132
Chand, Tara, 133
Chāndogyopanisad, 311
Chandra Roy, Pratab, 134
Chaterjee, Ashok Kumar, 135, 136, 546
Chatterjee, K.N., 137
Chatterjee, Margaret, 143
Chatterjee, Satischandra, 138, 139, 140
Chatterjee, Tara, 141
Chatterji, D.C., 217
Chatterji, Jagdish Chandra, 142
Chattopadhyaya, Debiprasad, 144, 145, 146, 147, 257
Chattopadhyaya, Narayan Kumar, 148
Chaudhuri, Anil Kumar Ray, 149, 150
Chaudhuri, Roma, 151
Chavan, Y.B., 152
Chemparathy, George, 68, 153, 154
Chethimattam, John B., 155
Chi, Richard S.Y., 156
Christie, Elizabeth, 157
Citsukhī (Citsukha), 61
Cittavajrastava (Nāgārjuna), 816
Cleveland, Harland, 520
Clooney, Francis X., 158
Cole, Colin A., 159
Collins, Steven, 160
Conio, Caterina, 161
Conze, Edward, 162, 163, 164, 283, 331, 405
Coomaraswamy, Ananda Kentish, 165, 166, 167, 420
Cousins, L.S., 168
Cowell, E.B., 429, 824
Creel, Austin B., 169
Currell, Melville, 561

Damle, P.R., 170
Dandekar, R.N., 171, 172
Daniel, E. Valentine, 373, 549, 558
Danielou, Alain, 173, 679
Das, A.C., 174
Das, Manmath Nath, 175
Das, Rasvihary, 519
Das, Saroj Kumar, 176
Das, Sudhendu Kumar, 177
Dasgupta, Shashi Bhusan, 178
Dasgupta, Surama, 179
Dasgupta, Surendranath, 180, 181, 182, 183, 184

Datta, Dhirendra Mohan, 119, 140, 185, 186, 187
Davis, Lawrence, 188
Day, Terence P., 189
Daye, Douglas D., 190
De, Sushil Kumar, 191
De Bary, William Theodore, 192
De La Vallée Poussin, Louis, 874
Della Santina, Peter, 193
Denwood, Philip, 586
Derrett, J. Duncan M., 194, 195, 415
Desai, M.D., 830
Desai, S.M., 196
Desai, Sunderlal T., 513
Deśanastava (Candragomin), 123
Deśanastavavṛtti (Buddhaśānti), 123
Descartes, René, 628
Deshpande, D.Y., 197
Deshpande, Madhav, 198
Deussen, Paul, 199, 200
Deutsch, Eliot, 201, 202
Dev, Govind Chandra, 203
Devanandan, Paul David, 204, 386
Devaraja, Nand Kishore, 205, 206
Devasenapathi, V.A., 207, 208
Devasthali, G.V., 209
Dhammasaṅganī, 555
Dhar, Niranjan, 210
Dharmakīrti, 211, 212, 213, 274, 292, 356, 537, 586, 704, 735, 779, 818, 819, 820, 869, 870
Dharmottara, 779
Dhavamony, Mariasusai, 214
Dhawan, Gopinath, 215
Dignāga, 156, 216, 217, 290, 291, 292, 537, 639, 675, 680, 735, 815, 818, 819, 820, 821, 822, 870
Dimock, Edward, 289
Dixit, Krishna Kumar, 218, 827
Doctor, Adi Hormusji, 219
Donner, Neal, 349
Dragonetti, Carmen, 813, 814, 815, 816, 817
Dravid, N.S., 220
Dravid, Raja Ram, 221
Dube, S.C., 221
Dube, S.N., 222
Dumont, Louis, 224
Dunuvile, Rohan A., 225
Durai, J. Chinna, 226
Dutt, Nalinaksha, 27, 228
Dvātriṃśika (Siddhasena Nyāyāvatāra), 830
Dwivedi, C.B., 229

Eckel, M. David, 230
Eckehart, 535
Edgerton, Franklin, 231, 232, 233
Elder, George, 868
Eliade, Mircea, 235
Embree, Ainslie T., 236

Faddegon, Barend, 237
Farqhar, J.N., 238, 239
Feigl, Herbert, 626
Fenner, Peter G., 240, 241
Feuerstein, Georg A., 242
Fichte, Johann Gottlieb, 49, 801
Filliozat, Pierre Sylvain, 243
Fisher, Margaret W., 761
Franco, Eli, 244
Frauwallner, Erich, 42, 245, 246
Frege, Gottlob, 730, 733
Frenkian, A.M., 247
Freud, Sigmund, 487

Gächter, Othmar, 248
Gādādhara Bhaṭṭācārya, 249
Gadamer, Hans-Georg, 248
Gajendragadkar, K.V., 250
Gajendragadkar, Prahlad Balacharya, 251
Galanter, Marc, 252
Gambhirananda, 253
Gandhi, Kishor, 254, 255
Gandhi, Mohandas K., 30, 55, 80, 102, 143, 185, 215, 321, 434, 479, 527, 577, 656, 664, 671, 807, 843, 845
Gangadhara, S., 256
Gangadharan, N., 669
Gaṅgeśa, 28, 88, 496, 694, 706, 851, 856
Gangopadhyaya, Mrinalkanti, 258
Ganguli, Hemanta Kumar, 259
Garbe, Richard von, 782
Gard, Richard A., 260
Gaudapāda, 90, 92, 159, 161, 203, 299, 432, 445, 680, 790

Gaudapādakārikās. See Māndūkyakārikās
Gaudapādakārikābhāṣya (Śaṃkara), 161
Gettier, E., 651
Ghoshal, Upendra Nath, 261
Gillon, Brendon S., 262
Gītā Rahasya (B.G. Tilak), 111
Glasenapp, Helmuth von, 263
Goekoop, C., 264
Gokhale, Balkrishna G., 265
Gokulanātha Upādhyāya, 692
Gore, N.N.S., 266
Gough, A.E., 429
Govardhana, 14
Griffin, Ralph T.H., 267
Griffiths, Paul J., 268, 269, 270, 271
Guenther, Herbert V., 272, 768
Guha, Dinesh Chandra, 273
Gupta, Rita, 274
Gupta, Sanjukta, 275
Gupta, Shanti Nath, 276
Gupta, Sisir Kumar, 277
Guthrie, W.T.K., 468

Hacker, Paul, 124, 278, 279
Halbfass, Wilhelm, 280, 281
Haldar, Aruna, 282
Hall, Fitzedward, 266
Hanayama, Shoyu, 283
Hardy, P., 582
Haribhadra Sūri, 196, 284
Haridāsa Nyāyālaṃkāra, 824
Hariharānanda Āraṇya, 285
Harvey, Peter, 286
Hasurkar, S.S., 287, 288
Hastamālā (Dignāga), 815
Hattori, Masaaki, 289, 290
Hayes, Richard P., 291, 292
Hegde, R.D., 293
Hegel, G.W.F., 515
Heidegger, Martin, 535, 801
Heimann, Betty, 294, 295
Helarāja, 55
Hemacandra, 677
Herman, Arthur L., 97, 296, 297, 298
Herzberger, Hans, 727
Hetubindu (Dharmakīrti), 274
Hetucakradamaru (or -nirṇaya) (Dignāga), 216

Hino, Shorun, 299
Hintikka, Jaako, 460
Hiriyanna, Mysore, 300, 301, 302, 303, 304, 305, 306, 668, 792, 860
Hoffman, Berngt R., 307
Hoffman, F.J., 308
Hopkins, E. Washburn, 309, 310
Hume, David, 162
Hume, R.E., 311
Huntington, C.W. Jr., 312
Husain, 671
Husserl, 498

Iida, Shotaro, 313, 349, 768
Ingalls, Daniel Henry Holmes, 274, 314, 315, 316, 317, 463
Iqbal, 671
Īśā Upaniṣad, 311
Īśopaniṣadbhāṣya (Śaṃkara), 253
Iṣṭasiddhi (Vimuktātman), 788, 860
Iṣṭasiddhivivaraṇa (Jñānottama), 860
Īśvarapratyabhijñāhṛdaya (Utpāla), 567
Īśvarapratyabhijñāhṛdayabhāskarī (Bhāskara), 567
Iyengar, P.T. Srinivasa, 318
Iyer, K.A. Subramania, 55, 319, 450
Iyer, M.K. Venkatarama, 320
Iyer, N. Raghavan, 321
Iyer, V.S., 884

Jacob, G.A., 792
Jacobi, Hermann, 322, 323, 782
Jagadīśa, 137, 198, 730
Jagirdar, P.J., 324
Jaimini, 158, 325
Jain, Champath Rai, 326
Jain, S.C., 327
Jain Tarkabhāṣā (Yaśovijaya), 882
Jaini, Padmanabh S., 328
Janacek, A., 329
Jaspers, Karl, 535
Javadekar, A.G., 119
Jayanta Bhaṭṭa, 293, 730
Jayarāśi, 225
Jayaratha, 646
Jayasena, 394

Jayatilleke, K.N., 330, 331
Jayatīrtha, 430, 643
Jha, Ganganatha, 332, 333, 667
Jha, Mitra Nandan, 334
Jīva Gosvāmin, 105, 181, 191
Jīvanmuktiviveka (Vidyāraṇya), 857
Jñānāmṛtam, 256
Jñānaprasthāna, 32
Jñānottama, 792, 860
Johannson, Rune E.A., 335
Johnston, Charles, 200
Johnston, E.H., 336, 337
Jones, Elvin, 374
Joshi, K.S., 174, 338
Joshi, Shanti, 340

Kabir, Humayun, 341, 342, 685
Kajiyama, Yuichi, 343, 374, 727
Kalghatgi, T.G., 344
Kalupahana, David J., 345, 346, 347, 348
Kambala, 417
Kaṇāda, 237
Kanakura, Yensho, 349
Kandaswamy, S.N., 350
Kane, P.V., 351
Kant, Immanuel, 162, 515, 769, 820
Kapadia, Hiralal Rasikdas, 556
Kaplan, Stephen, 352
Karmanirṇaya (Madhva), 528
Karmarkar, Raghunath Damodar, 353
Karmasiddhiprakaraṇa (Vasubandhu), 8, 9
Karunadasa, Y., 354
Karve, Irawati, 355
Kathālakṣaṇa (Madhva), 528
Kaṭha Upaniṣad, 311
Kathāvatthu, 223, 467, 865
Kaṭhopaniṣadbhāṣya (Śaṃkara), 253
Katsura, Shoryu, 356
Kattackal, Jacob, 357
Katz, Nathan, 358, 359, 535
Kaul, H.K., 360
Kaunda Bhatta, 361
Kauṣītakī Upaniṣad, 311
Kauṭilya, 362
Kavirāj, Gopinath, 75, 363
Kaw, R.K., 364
Kawamura, Leslie S., 767
Keenan, John P., 365
Keith, Arthur Berriedale, 366, 367, 368, 369, 370
Kena Upaniṣad, 311
Kennedy, Melville T., 371
Kenopaniṣadbhāṣya (Śaṃkara), 253
Kent, Stephen A., 372
Keyes, Charles F., 373, 549, 558
Khaṇḍanakhaṇḍakhādya (Śrīharṣa), 61
Kiraṇāvalī (Udayana), 802
Kierkegaard, Soren, 535
Kiyota, Minoru, 374
Kloetzli, Randy, 375
Klostermaier, Klaus, 376
Koelman, Gaspar M., 378
Koller, John M., 379, 380, 381, 382
Kothari, Rajni, 383
Kripke, Saul, 730
Krishna, Daya, 384, 385
Krishna, Raj, 386
Krishnamacharya, V., 430, 473
Krishnamurti, J., 387
Krishna Warrier, A.G., 388, 389
Kṣaṇabhaṅgasiddhi (Ratnakīrti), 466
Kumar, Shiv, 390
Kumārajīva, 661
Kumarappa, Bharatan, 93, 391
Kumārila, 58, 281, 290, 332, 648
Kundakunda, 392, 393, 394, 395
Kunhan Raja, C., 396, 397, 398
Kunjunni Raja, K., 399, 570
Kuppuswami Sastri, S., 400, 449
Kuppuswamy, B., 401
Kuranārāyaṇa, 161

Lad, A.K., 402
Lakṣaṇāvalī (Udayana), 802
Lal, P., 403
Lamotte, Etienne, 404
Lang, Karen, 19, 405
Laṅkāvatārasūtra, 445, 869, 870
Lannoy, Richard, 406
Larrabee, M.J., 407
Larson, Gerald J., 379, 408, 409
Laswell, Harold D., 520
Law, Bimala Churn, 410
Lazarus, F.K., 411
Lele, Jayant, 412

Lester, Robert C., 413, 421
Lindtner, Christian, 230, 414, 415, 416, 417
Lingat, Robert, 418
Lipner, Julius J., 419
Lipsey, Roger, 420
Lokacarya Pillai, 421
Lokātītastava, 816
Lott, Eric L., 422, 423
Love, Martha Lila, 262
Loy, David, 424, 425

Mabbott, I.W., 426
Macnicol, Nicol, 427
MacQueen, Graeme, 428
Mādhava, 429, 559
Madhusūdana Sarasvatī, 275, 277, 357, 541
Madhva, 161, 181, 430, 431, 528, 606, 643, 708, 711, 712, 835
Mādhyamakahṛdaya (Bhāvaviveka), 313
Mādhyamakakārikās (Nāgārjuna), 47, 81, 126, 426, 523, 529, 622, 781
Mādhyamakakārikā-Akutobhayā, 5
Mādhyamakāvatāra (Candrakīrti), 241, 242, 312
Mādhyamakavṛtti (Buddhapālita), 415
Madhyāntavibhāga (Asaṅga), 260, 365, 869, 870
Madhyāntavibhāgabhāṣya (Vasubandhu), 8
Mahābhārata, 403, 633, 832
Mahābhāṣya (Patañjali), 666
Mahadevan, T.M.P., 119, 121, 122, 432, 433, 434, 435, 436, 437, 605, 791, 795, 796, 797, 799
Mahāprajñāpāramitāsūtra, 375, 855
Mahāvibhāṣa, 806
Mahāyānābhidharmasūtra, 865
Mahāyānasūtrālaṃkāra (Asaṅga), 365
Mainkar, T.G., 438
Maitra, Susil Kumar, 439, 440, 441, 442, 443
Maitrī Upaniṣad, 311
Majumdar, A.K., 444
Majumdar, J.L., 445
Malhotra, Shadi Lal, 446
Malkani, G.R., 174, 447, 519
Mallik, B.K., 685
Mānavadharmaśāstra, 116, 507
Mandal, Kumar Kishore, 448
Maṇḍana Miśra, 287, 288, 449, 450, 590, 666, 810
Mandelbaum, David G., 451
Māṇḍūkyakārikās (Gauḍapāda), 90, 159, 161, 432
Māṇḍūkya Upaniṣad, 92, 311
Māṇḍūkyopaniṣadbhāṣya (Śaṃkara), 253
Maṇimekhalai, 350
Manu, Laws of. See Mānavadharmaśāstra
Marathe, M.P., 452
Marcel, Gabriel, 588
Marcus, John T., 453, 454
Marfatia, Mrudula I., 455, 703
Maslow, Abraham, 878
Masson, J.M., 289
Mathew, E.V., 456
Matilal, Bimal Krishna, 50, 119, 190, 289, 457, 458, 459, 460, 461, 462, 463, 464, 597, 727, 730, 733, 768
Matthews, Bruce, 465
Māyāvādakhaṇḍana (Madhva), 528
Mayeda, Sengaku, 124
McDermott, A. Charlene Senape, 374, 466
McDermott, James Paul, 465
McDougall, William, 487
McEvilley, Thomas, 468, 469
McGovern, William Montgomery, 470
Mees, Gualtherus Hendrik, 472
Meghanādari Sūri, 473
Mehta, Mahesh, 474
Mehta, Mohan Lal, 475
Mehta, P.D., 476
Menon, Y. Keshava, 477
Meykaṇṭa (Śāstra), 574, 731
Michael, Aloysius, 478
Milindapañha, 467
Mīmāṃsāsūtras (Jaimini), 158, 325
Mīmāṃsā(sūtra)bhāṣya (Śabara), 248, 667
Minor, Robert N., 479, 480, 481
Mishra, Ganeshwar, 482, 483, 546

Mishra, G.S.P., 484, 485
Mishra, Kamalakar, 486
Mishra, N., 487
Mishra, Umesh, 488, 489, 490, 491, 492, 493, 494, 495, 562
Misra. See Mishra
(Prapañca)Mithyātvānumāna-khaṇḍana (Madhva), 528
Mittal, Kewal Krishna, 659
Mohanty, Jitendra Nath, 119, 496, 497, 498, 592
Mokṣadharma, 231, 233
Monier-Williams, Monier, 500
Mookerjee, Satkari, 211, 501, 502, 503, 504
Moore, Charles A., 78, 133, 186, 505, 616, 636
Morehouse, Ward, 506
Motwari, Kewal, 507
Muhar, P.S., 508
Mukerji, Krishna Prasanna, 509
Mukherjee, Himangshu Bhushan, 510
Mukherji, Santi Lal, 511
Mukhopadhyaya, Pradyot Kumar, 512
Muktivāda (Gaṅgeśa), 694
Mulla, Dinshah Fardunji, 513
Muller, F. Max, 514
Muṇḍaka Upaniṣad, 311
Muṇḍakopaniṣadbhāṣya (Śaṃkara), 253
Murti, T.R.V., 515, 516, 517, 518, 519, 718, 768
Murty, K. Satchidananda, 284, 520, 521, 522, 523, 524, 525, 617
Muttarayan, K. Loganatha, 524

Nagao, Gadjin M., 374
Naga Raja Sarma, R., 528
Nāgārjuna, 5, 13, 47, 82, 107, 126, 414, 416, 426, 501, 523, 529, 530, 531, 581, 587, 661, 662, 680, 732, 734, 781, 783, 816, 817, 822, 855
Nagasaki, Hojun, 211
Nagatomi, Masatoshi, 211, 289, 532
Naiṣkarmyasiddhi (Sureśvara), 792
Naiṣkarmyasiddhicandrikā (Jñānottama), 792
Nakamura, Hajime, 533, 534
Nanajivaka, Bhikkhu, 535
Nanda, B.R., 536
Nandimath, S.C., 536
Nandy, Ashis, 537, 538
Narahari, H.G., 430, 539, 540
Narain, K., 541, 542
Na-Rangsi, Sunthorn, 543
Narasimhachari, M., 544
Naulakha, R.S., 545
Nayadyumaṇi (Meghanādarisūri), 473
Nayak, G.C., 546, 547
Nayakarṇika (Vinaya Vijaya), 830
Neevel, Walter C., 548
Nehru, Jawaharlal, 176, 760
Neufeldt, Ronald, 373, 549, 558
Nietzsche, 535
Nikam, N.A., 119, 550, 551
Nimbārka, 2, 59, 181, 492, 552, 623, 748
Niraupamyastava (Nāgārjuna), 816
Norman, K.R., 553
Northrop, F.S.C., 554
Nṛsimhāśrama, 799
Nyanaponika Thera, 555
Nyāyabindu (Dharmakīrti), 779
Nyāyabinduṭīkā (Dharmottara), 779
Nyāyabodhinī (Govardhana), 14
Nyāyacandrikā (Ānandapūrṇa Vidyāsāgara), 11
Nyāyacandrikā-Nyāyaprakāśikā (Svarūpānandamunīndra), 11
Nyāyakusumāñjali (Nyāyavijaya), 556
Nyāyakusumāñjali (Udayana), 68, 153, 824
Nyāyāmṛta (Vyāsarāya), 541, 707
Nyāyānusāra (Saṃghabhadra), 806, 874
Nyāyapraveśa (Śaṃkarasvāmin), 156, 262, 675
Nyāyaratna, Maheśa Candra, 824
Nyāyasūtras (Gautama), 107, 117, 692
Nyāyāvatāra (Siddhasena Divākara), 830
Nyāyavijaya, 556

Nyāyavivaraṇa (Madhva), 528

O'Brien, J. Devin, 734
O'Flaherty, Wendy Doniger, 373, 549, 558
Oldenberg, Philip, 782
Olivelle, Patrick, 559
Organ, Troy W., 560
Ostergaard, Geoffrey Nielson, 561
Ozanne, C.H., 238

Padārthadharmasaṃgraha (Praśastapāda), 237
Padārthatattvanirūpaṇa (Raghunātha Siromaṇi), 620
Padmapāda, 488, 562
Padmarajiah, Y.V., 563
Pal, Bipin Chandra, 508
Palmer, Norman D., 509, 564
Pañcadaśī (Vidyāraṇya), 651, 858
Pañcaprakrīya (Sarvajñātman), 377
Pāñcarātra (literature), 108, 179, 181, 633, 834
Pañcaskandhaprakaraṇa (Vasubandhu), 8
Pañcāstikāyasāra (Kundakunda), 393
Pañcavastukavibhāṣā (Dharmatrāta), 213
Pande, Hemaraja, 394
Pande, Susmita, 565
Pandey, Kanti Chandra, 566, 567, 647
Pandey, Sangam Lal, 568
Pandeya, Ram Chandra, 569, 570
Panikkar, Raimundo, 572, 573
Pāṇini, 131, 683
Paramārthastava, 816
Paranjoti, Violet, 574
Paranjpe, A.C., 575
Parīkṣāmukha (Maṇīkyanandin), 753
Parrott, Rodney J., 576
Pasandika, Bhikkhu, 530
Patañjali, 64, 234, 285, 329, 474
Patel, M.S., 577
Pattammal, Kumari R., 578
Perrett, Roy W., 579, 580, 581
Philips, C.H., 582
Phillips, Stephen H., 583, 584, 585
Piatigorsky, A., 586
Pind, O.H., 587
Pischel, 782
Plott, John C., 588
Ponniah, V., 589
Potter, Karl H., 281, 590, 591, 592, 593, 594, 595, 596, 597, 620
Prabhākara, 58, 301, 305, 332
Prabhavananda, 598
Prabhu, Pandharinath H., 599
Pradhan, R.C., 546
Prajñāpāramitā (literature), 164, 283
Prajñāpradīpa (Bhāvaviveka), 230
Prakāśānanda, 600
Prakash, Buddha, 601
Pramāṇalakṣaṇa (Madhva), 430, 528
Pramāṇalakṣaṇaṭīkā (Jayatīrtha), 430
Pramāṇamīmāṃsā (Hemacandra), 677
Pramāṇanayatattvālokālaṃkāra (Vādidevasūri), 831
Pramāṇapaddhati (Jayatīrtha), 643
Pramāṇasamuccaya (Dignāga), 290, 291
Pramāṇavārttika (Dharmakīrti), 211, 704, 869
Prameyakamalamārtaṇḍa (Prabhācandra), 753
Prasad, Hari Shankar, 602
Prasad, Jagat, 392
Prasannapadā (Candrakīrti), 260, 312, 501, 781
Praśastapāda, 237, 635
Praśna Upaniṣad, 311
Praśnopaniṣadbhāṣya (Śaṃkara), 253
Pravacanasāra (Kundakunda), 394
Pravacanasāratātparyavṛtti (Jayasena), 394
Pravacanasāratattvapradīpikā (Amṛtacandra), 394
Prebish, Charles S., 603
Puligandla, R., 573
Punyarāja, 55
Puruṣottama (the Dvaitin), 161

Purusottama (the Śuddhādvaitin), 720
Pusalkar, A.D., 14

Quine, Willard Van Orman, 597, 733
Quinn, Thomas, 349

Radhakrishnan, Sarvepalli, 120, 340, 376, 437, 478, 480, 606, 607, 608, 609, 610, 611, 612, 613, 614, 615, 616, 653, 671, 685, 696, 709, 790
Raghavachar, S.S., 617, 618
Raghavan, V.K.S.N., 619
Raghunātha Siromaṇi, 28, 620, 693, 730
Rahasyatrayasāra (Vedānta Deśika), 852
Raju, P.T., 621, 622, 623, 624, 625, 626, 627, 628, 629
Ramachandran, R.P., 630
Ramachandran, T.N., 826
Ramachandran, T.P., 631
Ramaiah, C., 632
Rāmakṛṣṇa, 357
Ramakṛṣṇa Rao, K.B., 633
Ramana Maharshi, 437
Rāmānuja, 125, 128, 181, 391, 411, 413, 419, 422, 548, 606, 618, 699, 708, 787, 834, 835, 836, 859, 881
Rāmānujācārya (the Mīmāṃsaka), 634
Ramanujam, 635
Ramaswami Aiyer, C.P., 636
Ranade, M.G., 110, 324
Ranade, R.D., 46, 340, 637, 638
Randle, Henry N., 639
Ranganathananda, Swami, 640
Rani, Vijaya, 641
Rao, M.A. Venkata, 642
Rao, P. Nagaraja, 643
Rao, Srinivasa, 644
Rao, Veluri Subba, 645
Rastogi, Navjivan, 646, 647, 648
Ratnaguṇasaṃcaya, 372
Ratnakīrti, 466, 715
Ratnāvali (Nāgārjuna), 523
Ratnayaka, Shanta, 649, 650
Ray, Roma, 651, 652
Ray, Santosh Kumar, 653
Rege, M.P., 654
Rhys-Davids, Carolyn A.F., 696
Rhys-Davids, T.W., 655
Richards, Glyn, 656
Riepe, Dale, 657, 658, 659
Robinson, Richard H., 660, 661, 662
Rouse, W., 678
Roy, M.N., 95
Roy, Ram Mohan, 334
Roy, S.S., 663
Rudolph, Susanne Hoeber, 664
Ruegg, David Seyfort, 665, 666
Rūpa Gosvāmin, 191
Russell, Bertrand, 259, 597, 730
Ryushin, Uriutso, 817

Śabara, 248, 332, 667
Śabdaśaktiprakāśikā (Jagadīśa), 137
Sadānanda, 668
Ṣaḍdarśanasamuccaya (Haribhadra Sūri), 284
Sadāśiva, Brahmendra Sarasvatī, 669
Saddharmapuṇḍarīka, 372
Saha, Sukharañjan, 670, 706
Saiyidain, K.G., 671
Saksena, S.K., 119, 672
Saleotre, Bhaskar Anand, 673
Samartha, S.J., 674
Samayasāra (Kundakunda), 395
Samayasāra-Ātmakhyāti (Amṛtacandra), 395
Saṃdhinirmocanasūtra, 365, 686, 869
Ṣaṃghabhadra, 874
Saṃkara(ācārya), 16, 25, 63, 82, 94, 104, 108, 122, 124, 200, 202, 203, 205, 253, 277, 278, 280, 288, 299, 300, 316, 317, 320, 340, 353, 357, 389, 445, 477, 482, 523, 545, 559, 596, 606, 628, 663, 681, 708, 724, 741, 745, 755, 789, 790, 801, 810, 835, 873, 884
Śaṃkarasvāmin, 675
Sāṃkhyakārikās (Īśvarakṛṣṇa), 279, 333, 370, 408
Saṃkṣepaśārīraka (Sarvajñātman), 682

Samtānāntarasiddhi (Dharmakīrti), 212, 586
Samtani, N.H., 546
Sanātana Gosvāmin, 191
Saṅgharaksita, 676
Sanghvi, Śukhlalji, 677, 827
Sankaranarayanan, P., 386
Saṅkhāpāni, 449
Sanmatitarka (Siddhasena Divākara), 830
Sanmatitarkatattvabodhavidhāyin (Abhayadeva), 764
Śāntaraksita, 289, 292
Śāntideva, 678
Sarasvatī, Hariharananda, 679
Sarkar, Anil Kumar, 680
Saroja, G.V., 437, 681
Sarvajñātman, 377, 682
Sartre, Jean Paul, 141, 535
Sarvadarśanasamgraha (Mādhava), 429
Sastitantra, 42, 370, 633
Śastri. See also Shastri
Śastri, K.S., Ramaswami, 11, 634
Śatadūsanī (Vedānta Deśika), 771
Śataśāstra (Āryadeva), 822
Satprābhrta (Kundakunda). See Astaprābhrta.
Satyadvayāvatāra (Atīśa), 414
Scharfe, Hartmut, 683
Schayer, Stanislaw, 684
Schilpp, Paul Arthur, 685
Schmithausen, Lambert, 686
Schopen, Gregory, 687
Schopenhauer, Arthur, 535
Schubring, Walther, 688
Schweitzer, Albert, 689
Scott, Keith, 767
Scott, Roland W., 690
Searle, J.R., 597
Sen, Debabrata, 691
Sen, Keshub Chandar, 95
Sen, Prabal Kumar, 692
Sen, Pranab Kumar, 706
Sen, Sachin, 693
Sen, Saileswar, 694
Sen, Sanat Kumar, 695
Sen, Sushanta, 696, 697
Sengupta, Anima, 698, 699
Sengupta, Bratindra Kumar, 700
Seth, Kirti Dev, 701, 702
Sextus Empiricus, 247, 469
Shah, Jethlal G., 703
Shah, Nagin J., 124, 704, 705, 728
Shah, Sukharanjan, 670, 706
Shamasastry, Rudrapatna, 362
Shanbhag, Dayanand N., 707
Sharma, Arvind, 708
Sharma, B.N., Krishnamurti, 709, 710, 711, 712
Sharma, Brij Lal, 713
Sharma, Candrahar, 714
Sharma, Dhirendra, 119, 715, 716
Sharma, Ishwar Chandra, 717
Sharma, L.N., 718
Sharma, Rakesa Ranjan, 719
Shastri, Arunchandra Devshankar, 720
Shastri, Dakshina Ranjan, 721
Shastri, Dhamendra Nath, 722
Shastri, Gaurinath, 723
Shastri, Hari Prasad, 858
Shastri, N. Aiyaswami, 724, 784
Shastri, P.S., 725
Shastri, S.N. Ghoshal, 726
Shaw, Jaysamkar Lal, 190, 597, 727, 728, 729, 730, 733
Siddalingiah, T.B., 731
Siddhāntamuktāvali (Viśvanātha Nyāyavāgīśa Pañcānana), 497
Siddhasena, 830
Siderits, Mark, 732, 733, 734
Śikṣāsamuccaya (Śāntideva), 678
Singh, Amar, 735
Singh, Avtar, 736
Singh, Balbir, 737
Singh, J., 738
Singh, Jaideva, 739, 850
Singh, Ramjee, 740
Singh, Ram Pratap, 741
Singh, Satyavrata, 742
Singh, Sheo Kumar, 743
Singh, Yogendra, 744
Sinha, Ajit Kumar, 745
Sinha, Braj M., 746
Sinha, Debabrata, 747
Sinha, Jadunath, 748, 749, 750, 751, 752, 753, 754
Sircar, M.L., 755
Sircar, M.N., 756
Śivāgrabhāṣya (Sivāgra Yogi), 589

Śivajñānasiddhiyār (Aruṇanti), 208
Śivāgra Yogin, 589
Şivananda, 479
Şivaprakāśa (Umāpati), 826
Ślokavārttika (Kumārila), 641
Smart, Ninian, 757, 758
Smith, Donald Eugene, 759, 760, 761
Smith, Wilfrid Cantwell, 582
Sogani, Kamal Chand, 762
Solomon, Esther A., 763, 764
Somānanda, 364
Sopa, Geshe, 374
Spandakārikās (Vasugupta), 850
Spellman, John W., 765
Sphoṭanirṇaya (Kauṇḍa Bhaṭṭa), 361
Sphoṭasiddhi (Maṇḍana Miśra), 450
Sponberg, Alan, 766
Şprung, Mervyn, 767, 768
Şrīdhara, 237
Şrīharṣa, 501, 581
Şrikaṇṭha, 151, 181, 567, 623
Şrīkarabhāṣya (Śrīpati), 774
Srīnivāsa, 552
Srinivasachari, P.N., 769, 770
Srinivasachari, S.M., 771
Srinivasan, G., 772
Şrinivasiengar, K.R., 773
Şrīpati, 623, 774
Srīvācanabhūṣana (Lokācārya Pillai), 421
Śrutisārasamuddhāraṇa (Toṭaka), 578
Staal, J. Frits, 727, 775, 776, 777, 778
Stcherbatsky, Th., 230, 557, 722, 779, 780, 781, 782, 820, 869
Steinkellner, Ernst, 587
Steinkraus, Warren E., 447
Strawson, Peter, 597
Streng, Frederick, 768, 783
Subba Rau, S., 431
Subhagupta, 784
Subrahmanian, N., 785
Subramanian, S.V., 786
Subrahmanya Sastri, S., 590, 857
Sukthankar, Bhalchandra Sitaram, 811
Sukhtankar, V.S., 787
Sundaram, P.K., 788, 789, 790, 861
Śūnyatāsaptati (Nāgārjuna), 416
Sureśvara, 25, 299, 449, 682, 791, 792, 793, 829
Suryanarayana Sastri, S., 794, 795, 796, 797, 798, 799
Sūtrasamuccaya (Nāgārjuna), 530
Suttapiṭaka, 114
Suzuki, Daisetz T., 800
Şvarūpānandamunīndra, 11
Svetāśvatāra Upaniṣad, 311, 337

Taber, John A., 801
Tachikawa, Musashi, 675, 802
Tagore, Rabindranath, 437, 508, 510, 671, 693
Tahtinen, Unto, 803
Taittirīya Upaniṣad, 311
Taittirīyopaniṣadbhāṣya (Śaṃkara), 253
Taittirīyopaniṣadvārttika (Sureśvara), 793
Takakusu, Junjiro, 804
Tahlib, Gurbachan Singh, 805
Tanaka, Kenneth K., 806
Tandon, Vishwanath, 807
Tantrāloka (Abhinavagupta), 646
Tantrālokaviveka (Jayarātha), 646
Tantrarahasya (Rāmānujācārya), 634
Tarkajvālā (Bhāvaviveka), 313
Tarkasaṃgraha (Annambhaṭṭa), 14, 403
Tarkaśāstra (Vasubandhu), 821
Tatia, Nathmal, 808, 809
Tattvacintāmaṇi (Gaṅgeśa), 88, 264, 694, 706, 851, 856
Tattvacintāmaṇīdīdhiti (Raghunātha Siromaṇi), 692
Tattvacintāmaṇigadādharī (Gadādhara), 249
Tattvaprakāśika (Aghoraśiva), 225
Tattvārthasūtra (Umāsvati), 827
Tattvasaṃkhyāna (Madhva), 431, 528
Tattvaviveka (Madhva), 528
Tattvodyota (Madhva), 528

Tattvopaplavasiṃha (Jayarāśi), 244
Tatz, Mark, 123
Täuscher, Helmut, 587
Teilhard de Chardin, Pierre, 642
Thomas, M.M., 386
Thrasher, Allen W., 590, 810
Tilak, Bal Gangadhar, 111, 437, 681, 811
Tiwari, Kapil N., 812
Tola, Fernando, 813, 814, 815, 816, 817
Toṭaka, 578
Triṃśika (Vasubandhu), 8, 666, 869
Tripathi, Chhote Lal, 818, 819, 820
Trisvabhāvanirdeśa (Vasubandhu), 8

Udayana, 7, 68, 153, 503, 802, 824
Uddyotakara, 117
Ul-Hak, Mahbub, 825
Umapati, Devanayanar, 731, 826
Umāsvati, 827
Upādhikhaṇḍana (Madhva), 528
Upadhyaya, Kashi Nath, 828
Upadhyaya, Veermani Prasad, 829
Upadhye, A.N., 830
Upāyahṛdaya (Nāgārjuna), 821
Utpaladeva, 364, 567

Vācaspati Miśra, 72, 117, 288
Vādavidhi (Vasubandhu), 8, 821
Vādidevasūri, 831
Vaiśeṣikasūtras (Kaṇāda), 237
Vākyapadīya (Bhartṛhari), 55, 319
Vākyapadīyaprakīrṇaprakāśa (Helarāja), 55
Vākyapadīyaṭīkā (Puṇyarāja), 55
Vallabha, 57, 181, 455, 703, 748
Vaṃśadhara, 692
Van Buitenen, J.A.B., 124, 202, 832
Varadachari, K.C., 833, 834, 835, 836
Varadachari, V., 837
Varma Vishwanath Prasad, 838, 839, 840, 841, 842, 843, 844, 845, 846, 847, 848, 849
Vasubandhu, 8, 9, 272, 292, 328, 365, 870, 874
Vasugupta, 850
Vattanky, John, 851
Vedānta Deśika, 12, 742, 771, 852
Vedāntakaustubha (Śrīnivāsa), 552
Vedāntapārijātasaurabha (Nimbārka), 552
Vedāntasāra (Sadānanda), 668
Vedāntasiddhāntamuktāvali (Prakāśānanda), 600
Vedārthasaṃgraha (Rāmānuja), 787
Veezhinathan, N., 682, 853, 854
Venis, Arthur, 600
Venkata Ramanan, K., 855
Vibhramaviveka (Maṇḍana Miśra), 287
Vidyabhusana, Satis Chandra, 830, 856
Vidyāraṇya, 357, 483, 596, 651, 857, 858
Vidyarthi, P.B., 859
Vigrahavyāvarttanī (Nāgārjuna), 501, 531, 822
Vijayalakshmi, R., 786
Vijñānabhairava, 739
Vijñānabhikṣu, 89, 148, 181
Vijñānadīpikā (Padmapāda), 488, 562
Vijñānakāya, 32, 865
Viṃśatikā (Vasubandhu), 8, 869
Vimuktātman, 860
Vinaya Vijaya, 830
Viraraghavacarya, T., 473
Viśuddhimagga (Buddhaghoṣa), 227, 260, 650, 808
Viśvanātha Nyāyasiddhānta Pañcānana, 497
Vivekananda, 18, 357, 437, 511, 701
Vyāsa (author of Mahābhārata), 403
Vyāsa (author of Sāṃkhyabhāṣya), 287
Vyāsarāya, 541
Vyāsatīrtha, 707
Vyavahārasiddhi (Nāgārjuna), 416
Vyomaśiva, 635

Wadia, A.R., 685

Walhout, Donald, 594
Walker, Benjamin, 862
Warder, A.K., 768, 863, 864
Watanabe, Fumimaro, 865
Watts, Jeffrey D., 866
Wayman, Alex, 162, 867, 868, 869, 870
Weber, Max, 871
Welland, B.C., 238
Werner, Karel, 872
Wesley, John, 650
Widengren, Geo, 867
Wiebe, Donald, 757
Wilkinson, Lancelot, 874
Williams, Michael A., 596
Williams, Paul M., 874, 875
Williams, R., 876
Wiltshire, Martin G., 877
Windelband, Wilhelm, 629
Winthrop, Henry, 878
Wittgenstein, Ludwig, 13, 34, 259, 312, 330, 644
Wood, Ernest, 879

Yāmuna, 181, 544, 837
Yamunacharya, M., 881
Yāska, 683
Yaśovijaya, 882
Yogabhāṣya, 132
Yogabindu (Haribhadra), 196
Yogācārabhūmi (Asaṅga), 686, 821, 869
Yogadṛṣṭisamuccaya (Haribhadra Sūri), 196
Yogasūtras (Patañjali), 285, 329, 584
Yoga(sūtra)bhāṣya (Vyāsa), 285
Yogasūtrabhāṣyavivaraṇa (Śaṃkara?), 280
Yogavārttika (Vijñānabhikṣu), 148
Yogavāsiṣṭha, 181, 398, 540, 857
Yuktidīpikā, 132
Yuktiṣaṣṭikā (Nāgārjuna), 416, 817

Zeno, 426, 734
Zimmer, Heinrich, 883
Zimmerman, R., 884

Subject Index

ābhāsavāda, 566
Abhidharma Buddhism. See Hīnayāna
absence (abhāva), 33, 504
absolutism, 135, 501
Acintyabhedābheda philosophy, 105, 191, 238, 371, 610, 748
action, 70, 151
activism, 621
Advaita Vedānta, 24, 25, 35, 45, 140, 161, 176, 181, 200, 201, 275, 278, 280, 288, 320, 353, 435, 445, 518, 568, 578, 590, 604, 610, 644, 663, 700, 741, 748, 754, 789, 801
-bibliography of, 11
-epistemology, 27, 61, 128, 149, 187, 205, 287, 340, 519, 617, 630, 670, 724, 745, 752, 788, 829
-liberation in, 104, 174, 388, 425, 483, 488, 596, 853
-logic in, 124, 580
-translations of texts of, 11, 82, 202, 253, 277, 377, 432, 449, 562, 600, 616, 668, 669, 681, 682, 791, 792, 793, 799, 857, 858, 860, 861
aesthetics, 406, 420, 630, 631, 726, 751
affective quality or states, 17, 65, 305, 359, 751. See also frustration; pleasure
āgamas, Jain, 218
aggregates (skandhas), 99, 240
agnosticism, 375
ahiṃsā. See nonviolence
aims of man (puruṣārtha), 276, 803. See also dharma
ajātivāda, 445
Ājīvika philosophy, 38
ākāra (form)
-sākāra vs. nirākāravāda, 691
Ālaṃkārika philosophy, 29, 131
Ālvārs, 181, 391
altruism, 151
anāditva (beginninglessness), 813
analysis (vicāra), 241
anekāntavāda (nonabsolutism), 458, 504
antaḥkaraṇa, 3, 75, 229, 271
anthropocentrism, 158
anthropology, 355, 373
anvaya (positive concomitance), 124
apabhraṃśa, 130
apoha, 289
arhat, 99, 100, 286
-desire to become an, 359
-arahattaphala, 872
art, philosophy of. See also aesthetics
-Tantric, 87, 565
arthāpatti, 44
Arvars. See Ālvārs
aryasatya, 228
ascetic(ism), 234, 664
asparśayoga, 159
atheism, 145, 233
atomic theory, 31, 38, 70, 257, 367, 489, 705
attitudes, sublime (brahmavihāra), 17

authoritarianism, 838
authority, 314, 483, 713
-scriptural, 94
-spiritual, 167
avacchedyāvacchedakavāda, 24
avayavipratyakṣa, 499
avidyā. See ignorance; māyā
awareness (jñāna), 3, 76, 438, 691. See also consciousness
-empirical, 51
-in Nyāya, 37, 460
-object of, 216
-path of. See jñānayoga
Āyurveda, 65

beauty, 631
beginninglessness (anāditva), 813
Bhagavadgītā, philosophy of the, 45, 165, 181, 297, 491, 610, 622, 748, 883
-and Buddhism, 828
-commentaries on studies of, 438, 681, 708
-ethics of, 769
-modern interpretation of the, 111, 479, 811
-philosophy of history in the, 844
-selections from the, 202, 231
-translation of, 616
-yoga in the, 879
bhakti (devotion), 412, 438, 565, 833
-in Advaita, 275
-as highest value, 442
-path of, 12, 630, 833
-in Saiva Siddhānta, 214
-in Viśiṣṭādvaita, 548, 588, 742, 852
bhaktiyoga, 12, 138, 173, 214, 833
Bhāṭṭa Mīmāṃsā, 58, 280, 634
Bhedābheda philosophy, 300, 610
-translations of texts of, 303, 774
bimbapratibimbavāda, 24
biology, 294
bliss, 62
bodhi, 872
Bodhisattva, 62, 872
body, 271
-subtle body, 318
bondage, 138
Brahman, 2, 59, 200, 431, 438, 583, 725
-saguṇa, 389
Brāhmaṇas, 46
brahmavihāra, 17
breaths, vital, 318
breathing, 44
buddhavipariṇāma, 666
buddhi. See will
Buddhism, 62, 141, 163, 165, 181, 245, 296, 366, 470, 491, 603, 610, 676, 743, 748, 804, 863, 876, 883. See also philosophy, Indian: general works about; philosophy, Indian: introduction to
-general analysis of, 91, 260, 345, 366, 440, 470, 546, 610, 641, 864, 868
-compared with other philosophies, 49, 162, 358, 500, 696, 873
-early (Tripiṭaka, etc.), 40, 146, 302, 331, 335, 425, 553, 828, 872
--catuṣkoṭi in. See catuṣkoṭi
--causation, theory of in, 347, 425, 866
--epistemology in, 330
--karma theory in, 467, 842
--in the nikāyas or Suttapiṭaka, 114, 168, 286, 865
--suicide in, 873
--time in, 684
-epistemology in, 259
-history of researches in, 86
-idealism in, 182
-metaphysics in, 220, 221, 228, 257, 346, 375, 502, 632, 658, 782
-moral philosophy in, 179, 309, 485
-mysticism in, 180
"Buddhist Logic" theory, 459, 639, 722, 735, 779, 821, 869
-catuṣkoṭi in, 51
-epistemology of, 27, 532
-logic in, 156, 818
-negation in, 716, 727

-translations of texts of, 211, 212, 216, 217, 262, 466, 586, 675, 704, 715, 817, 822
-truth, theory of in, 356

Cārvāka philosophy
-analysis of, 244, 293, 580, 581, 610, 658, 721
-history of, 245, 429, 491, 748
-introduction to, 140, 146, 396, 805
-selections from texts of, 616
caste, 355
catuṣkoṭi (fourfold negation), 51, 247, 308, 587, 662
causation, causality, 31, 54, 74, 348
-in Advaita, 794
-in Buddhism, 346, 347, 348, 425, 806, 866
-in Dvaita, 542
-the one and the many, 16, 29, 407
-in Sāṃkhya, 444, 652
cessation (*nirodha*)
-attainment of (*samāpatti*), 271
-of the world, 359
cit, 747. See also consciousness
change, 4, 632, 761
-illusory, 666
-technological, 152
Christianity, 307, 456, 650
-concept of law, 533
-tenets, 225
cittaviśuddhi, 227
cognition. See knowledge
comparison. See *upamāna*
compassion, 62, 359, 532
compounds in speech, 131
concentration, 44
conception. See *vikalpa*
conflict, 102
-group conflict, 527
Confucian concept of law, 533
consciousness, 155, 453, 672. See also awareness
-in Advaita, 63
-as *puruṣa*, 409
-stream of. See *saṃtāna*
-witness (*sākṣin*), 141
-in Yoga, 4
constitution of India, 251
contradiction, 581, 587, 777
cosmology, 38, 200
-Buddhist, 375, 470, 630
creation, 31, 94
culture, Indian, 22, 551

death, 101, 104
debate, theory of, 764
definition, 37
democracy, 15, 384, 760, 785
designation, related, 733
determinism, 794, 842. See also fate; karma
development, 152, 825
devotion. See *bhakti*
dhammas (or dharmas) in Buddhism, 168, 328, 555, 684, 780, 782, 865
dharma
-in ethics, 22, 31, 103, 138, 169, 280, 301, 379, 433, 509, 607, 608
-*dharmaśāstra*, 351, 558
-and society, 472
dhvani, 399
dialectics, 66, 716, 764, 783
difference (*bheda*), 1, 431, 504, 542, 643, 788, 799
doctrinalism, 292
domestic strategy, 152
doubt (*saṃśaya*), 497
dream, 65, 490, 836
dṛṣṭisṛṣṭivāda, 24
dualism, 243, 579, 584
duḥkha. See frustration
Dvaita Vedānta, 11, 23, 161, 181, 302, 542, 610, 707, 710, 711, 712, 748, 756, 835
-dating of authors of, 11
-epistemology of, 643
-logic in, 23
-translations of texts of, 430, 431, 473, 528, 541, 616
Dvaitādvaita Vedānta, 239, 492, 610, 756
-translations of texts of, 552

-economic philosophy, 186, 219, 222, 690, 825
ecstacy, 234

education, philosophy of, 56,
   342, 671, 702
-Gandhi's, 56, 577, 671
-modern, 341, 387, 839
-Radhakrishnan's, 671
-Tagore's, 510, 693, 761
-Vivekananda's, 701
-in Yoga, 65
ego and self, 679
egoism, 15
emanation, 279
embarrassment, 51
emotion, 3, 65, 751
emotionalism, 427
empathy, 757
empiricism, 298, 347. See also
   logical positivism
Epics, 748. See also
   Bhagavadgītā
-devotion in the, 565
-omniscience in the, 740
epistemology, 41, 76, 165, 459,
   461, 464, 595, 740, 756
-in Advaita, 61, 187, 205, 275,
   630, 751, 788, 801, 829
-in Buddhism, 259, 676, 704,
   722, 732, 784, 819
-in Dvaita, 542, 643
-in Jainism, 218, 504, 831, 882
-in Nyāya-Vaiśeṣika, 37, 139,
   457, 496, 597, 722, 729
-in Pūrvamīmāmsā, 58
-in Saiva philosophy, 256
-in Viśiṣṭādvaita, 12, 699, 836,
   859
-in Vyākarana, 259
error, theory of (khyātivāda),
   306, 860
-in Advaita, 287, 340, 435, 670,
   745, 763, 788
-in Cārvāka, 244
-in Kashmir Saivism, 648
-in Prābhākara Mīmāṃsā, 651
eschatology, 294
eternity, 122
ethics, 31, 129, 169, 179, 309,
   433, 471, 526, 717, 737, 764.
   See also punishment; social
   philosophy: ethics
-in Advaita, 357, 630, 812
-in Buddhism, 485, 678, 828
-in Dvaita, 542

-ethical (non)naturalism, 594
-and international studies, 550
-in Jainism, 129, 762, 805
-and politics, 509, 520
-recent views, 185, 321, 478
-and religion, 462
-in Viśiṣṭādvaita, 699, 742
evil, problem of, 94, 151, 462,
   547
evolution. See causation: in
   Sāmkhya
existence
-historical, 454
-social, 20
existentialism, 340, 453, 498,
   680, 772
experience, sub- and superconscious, 3

fallacies, logical (hetvābhāsa),
   28, 764
falsity, 128, 150. See also
   error, theory of
-of falsity, 128
-of the world, 203
family, joint, 226
fatalism, 38
fate, 38
feelings. See emotion
forces (in Buddhism). See
   samskāra
freedom, 235, 521, 795
-of the will, 78, 318
frustration (duḥkha), 298, 462,
   738, 751
functions, truth, 37

game theory, 262
God (īśvara), 31, 106, 138, 153,
   391, 423, 427, 834. See also
   theism, theology
-in Advaita, 94, 200, 389
-arguments against the existence
   of, 68, 145, 824
-in Dvaita, 542, 643
-love of, 213
-in Nyāya-Vaiśeṣika, 68, 117,
   153
-in Saiva Siddhānta, 225
-in Sāmkhya, 106
-in Viśiṣṭādvaita, 125, 413,
   419, 422, 699, 834

gods (deva), 38
government, theory of, 167
gradation, synthetic, 495
grammar, 294, 459, 683, 778
-philosophy of, 130, 131, 259, 683
Grammarian philosophy. See Vyākaraṇa philosophy
grasping, 359
Greek philosophy, comparisons with, 370, 402, 468, 469, 522, 775
guṇa
-in Sāṃkhya-Yoga, 782
-in Vaiśeṣika, 281
-in Vedānta, 318, 782

happiness. See pleasure
haṭhayoga, 173, 234, 474
hedonism. See pleasure
hermeneutics, 248, 268, 419
hetucakra, 156, 217
hetvābhāsa. See fallacies, logical
Hīnayāna Buddhism, 272, 354, 555, 780, 865. See also Buddhism: early; Sarvāstivāda; Sautrāntika; Theravāda
-analysis of dharmas. See dhammas (or dharma) in Buddhism
-causal theory of. See causation
-karma in, 467
-ontology in, 874
-psychology in, 282, 359
-time in, 746
-translations of texts of, 328
history, philosophy of, 113, 119, 454, 484, 521, 524, 551, 601, 642, 674, 725, 840
-in Aurobindo, 118, 120, 847
-in the Bhagavadgītā, 844
-of T.M.P. Mahadevan, 121
-in Radhakrishnan, 121
holism, 121, 242
holography, 352
humanism, 671, 878

idealism, 31, 182, 622, 624, 839
-in Advaita, 24, 747
-in Buddhism, 135, 136, 417, 686, 784, 818
-in philosophy of education, 702, 839
-in Sāṃkhya, 49, 409
-transcendental, 732
identity, 632
-in difference (bhedābheda), 1, 623, 774
-theory of prejudice, 575
ideology, 152, 599
ignorance (ajñāna, avidyā), 104, 149, 316, 483. See also māyā
imagination, poetic. See pratibhā
immorality, 62
immortality, 235, 263
indefinite, 504
indeterminism, 794
individual, 78
induction, 23, 37, 580
industrialization, 625
ineffable, ineffability, 462, 504
inexpressible. See ineffable
inference, theory of (anumāna), 37, 156, 190. See also anvaya; fallacies; tarka
-for oneself (svārtha), 291
-as a pramāṇa, 818
infinite regress, 23
insight (prajñā), 241
-concentration on, 269
integration, national, 115
intellect, 229
intellectualism, 427
international relations, 550
intuition (pratibhā), 65, 157, 289, 626, 750
invalidity. See validity and invalidity of inference
Islam, 192, 744, 761

Jainism
-analysis of philosophy of, 129, 323, 326, 458, 504, 563, 658, 677, 688, 704, 752, 809
-atomism in, 257
-dialectics in, 764
-ethics in, 129, 179, 762

-history of and introductions to philosophy of, 27, 50, 69, 70, 140, 181, 245, 344, 475, 491, 610, 748, 883
-karma and rebirth in, 558
-logic in. See logic: in Jainism
-metaphysics of, 70, 218, 221, 705, 753
-selections from, 192, 616
-self or soul in, 327
-translations of works of, 392, 393, 394, 395, 556, 827, 830, 831, 882
-truth in, 69
jātismara, 687
jīvanmukti (liberation while living), 104, 174, 596, 668, 669, 854, 857
jñānayoga, 12, 111, 138, 173, 300, 791, 853

kalpa, 318
kāraka, 131
karma, 10, 238, 301, 318, 351, 373, 398, 427, 438, 467, 471, 543, 549, 785
-Advaita on, 174, 562, 853
-Buddhism on, 467, 543, 655, 842
-law of, 138, 151, 447, 476, 572
-and liberation. See liberation
-theory of, 117, 200, 270, 547, 558, 594
karmayoga, 12, 111, 138, 173, 300, 791, 792, 853
Kashmir Śaivism, 4, 142, 364, 566, 610, 646, 647, 718, 748, 797
-epistemology in, 648
-śakti in, 177
-translations of texts of, 567, 850
-yoga in, 494
khyātivāda. See error, theory of
kleśa, 329
knowledge. See awareness
kośa. See sheaths
Krama theory of Kashmir, 647
kuṇḍalinī, 474, 879

Lakulīśa Pāśupata, 567
language, 534
-formalized, 37
-noncognitive, 767
-and perception, 459
-prefixes, 295
language, philosophy of, 229, 294, 459, 461, 570, 764, 776
-in Advaita, 482
-in Buddhism, 135, 715, 727
-in Pūrvamīmāṃsā, 209, 248, 733
-in Vaiyākaraṇa, 723
law, philosophy of, 186, 195, 533
-Buddhist concept of, 533
-compared with Western, 326
-and legal systems, institutions of, 133, 513, 636
-in modern India, 193, 195, 210, 456, 513
-moral ideas in, 309
-traditional Indian, 116, 194, 210, 252, 314, 418, 513, 533, 862
layayoga, 173
legal philosophy. See law, philosophy of
liberation (mokṣa), 31, 35, 127, 138, 200, 272, 275, 318, 398, 402, 427, 438, 483, 595, 788. See also nirvāṇa
-in Advaita, 353, 388, 424, 596, 771, 792, 853
-desire for, 269
-while living. See jīvanmukti
-and omniscience, 70
-path to, 12, 114, 138, 241, 494, 559
-in Śaiva Siddhānta, 526
-in Yoga, 338, 584
limitationism. See avacchedyāvacchedakavāda
literature
-Indian, 764
-Jain, 805
logic, 36, 98, 247, 294, 459, 461, 534, 595, 764, 856. See also inference, theory of; relations: logic of; tarka
-in Advaita, 84
-in Ājīvika, 38
-in Buddhism, 47, 241, 639, 676, 704, 818

-formal, 51, 156
-history of, 23, 37, 95, 246
-of induction, 580
-in Jainism, 50, 704
-and language, 130, 776
-in Nyāya-Vaiśesika, 14, 33, 37, 67, 273, 367, 639
-symbolic, 262, 264, 802
logical positivism or empiricism, comparisons with, 340, 459, 460, 462, 464, 482, 512, 592, 597
Lokāyata philosophy. See Cārvāka
love, 17
-loving-kindness, 359

Mādhyamaka Buddhism, 135, 193, 283, 459, 515, 661, 665, 783. See also Prāsañgika; Sautrāntika
-analysis of, 6, 47, 81, 126, 241, 732
-comparisons with other philosophies, 13, 107, 312, 426, 468, 469, 734, 766
-language in, 767, 875
-svabhāva in, 6
-translations of texts of, 5, 19, 230, 240, 313, 415, 416, 529, 530, 531
magic, 41, 62
mahābhūtas, 652
Mahāyāna Buddhism
-general, 165, 622, 800, 880. See also "Buddhist Logic" theory; Mādhyamaka; Yogācāra
-bodhisattva in, 872
-jātismara in, 687
-origins of, 40, 372
-pratibhāna in, 428
-translations of texts of, 423, 678
-via negativa in, 405
maṇḍala, 823
mantra yoga, 173
Marxism, 144, 145
materialism, 146, 293
-transcendental, 522
mātikās, 865
matter, 70, 354, 489
māyā, 31, 149, 197, 203, 204, 303, 352, 483, 790. See also ignorance
meaning. See also language, philosophy of; sentences: meaning of; words: meaning of
-Buddhist, 227, 269, 271, 272, 286, 374
-highest, 9
-"signless," 286
memory, 9, 687, 750
metalanguage, 37
metaphysics, 10, 36, 48, 294, 339, 440, 461, 512, 595, 756. See also cosmology
-in Advaita, 84, 275, 630, 747, 771, 812, 861
-in Buddhism, 676, 722, 828
-in Dvaita, 542
-in Jainism, 70, 218, 504, 563, 831
-metaphysical correlates of social system, 166
-in Nyāya-Vaiśesika, 722, 802
-and politics, 509, 849
-in recent Indian philosophy, 118, 420
-in Viśiṣṭādvaita, 419, 699, 771
-in Yoga, 584
Mīmāṃsā, Pūvamīmāṃsā, 140, 181, 332, 368, 397, 398, 610, 621, 748. See also Bhāṭṭa Mīmāṃsā; Prābhākara Mīmāṃsā
-dream theory in, 490
-epistemologies of, 27, 752
-metaphysics of, 29, 221, 257, 684
-moral philosophy in, 179
-negation in, 716
-philosophy of language of, 131, 209, 248, 450
-relation to Advaita, 791, 792
-relation to dharmaśāstra, 351
-theory of sacrifice, 158
-translations of texts of, 325, 616, 667
mind, 229, 272, 318
-mind-body problem, 271
modernization, 744
momentariness (kṣaṇikavāda), 274
monastic rules, 62
monism, 16

morals, moral philosophy. See ethics
motion, 426, 734
-arguments against, 81
-and rest, 70
mysticism, 47, 180, 584, 585
myth, mythology, 235, 883
-sociological analysis of, 146

names, proper, 730
Nandikeśvara Saivism, 567
nationalism, 110, 693
naturalist, 79, 658
nature, personalistic conception of, 444
Navya-Nyāya, 64, 67, 273, 315. See also Nyāya; Nyāya-Vaiśeṣika; Vaiśesika
-epistemology of, 198, 457, 496, 592, 597, 600, 730
-fallacies in, 28
-negation in, 33, 463
-pervasion in, 88, 776
-translations of texts of, 249, 400, 496, 616, 620, 706
naya (aspect), 50
necessity, 462, 866
negation, theory of, 37, 71, 77
-triple, 33
negativism, absolute, 504
neo-Platonism, 775
neo-Vedāntism, 446
nikāyas, 168, 865
nimitta (sign), 286
-nimittakārana, 652
nirvāna, 62, 99, 168, 424, 425, 655, 781
-anupadiśesa, 99
niyati (fate), 38
niyoga, 301
nominalism, 753
nonattachment as a requirement for liberation, 151, 559, 812
nondualism, 579
nonviolence (ahimsā), 93, 280
Nyāya, 7, 400, 440, 692. See also Navya-Nyāya; Nyāya-Vaiśeṣika; Vaiśeṣika
-dreams in, 490
-epistemology in, 96, 107, 139, 460, 499
-grammar in, 131
-tarka in, 23, 52, 188
-translations of texts of, 14, 639, 779, 802, 824, 851
Nyāya-Vaiśesika, 140, 181, 245, 363, 367, 398, 491, 593, 610, 632, 722, 748. See also Navya-Nyāya; Nyāya; Vaiśesika
-epistemology in, 27, 29, 72, 497, 728, 732, 752, 819
-logic in, 580, 581, 639, 728, 729, 856
-meaning, theory of, 450
-metaphysics in, 54, 257, 489, 560, 602
-moral philosophy in, 179
-salvation in, 694
-theism in, 68, 117, 153, 851
-universals in, 221, 504

obedience, 713
omniscience, 70, 740, 795
ontology. See cosmology; metaphysics

pain. See frustration
Pakistan, 761
particularism, absolute, 504
pāramārthika truth, 630
pariṇāmavāda, 652
parts, 499
Pāśupata Saivism, 567
path
-eightfold, 114
-in Buddhism, 655
-to liberation. See liberation: path to
perception (pratyakṣa), 190, 459, 749, 750
person, 240
phenomenology, 340, 425, 453, 498
philology, 269
philosophy, Indian
-general works about, 53, 138, 147, 165, 349, 380, 381, 437
--comparative study, 79, 654
--critique of studies of, 659
--foundations of, 737
--refutation of, 266
--synthetic gradation in, 495
--ways of thinking of, 534, 796

-history of, 73, 181, 245, 491, 748
--early period (Vedas, Upaniṣads), 46
-introduction to, 31, 97, 140, 170, 284, 297, 302, 304, 318, 339, 429, 441, 514, 516, 595, 610, 627, 629, 714, 758, 883
--Buddhist philosophy, 163
--Hindu philosophy, 171
physics, 745
play (līlā), 94
pleasure, 65, 127, 751
poetics, Indian, 53
political philosophy, 93, 110, 112, 186, 509, 524, 564, 571, 582, 759, 761, 841, 849, 862. See also sarvodaya
-of Aurobindo, 20, 21, 22, 144, 254, 360, 481, 508, 846, 848
-of Gandhi, 30, 80, 102, 112, 185, 215, 321, 656, 664, 843, 845
-institutions in contemporary India, 133, 167, 222, 334, 383, 520, 537, 538, 841
-of Nehru, 760
-of neo-Vedānta, 446
-of B.C. Pal, 508
-of Radhakrishnan, 653, 685
-of M.G. Ranade, 110
-of Tagore, 508, 693
-traditional, 103, 261, 362, 672, 765
-of Vivekananda, 18, 511
positivism, logical. See logical positivism
postures, 44
poverty, 825
power. See also skandhas
-divine, 177
-temporal, 167
Prābhākara Mīmāṃsā, 301, 305, 634, 651, 733
pragmatism, 312, 356
prajñā, 269
prajñaptisat, 875
prakāśa, svataḥ vs. parataḥ, 672, 691
Prakrit, 130
pralaya, 318
pramā (knowledge), 27
pramāṇa (instrument of knowledge), 27, 398, 430, 440, 764. See also inference, theory of; perception
-in Advaita, 187, 788
-in Cārvāka, 293
-in Jainism, 50
-in Nyāya-Vaiśesika, 139, 188
prapatti, 12, 548, 852
Prāsaṅgika school of Mādhyamaka Buddhism, 193, 343
pratibhā. See intuition
pratītyasamutpāda (dependent origination), 135, 228, 335, 348, 808, 866
pratyāya, 348
preexistence, 31
prefixes, 295
prejudice, 575
presupposition. See arthāpatti
progress, 605
propositions, 37
psychoanalysis, 44
psychology, 3, 84, 750, 751, 878
-Advaita, 200
-Buddhist, 555
-Viśiṣṭādvaita, 859
-Yoga, 44, 65, 184, 235
punishment, 189
Purāṇas, 181, 391, 565, 740, 748
purity, original, 365
puruṣa. See self; consciousness
puruṣārtha. See aims of men
Pūrvamīmāṃsā. Mīmāṃsā, Pūrvamīmāṃsā

question-begging, 23

rājayoga, 138, 173
Ramakrishna Mission, 640
Raseśvara Śaivism, 567
rationality, 51, 308
realism, 517
reality, 50, 109, 155, 542, 606, 788
-criterion of, 542
reason, 36, 280, 313, 617
rebirth, 44, 138, 200, 263, 351, 398, 471, 543, 549, 558, 562, 579, 595, 606, 785, 814
recognition, 364
reflection, 36

reflectionism. See bimbapratibimbavāda
relations, 77, 220, 348, 504
-logic of, 37
religion, 166, 177, 195, 476, 505, 757, 783
-in Advaita, 357, 630
-religious belief, 462
-in Jainism, 805
-plurality of traditions in, 280
-in recent Indian thought, 143, 614
-Tantric, 87
-in Viśiṣṭādvaita, 852, 859
renunciation, 559
-of the world, 224
retribution, 263
revelation, 41
-Vedic, 280

śabda (verbal cognition, language), 198, 248
-as instrument of knowledge (pramāṇa), 187, 198, 525
sacrifice, theory of, 158, 332
sādhaka (seeker), 12
sādhana, 12, 833
sādṛśya. See similarity
Śaiva Siddhānta philosophy, 181, 207, 208, 214, 225, 243, 567, 574, 610, 731, 786, 797
-epistemology of, 256, 589, 798
-ethics in, 526
-translations of texts of, 225, 826
Śaivism, 4, 75, 243, 739, 797. See also Kashmir Śaivism; Śaiva Siddhānta; Vīra-Śaiva philosophy
sākṣin (witness). See consciousness; witness
Śakti, 177
Śāktism, 474, 748
salvation, 263, 465
samādhi, 227, 269
samāpatti, 99
śamatha (meditation), 286
samjñā, 282, 875
Sāṃkhya philosophy, 42, 44, 49, 83, 132, 140, 146, 181, 233, 245, 279, 333, 336, 337, 370, 398, 408, 610, 632, 658, 698, 748, 752, 883
-compared with Jainism, 323
-compared with Vedānta, 84, 233
-dharmaśāstra's relation to, 351
-epistemology of, 27, 72, 229, 576
-metaphysics of, 440, 560, 652, 746, 782
-moral philosophy in, 179
-theism in, 106, 108, 633
-translation of text of, 616
saṃnyāsa, 438, 596
saṃsāra, 31, 424
saṃśaya. See doubt
saṃskāra(skandha), 282, 487, 655
-in Yoga, 487
saṃtāna (stream of consciousness), 9, 212
-saṃtānāntara (other stream of consciousness), 586
saṃvṛti (convention), 228
saptabhaṅgī. See sevenfold predication
Sarvāstivāda Buddhism, 32, 107, 347
sarvodaya, 93, 219, 434, 561, 845
satyāgraha, 527
Sautrāntika Buddhism, 193, 347, 684, 820
science, 222, 506, 745
scriptural authority, 94
self (jīva, ātman), 76, 138, 318, 516, 560, 606, 679
-in Advaita, 150, 200, 340, 483
-in Ājīvikas, 38
-and Brahman, 353
-in Dvaita, 542
-in Jainism, 70, 395
-in Nyāya-Vaiśeṣika, 489
-in Suddhādvaita, 2
-transmigration of the. See karma
-in the Vedas, 539
-in Viśiṣṭādvaita, 422
self-control, 664
self-determination, 21
self-identity, 453
self-refutation, 581
senses, sense-organs, sensation, 229, 318

sentences, 130, 131, 645
-cognition in, 198
-meaning of, 198, 399
sevenfold predication (saptabhangī), 50, 452, 504
sex, 532, 751
sheaths, 615
signless (animitta), 286
similarity (sādrśya), 29
simplicity (in logic), 23
simultaneous relation (sahabhūhetu), 806
Śivādvaita Vedānta, 151
śivayoga, 173
skandhas, 99, 240, 282
skepticism, 462, 628
socialism, 15, 761
solipsism. See drṣṭisṛṣṭivāda
soteriology, 159, 312
soul. See self
social philosophy, 115, 166, 172, 206, 355, 381, 385, 406, 451, 472, 785, 825. See also sarvodaya
-of Aurobindo, 20, 21, 22, 144, 254, 255, 360, 382, 481
-Christian, 307
-classical, 116, 265, 362, 384, 507
-ethics, 206, 386, 640, 690, 695
-of Gandhi, 30, 56, 80, 102, 185, 258, 321, 527, 656
-justice, 152
-of Nehru, 175
-of neo-Vedānta, 446
-of Radhakrishnan, 376, 480, 685
-of M.G. Ranade, 324
-of Vivekananda, 18, 511
social control, 30
social institutions, 39
social order, 93, 611
social organization, 599
social problems, 825
social progress, 121, 122
social responsibility, 612
social structure, 30
sociology, 507, 744, 842
-sociological foundations of education, 56
sound, 705
-evolution of, 130
-physical theory of, 493
space, 70, 448, 705
speech
-acts, 597
-inspired (pratibhāna), 428
-origin of, 130
-parts of, 130, 131
sphoṭa, 66, 131, 361, 399, 450
śruti, 154, 795
state, the, 15
-secular, 759
-statecraft, art of, 362
stream of consciousness. See saṃtāna
subjectivism, 203
Suddhādvaita Vedānta, 57, 161, 238, 443, 455, 610, 703, 720, 748, 756
suicide, 877
śūnyatā (emptiness), 9, 240, 313, 415, 587, 783
śūnyavāda, 9
superimposition, 435
svabhāva, 6
svalakṣaṇa, 6, 820
syādvāda. See sevenfold predication
sympathy, 17

Tamil literature, 558
tanmātra, 318
tantra, 4, 87, 178, 234, 250, 486, 739
-Buddhist, 558
-krama tantricism, 647
tarka (reductio reasoning), 23, 52, 188
tathāgatagarbha, 365
tathatā, 424
technology, 625, 825
-Indian, 222, 744
theism, theology, 125, 153, 200, 225, 419
Theravāda Buddhism, 160, 223, 331, 410, 553, 650. See also God
-arhat in. See arhat
-bodhisattva in. See Bodhisattva
-causation in, 808
-death in, 101, 543
-karma in. See karma
-matter in, 354

-selections from, 192
-translations of complete texts of, 9, 213
time, 26, 113, 436, 448, 573, 684, 746
-in Advaita, 122
-in Buddhism, 274, 407, 425
-in contemporary philosophy, 122
-in Jainism, 70, 705
-in Nyāya-Vaiśeṣika, 602
tolerance, 480
traces, mental. See saṃskāra
trairūpya (threefold mark), 217
transcendence (religious), 158, 483
transcendental thinking, 838
transformative philosophy, 801
transmigration. See rebirth
Trika system of Kashmir Saivism, 566
Tripiṭaka. See Buddhism: early
tripuṭi, 305
tṛṣṇā (thirst, craving), 465, 751
truth (prāmāṇya), 306, 592, 672
-in Advaita, 630, 788, 884
-in Buddhism, 356, 414, 767
-in Cārvāka, 244
-in Jainism, 69
-in Nyāya-Vaiśeṣika, 37, 496
-three-truths, 313
-two-truths, 13, 312, 313, 768

uncertainty principle, 745
unconscious, 65
universals (sāmānya, jāti), 37, 221, 459, 512, 697
-in Jainism, 504, 753
-in Nyāya-Vaiśeṣika, 281, 463
upādhi (in logic), 37
upamāna (comparison), 390
Upaniṣads
-Advaita in the, 568
-devotion in the, 565
-God in the, 389, 391, 834
-idealism in the, 182
-moral philosophy in the, 179, 309
-mysticism in the, 180
-philosophy of the, 45, 46, 165, 181, 199, 200, 245, 250, 369, 473, 491, 610, 637, 748, 883
-Sāṃkhya in the, 233, 633
-selections from, 202, 231, 297, 616
-translations of, 253, 311, 613

Vaibhāṣika Buddhism. See Theravāda
Vaiśeṣika, 237, 635, 658. See also Navya-Nyāya; Nyāya; Nyāya-Vaiśeṣika
-relations in, 220
-time in, 684
-translations of texts of, 616
-universals in, 503
validity and invalidity of inference, 28, 217, 438
value. See also aims of man
-ethical values. See ethics
-Indian and Western, 785
-metaphysics of, 741
-philosophy of, 803
-puruṣārtha, 276
-spiritual, 115
-theory, 36, 660
-traditional Indian, 384, 838
-ultimate, 30
Veda, 181, 245, 297, 369, 398, 491, 610, 883. See also Brāhmaṇasr; Upaniṣads
-Advaita in the, 24
-ātman in the, 539, 560
-bhakti in the, 565
-God in the, 834
-idealism in, 182
-interpretation of the, 154
-karma in the, 842
-moral philosophy in the, 179, 309
-mysticism in the, 180
-relevance of the, 31
-revelation in the, 280
-Ṛg, 267
-śakti in the. See śakti
-selections from the, 231, 616
vedanā, 282
Vedānta philosophy, 45, 84, 398, 473, 598, 615, 622, 638, 756, 883. See also Advaita; Dvaita; Viśiṣṭādvaita
-atomism in, 257
-idealism in, 182, 624
-metaphysics in, 440

-moral philosophy, 179
-relation to Mīmāṃsā, 397
-and social reform, 386
-and Sri Aurobindo, 585
verbal authority as pramāṇa, 187, 198, 525
via negativa, 405
vijñāna(skandha), 282
vijñānapariṇāma, 666
Vijñānavāda. See Yogācāra
vikalpa (conception), 750, 875
violence, 102
vipassanā, 269
Vīraśaiva philosophy, 177, 181, 243, 536, 567, 610, 786
virodha, 587
viṣaya, 249
-saviṣaya/nirviṣaya consciousness, 691
viśeṣaṇa, 706
Viśiṣṭādvaita Vedānta, 12, 59, 140, 161, 181, 411, 544, 610, 619, 699, 742, 748, 770, 787, 835, 837, 881
-comparison with Western philosophy, 588
-epistemology, 859
-metaphysics, 59, 560, 771
-philosophy of religion, 125, 422, 423, 548
-Śaiva Viśiṣṭādvaita, 567
-translations of texts of, 473, 616, 618, 634, 852
vivartavāda, 666
voluntarism, 584
Vyākaraṇa philosophy, 130, 131, 259, 319, 459, 645, 683, 723, 748, 778
-similarity in, 29
-theory of sphoṭa of, 66
-translations of texts of, 55, 361, 450
-yoga in, 494
vyāpti (pervasion), 52, 88, 264, 776
vyatireka (negative concomitance), 124
vyāvahārika, 630

war, 21
welfare, 226
wholes and parts, 499
will (antaḥkaraṇa, buddhi), 3, 75, 751. See also freedom: of the will
witness. See sākṣin
women, place of in Indian thought, 53
words, 645, 666
-meaning of, 130, 131, 137, 450
world, the, 59, 138, 272, 353, 719, 802
-and creation, 542. See also cosmology
-falsity of. See falsity

yoga
-as path, 44, 310, 329
-as a philosophical concept, 310
Yoga philosophy, 44, 85, 108, 173, 181, 183, 233, 234, 235, 242, 245, 329, 378, 494, 610, 748, 879, 883
-change and identity in, 632
-epistemology in, 27
-kuṇḍalinī in, 474
-liberation in, 338
-moral philosophy in, 179
-mysticism in, 180
-origins of, 337
-psychology in, 65, 184
-relation to Sāṃkhya, 370
-saṃskāra in, 487
-self in, 560
-time in, 746
-translations of texts of, 148, 196, 285, 616
-compared with Vedānta, 84
Yogācāra Buddhist philosophy, 136, 719, 752, 766, 781, 819, 870
-attainment of cessation through meditation in, 271
-critique of, 230, 635, 724, 752, 819
-translations of texts in, 8, 9, 414, 417, 784
-compared with Western philosophy, 407
yogic practices, 44
yuga (age), 122, 642